Afghanistan, 1900-1923

Published under the Auspices of the
Near Eastern Center
University of California
Los Angeles

Ludwig W. Adamec

Afghanistan, 1900-1923

A Diplomatic History

UNIVERSITY OF CALIFORNIA PRESS · 1967
Berkeley and Los Angeles

University of California Press
Berkeley and Los Angeles, California
Cambridge University Press
London, England
© 1967 by The Regents of the University of California
Library of Congress Catalog Card Number: 67-24832
Designed by Jorn Jorgensen

Acknowledgments

I gratefully acknowledge my obligation to the many who were helpful at one stage or another during my research. While I cannot here thank them all individually, I wish to thank them, no less cordially, collectively. Officials of the American Embassies in Afghanistan, India, and England were very kind and helpful. Professor G. Hasan Mujadidi, Dean of the Faculty of Letters of the Kabul University, as well as the Assistant Dean, Professor Mir Husayn Shah, and other members of his department were helpful with advice and much needed information. Officials of the ministries of Press and Education obtained permission for me to see material in various Afghan libraries.

In India I owe thanks to the Director and the Assistant Director of the National Archives of India, Dr. S. Roy and Dr. S. V. Desika Char, as well as to Mr. B. N. Das Gupta and Mr. P. R. Malik of the Research Room. I must further thank Dr. S. Gopal, Director of the Historical Division of the Indian Ministry of External Affairs, and Dr. B. K. Basu, Dr. A. K. George, and Dr. N. Abidi of the same ministry.

The Librarians of the India Office Library in London were also most helpful to me.

Members on the staff of the Near Eastern Center and allied departments of the University of California at Los Angeles have been helpful with advice and criticism for which I want to thank especially professors Amin Banani, Janos Eckman, Moshe Perlmann, Andreas Tietze, and Stanley Wolpert. Mr. John Bedrosian, now with the United States Department of State, read the manuscript and gave me the benefit of his opinion. Mrs. Teresa Joseph, editor with the Near Eastern Center, has my gratitude for her editorial assistance. For similar assistance and help in the preparation of the final manuscript I want to thank Mrs. Grace H. Stimson and

Vincent J. Ryan of the University of California Press at Los Angeles.

I also express my gratitude for a number of fellowships and for a Fulbright-Hays research grant for 1964–1965, given by the United States Office of Education, and for similar financial assistance extended by the Near Eastern Center of the University of California at Los Angeles. To Professor G. E. von Grunebaum, Director of the Near Eastern Center, UCLA, go my thanks for his advice and assistance in the completion of this work.

L. W. A.

Contents

	Introduction	1
1	Abdur Rahman	14
	Building a Nation 14	
	Formulation of a Foreign Policy 17	
2	Habibullah	28
	Accession to Power and Consolidation 28	
	Russian Pressures on Afghanistan 31	
3	The Dane Mission	39
	Formulation of British Demands 39	
	Negotiations 49	
4	Anglo-Russian Convention and Relations As Usual	65
	Habibullah's Visit to India 65	
	Afghan Reaction to the Convention 67	
	Afghan Relations as Usual 76	
5	World War I and Neutrality	83
	The Niedermayer Expedition 83	
	Incitement of the Tribes 96	
	The Sirāj al-Akhbār 100	
	The Aftermath 103	
6	Amanullah	108
	The Third Anglo-Afghan War 108	
	Peace Negotiations 123	
7	The Settlement	136
	Preliminaries to Mussoorie 136	
	Russo-Afghan Relations 142	
	The Mussoorie Conference 148	
	Kabul Mission—The Settlement 157	
	Conclusion	167
	Appendixes	169
	Notes	213
	Bibliography	233
	Index	239

Introduction

The conquests by European powers during the nineteenth and early twentieth centuries threatened the cultural and political existence of the Islamic world, and it seemed only a matter of time before the last independent Muslim country would disappear from the political map. For Afghanistan the situation became critical late in the nineteenth century, when the Russian and British empires advanced in Central Asia until they were separated only by the area of Afghanistan.

Afghanistan became a national entity in 1747 when Ahmed Shah united the Afghan tribes under his leadership. Ahmed Shah's power was consolidated in consequence of an aggressive foreign policy aimed at the conquest of large portions of northern India. But by the end of the eighteenth century the hope of Afghan rulers to increase their domain was definitely foiled. Lord Mornington, Governor of Bengal (1798–1805), initiated a policy of containment of Afghanistan, and Lord Auckland (1836–1842) began to interfere directly in the affairs of that country, bringing about the First Anglo-Afghan War (1839–1842). The failure of Britain to obtain her objectives in this war led to a temporary disengagement, but Britain's forward policy was not to be stopped, and the arrival of a Russian mission in Afghanistan became the cause of the Second Anglo-Afghan War (1878–1879).

The fact that Anglo-Russian advances in this area were definitely stopped, with Afghanistan remaining a national entity, was the result of such factors as her geographical situation; the rivalry between Russia and Britain, which prevented the one from advancing at the expense of the other; and the skill of the Afghans in guerilla warfare. The most important factor to which Afghanistan owed her national survival, however, was the skillful policy of her rulers. Much has been written about Afghanistan's international relations, but this aspect—the policy of her rulers—has generally been neglected.

It is my contention that Afghan rulers followed a conscious policy, first formulated by Abdur Rahman in the late 1890's, which rested on the premise that Afghanistan's neighbors were essentially hostile and bent on territorial annexation. To deter his neighbors from aggression, Abdur Rahman relied on a policy of militant independence, strict isolationism, and a middle-course balancing of powers which attempted to check pressures from one of his neighbors by obtaining support from the other. To conduct such a policy successfully, the Afghan ruler had to be careful not to provoke either of his two neighbors: Britain, with whom he had a cautious alliance, and Russia, from whom he isolated himself in the arrangement with Britain.

My purpose is to present a history of Afghan foreign relations from the turn of the century to the early 1920's, and to describe and analyze Afghanistan's foreign policy from formulation to execution under three Afghan rulers.

This study provides new information that is needed for an understanding of the recent history of Afghanistan. It brings into focus certain trends in Afghan foreign policy which have persisted to this day. Having attained independence in 1919, Afghanistan gradually abandoned its isolationist policy; but Afghan rulers have continued to resist the peaceful penetration of their country and they have not granted foreigners any vital concessions or positions of power within their domain. The fate of the transborder Afghans continues to affect Afghanistan's foreign relations, and Afghanistan in the 1960's is a nonaligned nation which wants to be at peace with all and refuses to support either of the two power blocs in their ideological dispute.

Just as it describes Afghan foreign relations, this book also gives an example of European imperialist policy. It shows one of the many instances in the nineteenth and early twentieth centuries of the confrontation of West and East, the unequal battle between the industrial, expanding West and the undeveloped, traditional East. What is remarkable in our story is that Afghanistan survived this confrontation.

As a study of Afghan foreign relations, this book is essentially a diplomatic history of Afghanistan. It deals primarily with the actions and pronouncements of policy makers—the Afghan rulers and their advisers, and the officials of various other states. In the course of my research a number of questions arose: Who was in charge of conducting Afghan foreign relations? What were the objectives of Afghan policy? Were there any internal factors militating against a "sound" Afghan foreign policy? Were there factors of economics, or of ethnic or religious diversity, which seriously affected Afghan rulers in the conduct of their foreign affairs? These and similar questions are answered in the subsequent chapters.

Above all, it should be emphasized that the conduct of Afghanistan's foreign relations during the early twentieth century, the period of this study, was the exclusive right of the Afghan rulers. This function was the concomitant of sovereign power and could not be delegated. Furthermore, in a state that had emerged as a centralized entity only toward the end of the nineteenth century, and whose centrifugal forces of tribal, ethnic, and religious differences had not yet been completely eliminated, Afghan rulers could not in their best interests delegate the task of conducting foreign relations.

Afghan rulers always feared that their officials could be induced by judicious bribes to connive with their enemies to the detriment of Afghanistan's security and independence. Abdur Rahman and his two successors, therefore, resisted British and Russian demands for permitting direct relations between officials stationed along the Afghan border to secure the settlement of minor offenses and to curb raiding and frontier violence.

At times when Afghan officials were in contact with British officials, as during the Dobbs mission in 1903,[1] or during repeated attempts at settling frontier disputes or demarcating the Afghan boundaries, Afghan officials were never permitted to negotiate independently and always had to refer for orders to the amir. In only one instance was this rule bypassed: during the Mussoorie Conference in 1920 Mahmud Tarzi, the Afghan Foreign Minister, was given plenary powers, provided he did not endanger Afghanistan's primary objective, her absolute independence.[2] It goes without saying that no agreements were legal without having been ratified by the amir.

Prior to Abdur Rahman's reign, Afghans sought outside support to rule over Afghanistan. After Abdur Rahman was established in

1880, two men in exile—Ishaq Khan in Russia and Ayyub Khan in India—were biding their time, hoping to return to Afghanistan. Afghan rulers knew of the machinations of their rivals. Abdur Rahman was aware of secret negotiations between Ayyub Khan, then in occupation of Herat, and Colonel St. John, with the British forces in Kandahar.[3] And Habibullah knew of the intrigues of Bibi Halima, wife of Abdur Rahman, who sought British assistance to establish her son on the throne.[4]

Abdul Kuddus Khan, Prime Minister under Amanullah, appeared willing to negotiate independently with the British, when the events of the Third Afghan War threatened to endanger his position in Kabul.[5] And Nasrullah, imprisoned for his alleged complicity in the murder of Habibullah, attempted to treat with the British for his rescue. This sirdar, who was known for his utter dislike of the British, was willing to surrender considerable portions of Afghanistan in exchange for liberation by the British and investiture with the authority to rule over the remainder of Afghanistan.[6] But the Indian government itself discouraged such intrigues. Britain seemed to fear chaos in Afghanistan more than the unfriendliness of an Afghan ruler, for she preferred to deal with a strong Afghan ruler, who could be induced by subsidies and by British support—in short, by self-interest—to refrain from an aggressive policy, rather than rely on the uncertain benefit that might be derived from installing some other aspirant on the Afghan throne.

It is reasonably certain, therefore, that the Afghan ruler was in command of foreign relations and that even his foreign enemies preferred it that way.[7] It must be admitted, however, that there existed a number of factors that did influence Afghan rulers in the conduct of their foreign relations. Furthermore, certain conditions strengthened or weakened Afghan rulers in their dealings with the outside world.

One factor that was of great importance in keeping Afghanistan an independent state was the rugged topography of the country. Afghanistan has an area of about 250,000 square miles, of which about 85 percent is at an altitude of more than 6,000 feet.[8] The Hindu Kush (Hindu Killer) and a number of other mountain ranges, with peaks of more than 20,000 feet, in the Wakhan Corridor, fan out in a western and southwestern direction, posing an endless series of barriers to north–south communications. Only in the western part of the country did it appear possible for an invader from the north to pass from Herat in a southern direction, and, skirting the mountains, to gain access to Kandahar and the Indo-Afghan boundary.

Before the advent of aerial warfare, the mountains and deserts of Afghanistan were enough of a barrier to discourage invaders. Large invading forces could not easily support themselves in a country so barren of vegetation. Thousands of transport animals were required to supply the troops and keep open the routes of supplies. It was relatively easy for Britain to occupy certain key towns in eastern and southern Afghanistan, but it was difficult to hold these areas against vigorous attack by Afghan tribal forces. Two Anglo-Afghan wars showed Britain that it was easier to invade Afghanistan than it was to hold or evacuate the country.[9] Britain's experience may have served as a warning also to the Russian government, which was not impressed by the plans of some Russian military officials to invade India.[10] The persistent policy of Afghan rulers was that nothing be done that would improve communications in Afghanistan to the extent of facilitating invasion by foreign armies. They resisted the extension of railroad lines into Afghanistan because these would have weakened the country's natural defenses.

Another factor that helped deter foreign invasion was the rivalry between Russia and Britain. The possession of Afghanistan by one of these two powers would have endangered either the British hold over India or Russia's consolidation in Central Asia. Rather than permit the other to establish itself in Afghanistan, Britain and Russia were willing to accept Afghanistan as a buffer between their two empires. But to accomplish this, at least the tacit cooperation of the Afghan ruler was required. Afghan rulers had the power to upset any arrangement between Russia and Britain by joining one of them in an aggressive alliance against the other. Some British officials therefore saw it as inevitable that Britain would one day move into Afghanistan and establish her "scientific" frontier with Russia along the ranges of the Hindu Kush. That Britain never did so resulted in no small part from the Afghan rulers' skill in playing buffer-state politics and balancing Russia and Britain against each other.

In addition to its rugged terrain and the big-power rivalries, Afghan rulers counted on other assets in their dealings with their neighbors. One of these was the rise in the Islamic East of Pan-Islamism as an increasingly powerful challenge to domination by Christian imperialist powers. Both Russia and Britain had millions of Muslim subjects within their territories. Muslims in India and Central Asia were potential partisans of or at least sympathizers with the Afghans, and the destruction of Afghanistan by European powers might have led to serious repercussions in India and elsewhere. Afghan rulers, therefore, did all they could to propagate the image of themselves as "Islamic kings" and the defenders of the faith.

A similar source of strength for Afghan rulers was the existence in India of Afghan, or Pathan, tribes (these terms may be used interchangeably),[11] some of whom lived in semi-independence along the Indo-Afghan frontier. Afghan rulers considered this tribal belt to be Afghan territory; failing to gain it for Afghanistan, however, they wanted to see it established as a buffer zone between Afghanistan and India, a barrier to British penetration. Afghanistan, therefore, resisted British demands to sever relations with these Afghan tribes, and overtly or covertly they countered British measures of penetration of this area by their own measures of cultural and political penetration. These transborder Afghans were valuable allies in the event of Anglo-Afghan conflicts, for the amir's call for holy war, supported by financial and military assistance, could rally many of them against a British invader.

Finally, an important asset of Afghan rulers was that their country, poor as it was, was economically self-sufficient. Afghanistan was not burdened with any foreign debts; debts were unacceptable to Afghan rulers as a matter of principle.[12] The existence of a flourishing foreign trade merely meant a measure of prosperity; it was not vital to the survival of Afghanistan.[13] This economic self-sufficiency becomes apparent when one examines the use Afghan rulers made of the British subsidy. From the beginning Afghan rulers used the subsidy for the purchase of arms and ammunition, and for the machinery needed for their manufacture. Some money was also expended on projects of modernization, but none was needed to redress an unfavorable balance of trade or to provide services vital to the existence of Afghanistan. Furthermore, Afghan rulers kept large amounts of their subsidies deposited with the government of India. So large were these accounts that in 1903 Habibullah still held about 9 lakhs of rupees which were due his father and thus avoided the showdown that would have resulted by drawing on his own account of 24 lakhs, which Britain wanted to pay only after renegotiation of the Anglo-Afghan agreements.[14] Only after confirmation of the treaty in 1905 did Habibullah request 32 lakhs of an account that had risen to a total of 62.5 lakhs.[15] Finally, after the Third Afghan War, Amanullah was able to refuse the British subsidy when he felt that it would limit his power to conduct independent foreign relations.[16] In sum, it may be said that Afghanistan's economic position was not the kind likely to make the country vulnerable to economic pressures, such as an economic blockade or the stoppage of subsidy payments.

There existed, however, a number of internal Afghan factors that influenced Afghan rulers in the conduct of their relations with the outside world, and none of these was of greater importance than the Islamic sentiment of the Afghan people. Even so formidable a ruler as Abdur Rahman could not afford to disregard this sentiment. The "Iron Amir" had destroyed all his rivals, real or imaginary; he broke the power of the ulema and combined in his person the temporal and religious establishments. But there were limits even to his powers. Abdur Rahman could not permit even the merest suspicion that he had received his throne from the British, and he could show no friendship for either Russia or Britain which would exceed the limits of what was necessary in the national interest of Afghanistan. "If I showed any inclination towards the English," said Abdur Rahman in his biography, "my people would call me an infidel for joining hands with infidels, and they would proclaim a religious holy war against me." [17]

In the religious hierarchy the mullahs, the lowest sector, were a force the amir could not ignore. Following the concept of the Divine Ruler, the amir claimed the right to make final decisions in matters of religious interpretation. He reserved for himself the right to proclaim jihad, and he "nationalized" the waqf (*auqaf*), the religious endowments, thus making the higher religious officials dependent on the salary they received from the state. But he could not so easily control the lowest segments of this class, the wandering mullahs, who depended for their livelihood on the offerings of the pious and thus had preserved a certain amount of independence from the Afghan rulers. These mullahs were the perpetual preachers of jihad. They were often the tools of their amirs, but they were even prepared to turn against their king should he show any tendency of unwarranted friendliness toward Britain or Russia.[18]

Another factor, but merely of secondary importance in influencing Afghan foreign relations, was the existence of certain checks and balances within the ruling establishment of Afghanistan. The amir's Council of Advisers included men who held positions of power, the heads of the military and the religious sector, the courtiers, the members of the royal family, and others. This council was purely advisory during the time of Abdur Rahman, but it gained a certain measure of influence in subsequent years. Although the British at times wondered whether the amir was ruling the council or vice versa, it soon became apparent that he was not the captive of any clique.[19] There was also the Loe Jirgah, or Great Council, an assembly of tribal leaders and personalities from all parts of the country. It convened at times of national emergency, as for example for the declaration of war. Although it was no rubber-stamp assembly, experience has shown that the Amir always succeeded in winning it over to his point of view.[20]

During the reign of Habibullah there appeared a coalition of nationalistic forces which included, on the one hand, the "Young Afghans"—Afghan modernists, students, and some military and government officials at Kabul, who gravitated toward the personality of Sirdar Mahmud Tarzi, their chief propagandist and the editor of the *Sirāj al-Akhbār*—and, on the other hand, the traditional element, the mullahs and frontier tribes, who saw in Nasrullah, the Amir's brother, their protector and benefactor. The British soon dubbed this coalition the "war party" because of the inclination of its leaders to side with the Central Powers against Britain during World War I. This coalition put strong pressure on Habibullah, but it could not convince him (nor, perhaps, themselves) that Afghanistan should initiate a war against Britain without massive support from Germany and Turkey.

What mitigated the pressures exerted on the amir by his council, the war party, the "pro-British" element, or other potentially powerful groups was that their leaders belonged to the ruling establishment and therefore could not exceed certain limits if they did not want to run the risk of destroying themselves by destroying their ruler.

For various reasons, the commercial class in Afghanistan did not exert strong influence on the Afghan rulers in their relations with the outside world. First, part of the Afghan trade was in the hands of foreign merchants, who often possessed more capital than Afghans and had the inclination for that kind of occupation. It is true that trade (including smuggling) was one of the occupations of the Kutchis, the Afghan nomads, who during their yearly migrations traveled far into India, but their trade was, if important to them, not a vital factor in the Afghan economy. Second, Afghan rulers, after the time of Abdur Rahman, pursued a policy of economic self-sufficiency, often setting prohibitive customs rates to protect home industries or state monopolies. Foreign trade was therefore subject to erratic changes which were not conducive to the expansion of trade with Russia and India.[21]

Afghan rulers were not economists and, rather than strengthening trade, they often stifled it with such devices as state monopolies, excessive taxation, and the boycott of Anglo-Russian rail terminals at the Afghan frontiers. Afghan rulers were not hostile to trade; they merely seemed to prefer a poor Afghanistan which was their unchallenged domain to a state prospering with foreign trade, over which they might lose their control. Although the commercial class, such as it was in Afghanistan, was interested in peace, its feelings did not generally play an important role in influencing the amirs' decisions for war or peace.

Finally, the military class also was not able significantly to influence foreign political decisions. Afghan military commanders in the provinces were often checked by the amir's governors. The amir controlled the flow of new weapons and ammunition he purchased from abroad. Unlike the tribal armies of the border Afghans, the regular Afghan forces were often a pitiable lot.[22] The amir controlled the appointment of the highest military leaders, and it is surprising how quickly even they could be deposed or lose much of their influence. The fates of such high military commanders as

Abdul Kuddus Khan, Nadir Khan, and Saleh Muhammad illustrate this very well.

Like other Afghan groupings, the military as a class did not pose a serious challenge to the amirs' foreign political dealings. That the foreign policy of Afghan rulers was eminently successful was due in no small amount to the popularity it enjoyed among the Afghan people, especially the Pashtu-speaking majority, who gave it their wholehearted support. This popular support strengthened the amir in his dealings with Britain and Russia and made it impossible, without resorting to war, for foreigners to gain influence in Afghanistan. Often the deterrent to war with Afghanistan was the fact that the British, and at times also the Russians, feared a defeated and leaderless Afghanistan more than a hostile but neutral Afghan ruler.

The conduct of the foreign policy of Afghanistan was the exclusive right of the amir. Therefore, I examine in this study such tangible manifestations of Afghan policy as the correspondence of Afghan rulers, their pronouncements at court, their conversations and negotiations with officials of foreign powers, and last but not least their actions.

It is appropriate here to discuss briefly the available literature on Afghan foreign relations. It is hardly surprising that the great majority of sources are in English, written by Britishers whose country was so closely involved in the history of Afghanistan. There are diaries of veterans of the Afghan wars, accounts of world travelers and explorers, and writings about history, politics, geography, and other fields concerning Afghanistan. Russian writings appeared around the turn of the century and, like those of many British authors, they were often motivated by empire interests. German and French writings were stimulated by the events of World War I, the opening up of Afghanistan after the war, and by the arrival in 1923 of German and French representatives at Kabul.[23] Books in languages other than these draw heavily on sources in English.

This study of the trends in Afghan foreign policy from 1900 to 1923 was motivated by the fact that no comprehensive work on Afghanistan's foreign relations which draws on original sources and provides new information exists for this period. There is the excellent monograph by William Habberton, *Anglo-Russian Relations*

Concerning Afghanistan, 1837–1907, but as it was not based on archival material available in India, it stresses the policies of the two European powers and reflects Afghan policy merely on the basis of an occasional letter from the Afghan ruler. D. P. Singhal's *India and Afghanistan, 1876–1907,* a similar study of international relations, does not utilize material available in India; it tends for this reason to overemphasize the importance of the personality and character of certain statesmen.[24] Other works that utilize archival material in India, such as the books of D. K. Ghose, *England and Afghanistan,* and R. S. Rastogi, *Indo-Afghan Relations, 1880–1900,* deal with Anglo-Afghan relations only up to 1900. Sir Percy Sykes's *History of Afghanistan,* a standard text in view of its scope and structure, is at times incorrect or deals rather sketchily with the subject. W. K. Fraser-Tytler's excellent study, *Afghanistan,* is still a most reliable work, but it omits much of importance for *raisons d'etat.* Such works as the histories or handbooks by D. N. Wilber, *Afghanistan,* Arnold Fletcher, *Afghanistan: Highroad of Conquest,* and by Max Klimburg, *Afghanistan, das Land im historischen Spannungsfeld Mittelasiens,* are too large in scope to cover Afghan foreign relations in great detail.

Of Russian books there are the works of N. A. Dvoryankov *et al., Sovremennyy Afganistan;* L. B. Teplinskiy, *Sovetsko-Afganskiye Otnosheniya, 1919–1960;* M. G. Pikulin, *Afganistan: Ekonomicheskiy Ocherk;* N. A. Khalfin, *Proval Britanskoy Agressii v Afganistane;* and W. A. Romodin, *Istoriia Afganistana.* The last-named is an excellent work, but it and the other books are difficult to obtain. They also suffer from the fact that either they are not based on original archival sources or they are based on a conceptual framework in which the economic infrastructure is the determinant factor.[25]

The fact that no comprehensive study of Afghan foreign relations from 1900 to the mid-1920's has been undertaken is attributable mainly to the British regulation prescribing that foreign and political files of the British government remain secret for a period of fifty years. The archives up to 1922 are now open. In 1956 I received permission from the Ministry of External Affairs of the government of India to consult secret files up to 1923 from the National Archives of India in New Delhi. This material was supplemented from the files of the Foreign and Political Department of the India Office in London. For a clear and comprehensive view of German activities and relations with Afghanistan from 1914 to 1920, the political files of the Deutsche Auswaertige Amt have been examined. These German Foreign Office files are available in microfilm at the library of the University of Michigan and were obtained from that source. Some documents were obtained from the Hof- und Staatsarchiv in Vienna, Austria, but they were found to be also in the German political files.

This study is structured chronologically. Periods of foreign political crises and diplomatic confrontation were selected, and the course of a number of negotiations of the Afghans with representatives of Britain, Russia, and Germany are presented to reveal and define the workings of Afghanistan's foreign relations. Chapter 1 discusses the period of Abdur Rahman and defines the policy he instituted. Chapter 2 reviews Habibullah's struggle for British recognition; it further stresses the importance of the Russian Memorandum of 1900 which exerted great pressure on the Afghan ruler and set the stage for Anglo-Russian negotiations leading to a settlement over the head of the Amir of the "Afghanistan Question." Chapter 3 gives an account of the formulation of British demands from the Amir and describes the subsequent negotiations. New details of importance are brought out concerning Afghan willingness to conclude a defensive-offensive alliance with Britain. An illustration is also given of what was to become a familiar "technique of attrition" by which the Afghans successfully frustrated the British in endless negotiations, confronting them with the alternative of either acquiescing to Afghan demands or resorting to an ultimatum to force the Afghans to accept the British point of view. Since Britain was often unable to threaten military action, the Afghans enjoyed an advantage that balanced to some extent their inadequate bargaining powers. Chapter 4 concentrates on the hitherto neglected Afghan reaction to the Anglo-Russian Convention of 1907. Events in Afghanistan are examined to show that from 1907 until the beginning of World War I nothing had changed in Afghan foreign policy. Chapter 5 gives an account of the so-called Niedermayer expedition, its activities in Afghanistan, and its effects on Afghan foreign relations. Chapter 6 discusses the Third Anglo-Afghan War, but it is beyond the scope of this study to examine in detail the course of the war. Chapter 7 describes the events subsequent to the Third Anglo-Afghan War, the Mussoorie Conference, and the final settlement culminating in the Treaty of Kabul of 1921.

The system employed for the transliteration of foreign words avoids the use of phonetic symbols or diacritical marks. Foreign words listed in *Webster's Third New International Dictionary* are written as they appear there.

1. Abdur Rahman

BUILDING A NATION

When the British in 1880 reluctantly and with serious misgivings recognized Abdur Rahman as Amir of Kabul, Anglo-Afghan relations were burdened with the legacy of two wars, the loss of life and property and the ill will and distrust that resulted. Russia was extending her influence in Central Asia, soon to impinge on Afghan territory, and the stage was set for the battle of the Hindu Kush as the ultimate "scientific frontier" between the Russian and British Empires.

The new Amir was, to a certain extent, the creature of the two rivaling empires. He owed much of his political training and his understanding of power politics to almost twelve years of exile in Russian Turkestan. He ascended the throne with the sanction of both Britain and Russia. Russia permitted Abdur Rahman to establish himself in northern Afghanistan.[1] Lord Lytton, in a reversal of his forward policy, wanted to withdraw the British troops from their increasingly precarious occupation of southeastern Afghanistan and offered Abdur Rahman the entire country with the exception of Herat, which was to be ceded to Persia,[2] and Kandahar, which was to become an independent amirate under the protection of Britain.[3]

In his first pronouncement of foreign relations, Abdur Rahman conveyed to Lepel Griffin, chief British political officer in Afghanistan, his hopes for the country, saying:

> . . . as long as your Empire and that of Russia exist, my countrymen, the tribes of Afghanistan, should live quietly in ease and peace; and that these two States should find us true and faithful; and that we should rest at peace between them: for my tribesmen are unable to struggle with Empires, and are ruined by want of commerce; and we hope of your friendship that, sympathizing with and assisting the people of Afghanistan, you will place them under the honorable pro-

tection of the two Powers. This would redound to the credit of both, would give peace to Afghanistan, and quiet and comfort to God's people. This is my wish: for the rest it is yours to decide.[4]

But an independent Afghanistan under Anglo-Russian guarantees was not what Britain desired. Disturbed about the security of her possessions in India, Britain in 1869 had already extracted an assurance from Russia that Afghanistan was outside her sphere of influence. This assurance, later known as the Granville-Gorchakoff Agreement, was reiterated on a number of occasions.[5] To permit Russia to become a party to the Afghan settlement was therefore not acceptable to Britain.

In his correspondence with Abdur Rahman, Lepel Griffin gave assurances that Britain had no desire to interfere in the internal affairs of Afghanistan, but conceded it might be advisable that a Muslim agent of the British government should reside at Kabul. As for British policy toward Afghanistan, Griffin stated:

> ... since the British Government admits no right of interference by Foreign Powers within Afghanistan, and since both Russia and Persia [6] are pledged to abstain from all interference with the affairs of Afghanistan, it is plain that Your Highness can have no political relations with any Foreign Power except with the British Government. If any Foreign Power should attempt to interfere in Afghanistan, and if such interference should lead to unprovoked aggression on the dominions of Your Highness, in that event the British Government would be prepared to aid you, to such extent and in such manner as may appear to the British Government necessary, in repelling it: provided that Your Highness follows unreservedly the advice of the British Government in regard to your external relations.[7]

British policy had gradually changed during the negotiations between Griffin and Abdur Rahman from the originally planned unconditional surrender of the country to an Afghan ruler to the attachment of conditions for the control of Afghanistan's relations with foreign powers.[8] Abdur Rahman showed himself not at all anxious to accept the Kabul throne from the British, nor did he accept the British proposal to divide his country. Britain had already set a date for evacuation of her troops, and the increasing pressure of Afghan tribal forces threatened to make the withdrawal a somewhat undignified affair.[9] This was especially so when, after recognizing

Abdur Rahman as Amir of the country, the British troops of General G. R. S. Burrows were defeated at the Battle of Maywand on July 27, 1880, and Shir Ali, the British-imposed Amir of Kandahar, was forced into Indian exile. Abdur Rahman used the opportunity to extend his power over the whole of Afghanistan; he defeated Ayyub Khan, and by the end of 1881 he was in control of the entire country.[10]

Britain did not want to conclude a formal treaty with the Amir and merely indicated in two letters of June and July, 1880, her policy of supporting an independent ruler in Afghanistan and defending him from outside aggression, provided that the Amir had foreign relations only with the government of India. A letter of June 22, 1880, contained the Amir's reply and acceptance, in somewhat modified form, of the British conditions. These three letters constitute the Anglo-Afghan Agreement of 1880.[11] To strengthen the Amir against internal and external enemies, the government of India granted him, in 1882, a subsidy of 12 lakhs of rupees.[12]

Russian advances in Central Asia led to Anglo-Russian negotiations and the final demarcation of the Afghan border from Zulfikar to Khwaja Salih in an agreement ratified in 1887.[13] Russia solved a territorial dispute with Afghanistan over the Panjdeh district in March, 1885, by forcefully occupying the area. The fact that Britain did not live up to her obligation of assisting Afghanistan against this aggression has not been forgotten by subsequent Afghan rulers.

Afghanistan's northeastern boundary was demarcated with the assistance of Sir Mortimer Durand in 1893. At that time Afghanistan lost the northern provinces of Shignan and Rushan while she gained the cis-Oxus province of Darwaz and the unwanted Wakhan Corridor. The Indo-Afghan boundary was also defined, and, to overcome some of the Amir's opposition, his subsidy was increased by 6 lakhs of rupees. (For the administration of the Wakhan province, the Amir was given an additional sum of half a lakh of rupees in 1897.) Demarcation of the Indo-Afghan boundary was left to a later, mutually satisfactory settlement. The Amir was further assured that the government of India would raise no objection to the purchase and import by the Amir of arms and ammunitions. These assurances were incorporated in the Agreements of 1893 which were signed by Sir Mortimer Durand and the Amir of Afghanistan.

FORMULATION OF A FOREIGN POLICY

Abdur Rahman knew he owed his kingdom to the fact that two empires were approaching the borders of Afghanistan, and that he was set up to keep them apart. Russia had, at a time when she had not yet reached the banks of the Oxus, agreed to recognize this river as the southern limit of her sphere of interest. Britain, finding direct control over Afghanistan expensive and difficult, was willing to accept an independent, strong—though not too strong—Afghanistan as a barrier to conflict with Russia. Britain expected to control Afghanistan indirectly, by penetrating the country peacefully and establishing an influence over the Amir, her subordinate ally. But the policies of two empires, decisions of war and peace, and, in the end, the fate of India depended on the goodwill and cooperation of Abdur Rahman. The Afghan ruler's foreign political task was therefore clear: the preservation of an independent Afghanistan as a buffer state between two powerful imperialistic empires. Abdur Rahman knew that the powers that agreed to a buffer between their territories could also agree to divide the country; the existence of an independent buffer was desirable at that time, but not vital to his neighbors.

An Afghan foreign policy could soon be discerned, implicitly in the Amir's actions and explicitly in his pronouncements at durbar and in his writings. The pillars of this policy were: (1) assertion of national independence, (2) insistence on isolationism, and (3) promotion of a balance of power.

Assertion of National Independence

Abdur Rahman had always considered himself the independent ruler of an independent Afghanistan, subject to no interference by any foreign power in the internal affairs of his country and guided solely by his personal interest, which he equated with Afghanistan's national interest. "Abdur Rahman, Padshah of Afghanistan, by his own will and that of his own independent tribes," as he called himself defiantly in some of his letters to the government of India,[14] always disputed the claims of British Indian officials that it was they who put him on the throne of Afghanistan and gave him his country.¹⁵ Indeed, the British action was no more than a recognition of the de facto situation.¹⁶

Abdur Rahman soon began to interpret his contractual obligation not to have foreign relations with any power other than Britain to mean that he could conduct neighborly relations with others, provided he informed the government of India and sought its advice. Later, Abdur Rahman insisted that, after seeking the advice of the government of India, he could make his own, independent decision on the matter at hand.¹⁷

The Amir also did not see in the fact that he received British assistance an infringement of his sovereignty or independence. He saw the British subsidy as the result of an alliance in which the two partners cooperated in their common interest: the protection of their territories from Russian aggression. Afghanistan provided the manpower and Britain the arms and equipment.¹⁸ Abdur Rahman was nobody's servant. To Griffin he wrote in 1880: "I desire nothing in lieu of services rendered, nor do I demand favours in exchange for duties performed. But I have my claims on the desire of the Afghan nation." ¹⁹ When the British government presented the Grand Cross of the Order of Bath to the Amir, he objected to the word *khedmat* (service) in the accompanying document and wanted the order given in recognition of his friendship with Britain.²⁰ Furthermore, he preserved his independence in the use of his subsidy and gifts of arms and money. From the beginning (i.e., 1883) he disregarded British demands that he pay the salaries of his troops in Herat from his subsidy; he continued to use the money for the purchase of arms.²¹ Toward the end of his rule, the Amir became increasingly insistent on having his ambassador at the Court of St. James and representatives in various Muslim countries.²²

When the international picture began to change at the end of the century and Russia pressed for direct relations of a nonpolitical nature with her neighbor, Abdur Rahman increasingly maintained that he reserved the right to decide for himself whether or not he should accept the advice of the Viceroy.²³ The Amir sent emissaries to various Muslim countries, ostensibly on commercial missions, and maintained commercial representatives in Meshed, Bukhara, and Peshawar who were de facto representatives of Afghanistan.²⁴

Abdur Rahman united Afghanistan and kept all power and

authority in his hands. He soon set up a network of spies to keep him informed on the state of affairs in his country. Abdur Rahman created the prerequisites of a modern state; he negotiated definite boundaries for his state, and he established himself as the absolute ruler over his people. At a time when the technology of warfare could not yet surmount the barriers of a rugged terrain, it was possible for the Amir to arm his people into a force that posed a certain deterrent to outside aggression.

The Amir used, therefore, the larger part of his subsidy and the income he derived from his provinces for the purchasing of arms and the strengthening of his defenses. The Afghan desire for arms is proverbial, and no one will dispute Mahmud Tarzi's claim that "the Afghans in general and the frontier Afghans in particular have a deep love for arms, so much so that they dispose of their ploughs, bullocks and land to buy arms." [25] The Amir was no less an Afghan in this respect. In 1880 he had already demanded and obtained arms from the government of India to fight Ayyub Khan at Kandahar and to consolidate his power over Afghanistan.[26] From the beginning, Abdur Rahman insisted that Britain was under treaty obligation to assist Afghanistan with grants of arms and military equipment to be used for their common protection against Russian attack. But it was noted in India that some of the weapons and outdated guns, which were replaced with British assistance, tended to appear at the Indian frontier. British officials in India and England feared that an irredentist Afghanistan would one day use these arms to force Britain to make territorial concessions.[27] The frontier tribes, which were already difficult to control in spite of their antiquated weapons, might get a new impetus in their raiding propensities and prove intractable in their dealings with British frontier officials.

The government of India was, therefore, reluctant to lose all control over the import of arms into Afghanistan; the Amir, on his part, insisted that he required the weapons for his own safety and that of his allies in India. The oft-mentioned greed of Afghan rulers, which seemed a reassuring sign to British Indian officials, who hoped to solve all problems with money, appears to have been nothing but a manifestation of a vital need for arming the country for "an evil day." Unlike other Oriental potentates, the amirs of Afghanistan lived on a rather modest scale and devoted their incomes to the purchase of arms which they considered essential for their survival.

Insistence on Isolationism

The most prominent feature in Abdur Rahman's foreign relations soon appeared to be a consistent policy of isolationism. His agreement with Griffin isolated him from Persia and Russia and left the door for political relations open only to Britain. The government of India expected that a grateful Amir would be receptive to British guidance in matters not necessarily confined to foreign affairs, and that their effort of containing a common foe would lead to the kind of peaceful penetration so often resulting from an alliance of unequal partners. It was Abdur Rahman's achievement to resist the "friendly embrace," to prevent British influence from getting a hold in his domain without going to the point of provoking Britain to destroy her reluctant ally. His success in maintaining this unequal alliance by isolating himself from his partner was a main factor in the Amir's preservation of his independence.

In his agreement with Britain, Abdur Rahman accepted a Muslim representative at Kabul. He wrote to Griffin: "The Envoy which you have appointed in Afghanistan you have dispensed with, but what you have left to my wish is, that I may keep a Mussulman Ambassador, if I please. This was my desire and that of my people, and this you have kindly granted."[28] But in his circular letter to the tribes of Afghanistan, dated June 22, 1880, he misquoted Griffin's letter as saying: "No envoy will be maintained in Afghanistan by the British Government, but if at any time you wish to have one, a Muhammadan, he shall be sent to you; as long as you do not wish one, no one shall be sent on behalf of the British Government and there shall be no pressing about this matter."[29] As it turned out, the Amir did not wish to have one, and the British government began pressing him about it. As early as November, 1880, Sir Alfred Lyall, Secretary to the government of India, proposed sending a Muslim envoy to Kabul, and the Viceroy wrote to the Amir in March, 1881, suggesting a certain Muhammad Afzal Khan for this post (he was an intermediary in the Abdur Rahman–Griffin negotiations). The Amir accepted, but asked the government of India to wait until he had returned to Kabul from Kandahar. In October, 1881, the Viceroy again suggested that an agent, this time Mir Hashim Khan, be sent to Kabul. The Amir objected and requested that Afzal Khan be sent. But the Afghan Envoy in India suggested another delay, one of the reasons given being that "His Highness had one or more executions in hand" and was afraid that the British Agent would report the proceedings to India. It was not until June, 1882, that Colonel Muhammad Afzal Khan arrived in Kabul.[30]

If Afzal Khan expected to enjoy the status of ambassador of a friendly power at the court of the Amir, he was immediately disappointed. From the beginning the Amir isolated the Agent from the Afghan people. He did not even permit two of the Agent's brothers who were living in Kabul to receive him on his arrival at court. And when the Agent complained to the Amir about being a virtual prisoner in Kabul, Abdur Rahman did not hide his motives, saying, "Yes, certainly I have prohibited them [to have intercourse with you], and I do not wish that there should be two Darbars, one at my house and another at your place. As the late Amir Shir Ali allowed this, he was ruined."[31]

Subsequent agents did not fare better; they were restricted in their movements, were inadequately housed, and were not even permitted to establish contact with the British subjects residing in Kabul.[32] The agency maintained a hospital that was open to the Amir's subjects and could have been a valuable means of collecting news and intelligence, but the Amir did not generally permit his officers and soldiers to visit the hospital.[33] The Amir maintained a guard at the agency gates, and the British Agent was usually escorted or kept under surveillance by Afghan soldiers. The Amir claimed that this was for the Agent's protection and offered to remove the guards if the Agent would give him a statement in writing that the Amir would not be responsible for any harm that might result to the mission.[34] The problem of the British Agent could not be solved since the Amir never permitted him to be an important factor of British influence in Afghanistan.[35] Abdur Rahman conveniently pointed to the fate of Cavagnari, the British representative at Kabul who, together with the members of his mission, were killed by Afghans in 1879, and the Amir's argument seemed plausible if not honest.

Another factor of isolation from his British ally was the Amir's refusal to admit British troops and officers or to permit such strategically important means of warfare as railroads or telegraph lines within his country. The Russian occupation of Merv in 1884 had already stimulated the British to expand their railroad into the North-West Frontier,[36] and during the Amir's visit to Rawalpindi in the same year Lord Dufferin asked the Amir whether he would be inclined to favor the construction of a railroad from Kandahar to Herat. The Amir replied that he fully appreciated the advantages of such an undertaking, and would like to promote it, but thought that for the time being it would not be understood by his people. He hoped, however, to link his chief cities by rail sometime in the future.[37]

In a letter on July 20, 1887, Lord Dufferin told the Amir that he

> ... will merely observe that on many occasions Your Highness has shown a jealousy of our officers, a distrust of our intentions and an unwillingness to comply with our suggestions which was hardly consistent either with the kindness we have shown you or the friendship you profess towards us. You have even neglected my advice with regard to so slight a matter as the establishment of a telegraph between your capital and Peshawar, though it is evident that it would be very much to your advantage to be able to communicate quickly to me your wishes in relation to any difficulties which may arise between yourself and your neighbours.[38]

The Amir either ignored such letters or pleaded that innovations like railroads and telegraphs were unaminously opposed by his people. He protested the planned extension of the British railroad to Chaman as "leading to no good."[39] And when the New Chaman railroad was constructed, the Amir threatened with death any of his subjects using this section of the line.[40] His boycott was immediately successful in reducing by two-thirds the volume of goods shipped.[41]

Anglo-Afghan differences in this matter were again aired in a voluminous correspondence in 1899. The Amir reported on January 9 that the Russian commander of the Ashkhabad forces had sent the "good tidings" of the coming of the Russian railroad to Tanurah (Kushk). To the Amir this was bad news, and he urged the Viceroy that a "systematic arrangement" be made to protect him from Russian aggression. In his answer, Lord Curzon asked sarcastically in what respect the arrangements lacked system: whether it was in respect to railways or telegraphs, which had so long been recommended to the Amir. In a subsequent letter the Viceroy discounted the Amir's argument that Afghanistan was not sufficiently wealthy for constructing such facilities by saying that the cost of a telegraph line was very small.[42] He also contradicted the Amir's statements that other nations had suffered much evil and sustained heavy losses through such equipment by saying that, on the contrary, those countries that had refused railroads and telegraphs had grown weak because they could not move their troops quickly in the event of an emergency.

The Amir resisted the introduction of modern technology mainly because he feared it might result in the influx of large numbers of foreigners into his country. He also did not permit British military advisers or British troops to be stationed within his domain. When in times of crisis, such as the Ghilzay rebellion in 1887 or the revolt of Ishaq Khan in 1888, he proclaimed that British troops were waiting at the border for his call to come to his aid, it was obvious that his purpose was only to warn his enemies and that he would sanction the use of foreign troops in his country only when his possession of Afghanistan was seriously threatened.[43]

When he permitted the British Boundary Commission to proceed to Afghanistan in 1884, the Amir insisisted on curbing the size of the group,[44] and at first he did not accept Lord Dufferin's offer to use Sir Peter Lumsden and his officers to inspect Herat. Lord Dufferin complained that there was no precedent in the history of a small state accepting military aid from his neighbor but rejecting his officers. Abdur Rahman's only concession was that in case of war he would accept the stationing of two British officers in Herat.[45] In 1892 when Britain urged that he receive a British mission under Lord Roberts, the Amir suffered a series of "diplomatic ailments" that lasted longer than Roberts' assignment in India. The Amir explained in his biography that he would require a hundred thousand men to protect this general of the Second Afghan War and his escort of ten thousand troops.[46] The success of Sir Mortimer Durand's mission to Afghanistan in 1893 was in no small measure due to his decision to enter Afghanistan without any escort and as the guest of the Amir.[47]

Abdur Rahman did not seem to be unduly concerned over the xenophobia of his people and even reinforced it on occasion by publishing calls to vigilance and instructions on the obligations of jihad.[48] Lord Dufferin protested such proceedings in 1888 saying, "One would suppose that you were conferring a great favour in allowing the Government of India to spend sums of money . . . in demarcating your frontier. . . . But your mind is so constantly occupied by the idea of asserting your independence of all control in internal affairs, that you see interference in every British action."[49]

Promotion of a Balance of Power

By the end of the century it was possible to recognize a systematic Afghan foreign policy from the Amir's actions and pronouncements and, above all, from statements in his biography, which is his political testament. To Abdur Rahman the power-political situation was clear:

Russia was the more aggressive of his two neighbors. She wanted to see the Ottoman Empire, Persia, and Afghanistan destroyed to gain access to the sea.

Britain saw Russian intentions as a threat to her overseas possessions and a dangerous disturbance of the international balance of power. To contain Russian expansion, Britain had an interest in the existence of strong Islamic states along Russia's southern borders.

Therefore, the Islamic states, trying to preserve their independence, had a community of interest with Great Britain and should seek her alliance.

But since Britain was also an absorbing power which might respond to Russian aggression by helping herself to a portion of the land of the Islamic states, a "middle course" policy was required: an alliance with Britain, but not one that would lead to integration; hostility to Russia, but not to an extent as would result in provoking aggression; preservation of an equilibrium which would permit Afghanistan to remain independent if not neutral.

Abdur Rahman's relations with the more or less independent Muslim populations of the East were influenced by Pan-Islamic considerations. Since Afghanistan was one of the few remaining Muslim states which had not fallen under direct foreign control, the captive Muslims in Central Asia and India were looking to her for support and would be her allies if called to jihad. And by virtue of his position as the Islamic King, the Amir would try to maintain his influence over them and attempt to create tribal buffer states between Afghanistan and her powerful neighbors. Afghanistan had legitimate rights for expansion into these areas if a change in the international situation made this possible. To gain strength and to give strength to others, Afghanistan had to promote the causes of Pan-Islamism.

Abdur Rahman acquired his opinion about Russian intentions during his long Central Asian exile. To him, Russian policy was essentially that "rightly or wrongly, friendly or unfriendly, with peace or war, the Islamic kingdoms should be washed away from the face of the Asiatic continent." [50] Russia wanted to absorb and swallow Persia, Turkey, and Afghanistan, or she would try to obtain their friendship and draw them to herself. Failing in this effort, she would arouse them against Britain, with the result that in the ensuing hostilities Russia might assist the British in crushing them and dividing their countries between herself and Britain.[51]

Through his contact with Russian officials, Abdur Rahman was convinced that Russia intended to attack India. He claimed he saw Russian soldiers "jumping for joy at the idea that they might one day have a hand in plundering this rich country," and he thought Russia was quite satisfied when Britain responded to Russian aggression by merely helping herself to some territorial gain. Russia expected that an attack on India would be accompanied by a general uprising in that country, followed by a quick Russian victory, since Britain, as a sea power, was no match for Russia on land.[52]

By contrast, the Amir declared British policy fickle: "The ideas and notions of any statesman or leader who is in power in England, become, for the time being, the policy of the empire" to be changed when someone else is in charge of decisions. At least, Abdur Rahman saw one continuous trend, "namely, that the Islamic Governments, which are a barrier and strong wall between India and Asiatic Russia, should exist and have their independence strongly maintained, to continue as a strong barrier wall in the way of Russian advance towards India." [53] The Amir proposed the establishment of an Islamic alliance among Turkey, Persia, and Afghanistan, which would separate the two empires, "neither allowing Russia nor

England to take any part of our dominions." The Muslim states would then support those of their neighbors who respected their integrity and independence.[54]

The Amir declared that Afghanistan could lean on British support because she had no expansionist intentions that would require her to traverse Afghanistan. On the other hand, the friendship of Afghanistan was of no value to Russia unless she permitted Russia passage to India. Britain had arms and money and needed only Afghan fighting men, whereas Afghanistan had enough men but needed arms and money. It was therefore clear that Britain and Afghanistan were complementary. The Amir blamed Britain for not realizing this. Britain never ceased to ask herself whether Afghanistan's friendship was of any use or not, or whether the Afghans could be trusted and whether the benefits of their friendship compensated for the responsibility of protecting Afghanistan. Also, would Parliament authorize the decisions of India, and would the future British government agree to previous arrangements?[55] The Amir deplored that Britain never failed to extend her influence toward the Afghan border. He admitted that he had gained more by Britain's friendship than he had lost, but he maintained "though England does not want any piece of Afghanistan (as she constantly claims) still she never loses a chance of getting one—and this friend has taken more than Russia has!"[56] Since neither Russia nor Britain could take all of Afghanistan without arousing the hostility of the other, the Amir considered the presence of two powerful neighbors as not altogether a bad thing. He felt that although "these neighbours are a cause of much anxiety to Afghanistan yet, as they are pulling against each other, they are no less an advantage and protection for Afghanistan than a danger [and indeed] a great deal of the safety of the Afghan Government depends upon the fact that neither of these two neighbours can bear to allow the other to annex an inch of Afghan territory."[57]

The Amir's policy with regard to transborder Muslim populations was that they should be independent, if not under his influence, and serve as buffers between Afghanistan and his imperialistic neighbors. Although the Afghan borders were generally closed to Europeans, Afghan merchants crossed into Russian Turkestan, and thousands of Afghans moved seasonally into India.[58] They were the eyes and ears of Afghanistan, a significant factor in trade, and an important factor in arming the frontier with contraband arms. Since they lived under Christian rulers, the transborder tribes—especially on the Indian frontier—recognized Abdur Rahman as the Islamic king who should be obeyed in certain matters and whose call to jihad should be followed.

2. Habibullah

ACCESSION TO POWER AND CONSOLIDATION

The government of India was soon disillusioned with Abdur Rahman. It felt that it did not receive a fair return for its obligation of protecting the Amir from foreign aggression. His policy of isolationism and resistance to British penetration, which was first manifested in the liquidation of collaborators and spies of the British no less than those of Russia, and his attempts to spread his influence in the independent tribal areas were increasingly resented.[1] Ever since Abdur Rahman had crossed into Afghanistan in 1880 there were rumors that he was intriguing with Russia and in secret alliance with her. It was therefore not long before India felt that a more active forward policy was required to guarantee British interests and the defense of India. In Lord Lansdowne's government voices were heard advocating harsher treatment of the Amir.[2] Britain's moves, it was argued, should be guided by strategic and political needs, and not by the feelings of the Amir; it also was suggested that "it would for many reasons be safer and more advantageous to have a declared enemy than a secret one on the throne of Kabul."[3] But the "anomaly" of Anglo-Afghan relations was finally permitted to last for the duration of the Amir's life which was approaching a natural end on October 3, 1901.[4]

When Abdur Rahman had fallen ill previously, in October, 1894, contingency plans were worked out by the government of India in preparation for the Amir's death. Lord Curzon, in a memorandum of December, 1898, suggested that his son Habibullah, Abdur Rahman's choice for succession, was acceptable, but no pledge should be given by the government of India unless this was demanded by Abdur Rahman. British troops should, however, be prepared to move on Jalalabad in support of Habibullah if he should ask for such assistance. Afghan sirdars in British exile were to be kept under supervision.⁵ Should Habibullah succeed to the throne, the Russian government was to be told that from an international point of view Afghanistan remained in the same position as before. Since British engagements with Abdur Rahman were personal, new and substantially changed ones must be concluded.⁶ The home government accepted Lord Curzon's suggestions, including the proposal that a mission be sent to Kabul to arrange for a new agreement with Habibullah.

As to the conditions for continued support of the new ruler, the government of India in 1891 had suggested such measures as the rectification of the Afghan boundary in the area of Chaman and Shurawak and the evacuation of Chageh by the Afghans; the obtaining of facilities for railroad expansion, whenever it might become desirable, toward Kandahar and to Jalalabad; the establishment of a British officer at some convenient point near the Russian border; the construction of telegraph lines; and the removal of obstacles to commerce between Afghanistan and India.⁷

The Intelligence Branch of the government of India suggested in a note of July 22, 1901, that the following guarantees be obtained from the new Amir:

1. Rectification of the Indo-Afghan frontier for strategic purposes.

2. Arrangements for obtaining information regarding affairs in Afghanistan generally, such as movements of troops, distribution and strength of the army and its organization, and armament and equipment.

3. Control of the supply of arms in Afghanistan, and some guarantees that they would not be used against India.

4. Improvement of communications from India to Kandahar and Kabul, and information regarding roads and routes all over Afghanistan.

5. Real, as well as nominal, withdrawal of support from the tribesmen on the British side of the border with a view to their more speedy pacification and reduction of military garrisons on the frontier.

6. The deputation of British officers to assist in the preparation of schemes of defense against the Russians.

To this sanguine assessment of the needs of the time, E. W. S. K.

Maconchy, of the Department of Military Intelligence, added that the Amir might invite the British, either spontaneously or through a little coercion, to assist him in the organization of his military forces. If the Amir would do so, the Afghan army could be turned into a force similar to the Imperial Service troops in India, which would have Afghan officers with British counterparts as advisers. Most members of the Viceroy's council were skeptical about the probability of the Amir agreeing to integrate his armed forces in such a manner, but they agreed that the other suggestions were acceptable.[8]

Habibullah acceded to the throne without any difficulties; khutbah was read in his name on October 4, 1901, and the new Amir informed Britain of his father's death and his own accession to power. The Secretary of State was wary and he warned the Viceroy not to use this opportunity for a forward move on the frontier. The government of India sent condolences to Kabul but nevertheless hinted that a mission would be required to meet with the Amir to confirm the previous arrangements. Russia was informed that the death of Abdur Rahman brought no change in the status quo.[9]

In his reply, dated October 31, the Amir ignored the British hint, saying that he reciprocated the Viceroy's desire for even closer and more secure relations between India and Afghanistan, and promised that he would maintain the terms of the agreement made by his father with the British government "so long as the illustrious British Government firmly adhere to them."[10]

The government of India waited until February 7, 1902, when Lord Curzon again urged in a letter that a friendly discussion was necessary so that the alliance might continue even stronger. But the Amir considered the Agreement of 1880 quite strong enough and he reiterated that he would abide by it. He saw no need for revisions or amplifications and expressed the hope that nothing of the kind was intended. A visit to India, as suggested by the Viceroy, was desirable to prove to the world the existing friendship between the two countries, but the Amir felt himself unable to accept it at that time.[11]

Curzon was more blunt in his letter of June 6, and proceeded to specify some of the matters of "great portent" about which he wanted to talk with the Amir. He said that the late Amir had at times misinterpreted the agreement and, therefore, he wanted to know the new Amir's interpretation. The Viceroy claimed he did not mention the terms of the Agreement of 1880 because that agreement was personal and did not necessarily apply to the Amir's sons and successors; hence, neither a subsidy nor protection could be claimed by Habibullah until a new arrangement had been concluded.[12]

But the Amir remained stubborn. In his letters of November 27 and December 9, 1902, he replied that he could not leave Kabul owing to difficulties in settling the affairs of his kingdom. Habibullah complained of the Viceroy's insistence and said that, since it was not necessary to renew the alliance at the death of Queen Victoria, it was unnecessary to take such action now at the death of his father. He also demanded to know why the ammunition and military stores which he had ordered and paid for were detained by the government of India, and he showed himself disappointed that instead of generously helping Afghanistan during this crucial period the Viceroy threatened to withhold the Amir's subsidy.[13] Lord Curzon resented the Amir's attempt to gain time and he considered his arguments as neither quite candid nor respectful, but since there was "no hint of rupture or inclination to form new connections" on the part of the Amir, the Viceroy was willing to wait, especially since the Amir accepted a mission under A. H. McMahon to settle the Sistan dispute between Persia and Afghanistan.[14]

RUSSIAN PRESSURES ON AFGHANISTAN

The British position in 1902-1903 with regard to the Afghan ruler was rendered more delicate by the fact that British pressure on Afghanistan was offset by a new forward movement of Russia. The Russian Memorandum of 1900 was a direct challenge to Britain and her policy of isolating Afghanistan from Russian relations.

On February 6, 1900, M. Lesar, Secretary at the Russian Embassy in London, communicated to Lord Salisbury a memorandum on Russo-Afghan relations which said:

> Russo-Afghan relations have been defined by the Arrangements of 1872 and 1873, which Russia regards as still being in effect and as placing Afghanistan entirely outside her sphere of action. Although Russia's obligations only bind her to refrain from political action, she has, except in the case of transient deviation from the correct standard

of diplomatic action, consented in the past, from a feeling of friendly interest toward Great Britain, to forego even non-political relations. This attitude was formerly possible without material loss to Russian interests, but the situation has now become entirely abnormal owing to the creation in 1885 of a coterminous Russo-Afghan frontier of several hundred versts in extent, and to the completion of the Trans-Caspian Railway. The regular course of communications and business between limitrophe Powers can only be maintained "sous la fixation précise de leurs rapports réciproques," and the absence of such an organization creates an atmosphere of uneasiness and mistrust bound eventually to lead to regrettable complications. Moreover, attempts to settle questions by means of a reference to the British Government have proved abortive. The moment would accordingly appear to have come when a definite step should be taken in the regularization of these relations, and the Imperial Government considered it its duty to inform the Cabinet of London that it "regarde comme indispensable le réetablissement des rapports directs entre la Russie et l'Afghanistan. Pour ce qui concerne les affaires de frontière les rapports n'auront aucun charactére politique.[15]

Russian action followed, when on February 22, 1900, V. Ignatieff, Russian Political Agent at Bukhara, wrote to an Afghan trading agent in Bukhara. In answering to Afghan questions on the meaning of certain movements of troops in Trans-Caspia, he said that they had taken place in order to test the capacity of the railroad, and he added that they had attracted attention mainly because they occurred at a time when Britain "was suffering continual reverses, which still continue, in her war with the little State of the Transvaal." Ignatieff further noted that, from the time the boundaries between Russia and Afghanistan were fixed, no disagreements had arisen between the two countries. In conclusion he said he sincerely desired that his letter might be the first step toward the establishment of direct and friendly relations between Russia and Afghanistan and help to open up Afghanistan territory to mutual trade, which previously had been confined to petty trade at frontier posts. He hoped for some communication from the Afghans, which he promised to transmit to St. Petersburg.[16]

The government of India noted that Russia's admission that Afghanistan was outside her sphere of influence of action was renewed many times (1874, 1876, 1877, 1878, 1882, 1884, 1885, 1887, and 1888) and held that "rarely, if ever, has a formal and voluntary engagement been invested, by dint of constant reiteration, with greater solemnity or a more binding force."[17] The Russian reason for change, the claim of the inadequacy of British mediation efforts, was limited, according to Indian opinion, only to one such case—the Bosaga Canal incident in 1891 in which Russia's spontaneous action was to blame. It was feared that establishment of commercial relations with Afghanistan might lead to the establishment of a Russian agent at Kabul, and, if this agent were insulted, it would be a political injury, and the government of India was "most unwilling that Russia should incur this risk and its possible consequences."[18]

There followed a series of diplomatic discussions in which Britain wanted Russia to explain her intentions in order to ascertain if a mutually satisfactory solution could be found. On November 30, 1900, Sir Charles S. Scott, the British Ambassador at St. Petersburg, was instructed to mention to Count Lamsdorff the subject of Ignatieff's letter, and to state that the Amir had complained about its communication. After initially characterizing the letter as highly improper," the Russian Foreign Minister attempted to justify it as written in response to a question from the Amir's agent. The discussions continued, and on January 29, 1902, Scott was instructed to make the verbal declaration that "His Majesty's Government did not wish to contend that there was no force in the Russian arguments for direct communications on matters of local detail, but that, as having charge of Afghan foreign relations, they held that arrangements for the purpose could only be made with their consent." It was left to Russia to formulate proposals as to the change of the status quo and to give guarantees that any relations would remain of a nonpolitical character.

On December 19, 1902, the *Novoe Vremya* of St. Petersburg published a communique issued by the Russian Foreign Office, which read, in part:

> In regard to our relations to Afghanistan, it must be remarked that in this matter we made no request to the London Cabinet, but that we merely intimated our decision to enter into direct relations with Afghanistan in consequence of altered circumstances. No further explanations have taken place on this subject.[19]

The Russian Foreign Minister argued that it was impossible for Russia to be bound by old assurances given under different circumstances. He considered it hardly compatible with the dignity of an independent power to bind itself forever by engagements with another power placing limitations on its legitimate intercourse with a neighboring country.

An impasse had thus been reached: if the British government permitted direct relations between Russia and Afghanistan, the raison d'etre of its Afghanistan policy would no longer exist. On the other hand, it was both ineffective and impossible to demand that Russia should deal with the government of India in such matters of a nonpolitical character as the theft of a few sheep by Afghans.

Russia's diplomatic offensive was soon supported by action resulting in a series of incidents, which the Russian government wanted to see mediated in direct talks with the Afghan ruler. The Governor of Herat complained to the British Consul General at Meshed in September, 1902, that three frontier pillars had been removed by the Russians in the area between Chashme Gugerdak and Chaharsunak and that a canal had been constructed at the latter place 400 paces within Afghan territory. In December the Governor reported the destruction of seven more pillars between Kara Tappa and the Murghab. The government of India instructed Colonel Whyte to remonstrate with the Russian Commandant at Kushk, and to ask that the pillars be rebuilt. In the meantime, the Governor of Ashkhabad had complained in a letter reaching Herat in November, 1902, that there was a scarcity of water in the Murghab and Hari Rud rivers, and, since it must have been caused by new dams constructed in Afghan territory, the Afghan authorities were requested to see to it that the water supply was restored. But the Amir denied that any new dams had been constructed and claimed that the scarcity of water was attributable to the small amount of snowfall in recent years.[20] In April, 1903, the British Consul General at Meshed reported that the Russians at Kushk were selling wheat to Afghans, who were suffering from famine, offering them cheap rates on credit for which some Afghans were reported to be giving mortgages on their lands. In another case of direct relations, the Governor of Trans-Caspia addressed a long letter to the Governor of Herat in April, 1903, discussing the subject of Afghan representation in Trans-Caspia and various matters of irrigation. Turkoman troopers repeatedly visited Herat, bringing messages from the commandant at Kushk. They came to negotiate about horse thefts and similar border incidents, and attempted to solve these problems with local Afghan officials.[21]

The apparent effort of local Russian officials to force the question of direct relations, while the St. Petersburg and London governments were discussing the problem, aroused the government of India to the belief that it was necessary to check these contacts by establishing a permanent British representative at Herat. When Russia offered to restore the boundary pillars, the British Ambassador, Sir Charles Scott informed the Russian Foreign Minister on August 14, 1903, that, in response to an invitation of the Amir, His Majesty's government would send a British officer to the spot, who would be happy to cooperate with a Russian official of similar rank in the restoration of the boundary markers. In spite of Russian opposition to such a procedure, the government of India sent a British official to the area.

The question of direct relations between local officials on the Russian boundary was especially vexing for Britain, since such relations had not been permitted by the Amir along the Indo-Afghan frontier. Louis W. Dane, of the Indian Foreign Department, called attention to this "absurd position" in which "our letters should be returned by the Amir's frontier officials, and our officers arrested if they go a few yards across the border,[22] while Russian sowars are allowed free access to Herat, and Russian officer's letters are not only received but answered by the Governor of Herat."[23] Several members of the Viceroy's council urged that a British representative should be stationed at Herat, but Lord Curzon cautioned against such a move since it would frighten the Amir, who might resent Russian pressure just as much as he did British.[24]

In view of the delicate situation, the government of India decided not to send a mission to Kabul and to leave the question of renewing the Anglo-Afghan agreement to a future, more auspicious, occasion. It was felt that sending a mission at this time without the express invitation of the Amir would merely show weakness on the part of the government of India. During the existing period of pressure from the government of Russia, a mission could do no more than renew the existing agreement, and this was not what the government of India desired.[25]

In the meantime, H. R. C. Dobbs, a political officer, was delegated to Herat in the fall of 1903 to supervise, in cooperation with a Russian officer, the repair of the boundary pillars. The Russians, however, refused to have any dealings with Dobbs and ignored his presence while they invited the cooperation of the Afghan authorities; and when the Afghans did not respond to their request, the Russians themselves repaired some of the pillars.[26] Dobbs felt himself greatly obstructed also by the Afghan authorities, who refused to deal independently with him but referred all his requests to the Amir. Dobbs wanted to use this opportunity to inspect the entire Russo-Afghan boundary. But the Governor of Herat told Dobbs that the Afghan authorities had petitioned the Amir in connection with those damaged pillars which were located within the Herat district—the frontier between Khwaja Gugirdak and Dahna-i-Zulfikar—and not about the pillars in Afghan Turkestan. Since Turkestan was not under the jurisdiction of the Governor of Herat, he could not permit Dobbs to proceed to that place.[27]

The Amir then wanted Dobbs to leave Herat and Afghanistan by the same route he came, namely, by way of Meshed, and suggested that anything left to be done could be conveniently settled in the coming year when the weather would be better.[28] But the government of India demurred. As so often when it succeeded in getting one of its officials into Afghanistan, the government of India wanted to make the most of the opportunity to collect information on the terrain and the mood of the people, and establish the practice of delegating British officers as advisers in matters not necessarily limited to the conduct of foreign relations. The government of India insisted that Dobbs should stay in Afghanistan and carry out his program of inspections and repairs of boundary pillars from Andkhui to Zulfikar.[29]

Dobbs turned his attention to the problem of border relations, and he was soon convinced that direct relations on minor matters between Russia and Afghanistan could not be prevented. In a letter to Louis W. Dane, the Secretary to the government of India, dated January 7, 1904, he reported that letters on various subjects passed almost daily between the Russian authorities at Panjdeh and the Governor of Bala Murghab.[30] The nomads along the frontier were selling their wool and curd to the Russians, and because of the great number of remote passes, running through a wilderness of clay hills, it was impossible to patrol the border to stop cross-border trading. Dobbs, therefore, thought that the old policy of complete isolation of Afghanistan was no longer feasible and should give way to regularized commerce which could become a source of wealth and contentment for the country. He proceeded to devise a complex system of commercial intercourse for both the Russian and Indian boundaries, which required the presence of a British officer at the Russo-Afghan boundary and an Afghan trade boycott of Russia to force her adherence to this scheme. Lord Curzon dismissed Dobbs's suggestions as full of paradoxes, "which isolated officers have a tendency to design with most deplorable consequences." [31]

Habibullah's resistance to British pressure led to a worsening in Anglo-Afghan relations. The British refusal to pay Habibullah a subsidy without a renewal of the previous agreement had not yet affected monetary transactions, because Abdur Rahman had accumulated a sufficiently large deposit with the government of India from which Habibullah could draw funds without bringing up the question of the subsidy. Finally, however, angered at the Indian practice of showing his account as containing only the amount due Abdur Rahman, the Amir complained to the Viceroy of these proceedings.[32] If no subsidy was due him, the Amir wanted to know, under what agreement did the government of India insist upon controlling his relations with Russia. If the previous agreements were no longer valid, was not also the Durand Agreement no longer valid? This was indeed a difficult question for the government of India to answer.

In 1903 a series of incidents occurred on the Afghan border. Lieutenant Colonel A. C. Yate visited the frontier area and, "innocently galloping" on his horse into Afghanistan, he was arrested by Afghan soldiers and kept a prisoner for about two weeks. The government of India planned retaliatory action, including the arrest of Afghan merchants in India and military measures, but Yate was released and returned to India. This Afghan action was taken by some as due to Afghan excitement over Lord Kitchener's tour of the border and his presence in the vicinity. The Amir offered no apology for the incident and said that the Afghan official responsible for the arrest should be praised, not punished. The Amir claimed that

Yate was in attire that could not be recognized, and it was only thanks to good fortune that there had not been any Afghans of the Achakzay clan at the border, or the Colonel would have been in a critical situation.[33]

In 1903 there were also disputes on the Indian border over Shinpukh and Smatzai. The former seemed to be in British territory, but the latter was in Afghanistan according to the map attached to the Durand Agreement. Interference by the Afghan Sartip of Dakka into both areas was taken as a pretext by the government of India to sanction occupation of both areas.[34] Some of the ammunition ordered by the Amir was detained at the Indian border; the reason for this was, according to the government of India, that it was of a type prohibited by the Hague Convention.[35]

It was not surprising that, at a time like this, rumors of Afghan intrigues with Russia were not lightly dismissed. An article in the Cairo newspaper *al-Mu'ayyid* of April 2, 1902, quoted a London *Daily Mail* correspondent in St. Petersburg saying that "after a short time some events of importance will occur in Central Asia and that it has been confirmed that Amir Habib Allah wants to renounce the alliance with the English, and become an ally and friend of the Russians."[36] E. H. S. Clarke of the Foreign and Political Department of the government of India remarked to this that "straws show the way in which the wind is blowing."

3. The Dane Mission

FORMULATION OF BRITISH DEMANDS

Lord Curzon was greatly disappointed about his lack of success in persuading the Amir to come to India where he could meet him face-to-face, and convince him of the British government's good intentions and arrange new agreements with him. The Viceroy stopped arms deliveries to Afghanistan, acting contrary to recommendations from the home government, but to no avail.[1] Curzon's insistence upon putting Anglo-Afghan relations on a new footing and the pressures he brought to bear on the Amir were causes for alarm in the London cabinet. London wanted a continuance of the status quo and did not share the Viceroy's view of the existence of a "strange and sinister parallelism with 1876," the eve of the Second Afghan War.[2]

The government of India discussed at some length whether the Anglo-Afghan agreements were personal ones with the Amir or agreements concluded with the government of Afghanistan. There existed no doubt that the Agreement of 1880 was personal since it expressly recognized Abdur Rahman as Amir of Kabul. A subsidy of 12 lakhs of rupees was given the Amir in 1883 to permit him to consolidate his power within the country and to strengthen his forces. But in 1893 the Durand Agreement was signed, which set Afghanistan's eastern and southern borders with India and, apparently in exchange for territorial concessions or to make these more palatable to him, gave the Amir an additional subsidy of 6 lakhs of rupees as well as the promise that "the Government of India will raise no objection to the purchase and import by His Highness of munitions of war."[3] If the treaty was personal, then the articles dealing with the boundary question could not be considered perpetual and would have to be renegotiated. It was not difficult for the Viceroy's council to come to the conclusion that provisions of treaties are severable, some clauses being perpetual and others temporal. The Indian archives were searched, and a letter was discovered which Lord Lansdowne sent to Durand during the negotiations warning him against saying anything that might later on be construed to mean that the increase in subsidy was perpetual. But this letter, dated November 8, 1893, did not reach Durand in time to influence his decisions since the treaty had already been signed.[4]

The question of the validity of the engagements with the previous Amir was more or less an academic one. The desire of the government of India to renew the agreements with the new ruler was not motivated by doubts about their validity. It was rather motivated by the desire to conclude a new treaty that would permit India to extend her influence in Afghanistan in order to check any forward movement by Russia.

While Lord Curzon was in London in 1904, the question was again raised in India of sending a mission to Kabul to negotiate an agreement with the Amir. A definite break in the situation occurred when Louis W. Dane, Foreign Secretary to the government of India, reported that the Afghan Envoy in an interview with him suggested that a high officer be sent to discuss matters and settle all problems with the Amir.[5]

The sudden willingness of Habibullah to receive a British mission at Kabul was apparently prompted by the publication in the Allahabad *Pioneer* of General A. N. Kuropatkin's scheme to invade India. The Japanese successes in the Russo-Japanese war may also have contributed. What seemed to make the situation exceedingly grave was that Russia again tried to arrange direct contact with Afghanistan. The Governor General of Trans-Caspia ordered a Russian colonel to carry an important letter to the Governor of Herat, "with whom he is to confer about necessary matters affecting Russia and Afghanistan."[6]

The Amir finally agreed to the Viceroy, Lord Ampthill's, suggestion that a high British official be sent to Kabul. In his letter of September 22, 1904, the Amir also made the bellicose declaration that "now that Japan has broken Russia's leg, we must break her back; it is odd if England and Afghanistan cannot tackle Russia in her present condition."[7]

The government of India considered it urgent that the British mission be dispatched with a minimum of delay. The formulation of policy for future relations with Afghanistan and the preparation of instructions for the Kabul mission were made difficult by the fact that Lord Curzon was then in England conferring with the British government on the "Afghanistan Question." India informed the home government that the Amir had accepted a mission and requested instructions as to what policy had been devised in London. In the meantime, Lord Ampthill, Viceroy during Curzon's absence from India, and his government formulated their own program and tentative guidelines for his discussions with Habibullah.

Lord Kitchener, Commander-in-Chief in India, set the tone in a "Minute" demanding that military considerations be of primary significance. He laid down two propositions which were generally accepted by the Viceroy's council: (1) that the primary and principal object of a British alliance with Afghanistan was the defense of India, and (2) that the one-sided and indefinite agreement that had been concluded with the late Amir was wholly unsatisfactory.[8] Kitchener's conclusion was that military considerations should supersede all others in the agreement that Britain was about to negotiate with Habibullah. And if a treaty or agreement could not be secured which would give Britain the rights of an ally and enable her to formulate a definite scheme for the defense of the Empire, Kitchener would prefer to have no agreement at all, leaving Afghanistan to the natural and inevitable process of absorption between Russia and Britain.[9]

Kitchener warned that it had been held as a cardinal point in Russian policy that Afghanistan was the most important land frontier of the British Empire, and he believed it would be there that the struggle for the mastery of the Middle East would take place. Therefore, Kitchener wanted to impress on the Amir that India and Afghanistan had enormous mutual interests that should be preserved either by a "joint understanding and cordial working together" or by each party taking such measures as it considered necessary for the protection of its own interests without regard to the particular interests of the other.[10] Kitchener did not want this alternative to appear to be an ultimatum, but it is difficult to see how it could have seemed otherwise to the Amir.

Lord Kitchener wanted to convince Habibullah that it would be a long time before he could emulate the successes of the Japanese since the situation in Central Asia was profoundly different from that in the Far East. Railroad preparations by Russia north of Afghanistan were soon to reach a state that would permit her to move as many as half a million men into Afghanistan, against whom the Amir could not be successful. Having convinced Habibullah that his salvation lay in an intimate alliance with Britain, Kitchener wanted the British Envoy to discuss with the Amir how best to concert proper measures for mutual defense. Kitchener thought more active participation by Britain was needed. British and Afghan officers should jointly visit the various strategic points in the country and prepare on-the-spot schemes of defense. Britain should be in a position to advise the Amir generally as to the military measures deemed necessary. British troops should be permitted to enter and defend Afghanistan right from the beginning of a conflict, and not after Afghan troops had shown themselves unable to defend themselves from aggression. It would also be necessary for the Amir to improve all the main avenues of approach from India to Afghanistan. Border adjustments would be required to provide sites for British railroad terminals, and, since the Amir was so set against the introduction of railroads into Afghanistan, he should construct roads that would connect with the British railroad tracks and thus make possible the rapid laying of rails in case of a Russian attack.[11]

Lord Ampthill generally agreed with Lord Kitchener on the emphasis on military considerations in negotiations with Afghanistan, but he disagreed with the Commander-in Chief's conclusions that it would be better to have no agreement at all with the Amir than to continue the present unsatisfactory situation.[12] He feared that "instead of a lukewarm and suspicious ally, we should have an independent, neutral, or possibly an open foe on our borders, and instead of having a 'buffer state' to break the force of foreign invasion, we should either have to defend ourselves on our actual frontier or else invade Afghanistan." Hostility with Afghanistan would then arouse the tribes within the Indian North-West and, with such a two-front war, the actual defense of India would revert to the Indus River.[13]

Ampthill saw only three possible courses: (1) To continue as before, being content with the settlement of minor questions at issue and hoping for a change of attitude on the part of the Amir. (2) To make an agreement with the Amir whereby Britain was under no liability to defend Afghanistan. This could be framed so that by implication or otherwise Britain reserved its right of entering Afghanistan for the defense of India, while the Amir would continue to receive his subsidy and permission for the import of arms through India. (3) To put pressure on the Amir by refusing to make any agreement at all.

Lord Ampthill saw the third course as an all-or-nothing proposition and considered a combination of the first and second courses the best. If such a compromise were not possible, Lord Ampthill declared himself "pusillanimous enough to prefer the first course, that is 'to muddle on and trust to luck' in the good old British way."[14] Lord Kitchener gradually retreated from his all-or-nothing stand on a treaty by repeatedly modifying his statements until he was in virtual agreement with Ampthill.

The Viceroy then led the discussions in the council and contributed a proposal of his own to serve as the basis for further deliberations. He agreed with Kitchener's "moderate demands" that the Amir should consult with Britain on military matters generally, improve his communications, and permit visits to Afghanistan by British officers as advisers, and that British participation in Afghanistan should begin immediately on the commencement of hostilities.[15] Lord Ampthill felt that a formal treaty should be concluded; Abdur Rahman had wanted a formal treaty for a long time, until he realized that the advantages under the loose agreements were decidedly in his favor.

Ampthill saw a clear disadvantage in making a personal treaty with the ruler and not with the Afghan government, and he wanted a defensive alliance between the two governments.[16] As to the form of assistance Britain should render Afghanistan, Lord Ampthill suggested the following definition:

> Provided that the Amir unreservedly followed our advice in regard to his external relations, provided he gave us the stipulated facilities for concerting in peacetime a scheme of mutual defence and provided that on the outbreak of war he placed no restrictions on the time and

manner in which our assistance with military force should be rendered, we would aid him to the best of our ability to repel unprovoked aggression.[17]

Not explaining how he would induce Habibullah to sign a treaty that demanded so many concessions from the Amir without giving him anything in exchange, the Viceroy proceeded to outline the following provisions of a new treaty:

1. India and Afghanistan would proclaim the continuance of their alliance and friendship and disavow any mutually agressive intent. Both states would promise to defend each other against unprovoked aggression.

2. Both states would pledge not to interfere in each other's internal affairs and to respect the Indo-Afghan boundary.

3. The Afghan ruler would promise to follow British advice in his external relations and to accord peacetime facilities for a scheme of mutual defense in exchange for British protection of Afghanistan from outside aggression. The Amir would further pledge not to place any restrictions on the time or manner in which British assistance was to be rendered.

4. Britain would agree to pay a permanent subsidy to the state of Afghanistan or (if Lord Ampthill's suggestion were to prove unacceptable to his council or the home government) to the Amir personally. The subsidy was to be larger than the previous one, and its use was to be limited to the payment of troops, the import of arms, and the fortification of the country. The Amir would guarantee that no arms or ammunitions be sold or given to the tribes on the frontier.

5. The Amir would agree to provide facilities for British military officers to confer with their counterparts.

6. The frontier was to be demarcated in a manner that would permit India to construct strategic lines of communications up to the Afghan border without any interference from Afghanistan.

7. Satisfactory diplomatic relations were to be instituted. British officers were to be established, if not in Kabul, at least in such rural areas as Sistan and the Russo-Afghan border. They could be called "Consular Agents" to make their existence more palatable to the Amir, and some kind of honorific representation of the Amir at the Court of St. James could conceivably be granted.

8. A detailed customs and trade agreement was to be part of the new treaty or, if this might tempt Russia to demand a similar agreement, be part of a separate arrangement.[18]

This outline was the basis of discussion in the Viceroy's council, and suggestions were offered by several of its members. For example, Lord Kitchener would consider no less than five British officers necessary for inspecting the various strategic centers in Afghanistan. He also wanted a commitment from Habibullah regarding the extension of the British railways into Afghanistan immediately at the outbreak of war. The Amir would have to maintain the rails, but they would be removed again on the conclusion of hostilities. Afghan representation at London was deprecated by E. H. S. Clarke, and Lord Ampthill suggested bringing to the notice of foreign powers Britain's right to the control of Afghan foreign relations by obtaining a request from the Amir that British consular and diplomatic officers abroad act on behalf of Afghan subjects.[19] All these suggestions were submitted in a telegram of October 21, 1904, to His Majesty's Secretary of State. The government of India suggested that the military provisions of the new treaty be incorporated in a secret military convention. The subsidy was to be partly personal to Habibullah and partly permanent and, if necessary, the arrears of the subsidy were to be paid. No Afghan representative was to be permitted in London, and, since the existing conditions made the British military occupation of Afghan Sistan inadvisable, this matter was not to be mentioned to the Amir.[20]

The Foreign Secretary's reply made it apparent that the home government was not at all willing to "sacrifice the present loose, but generally satisfactory relations" with Afghanistan for changes the London cabinet doubted would be accepted by the Amir. Even if Habibullah were willing to accept the scheme recommended by Lord Kitchener, the generally antagonistic spirit among the tribes would prohibit its practical application. Furthermore, London held that any increase in the military strength of Afghanistan would be a danger to Britain since there was no certainty that the Amir would remain loyal "in all circumstances and under all temptations." The home government saw the real value of Afghanistan not in the efficiency of her army, but in the barrier against a Russian advance created by the geographical position and configuration of the country.²¹ London doubted that the Amir would be willing to accept such a treaty; if he resisted pressure to accept it, Britain would either have to modify her demands, which would involve a loss in prestige, or break off relations with the Amir, "leaving Afghanistan to the natural process of absorption between Russia and ourselves." In short, the risks were greater than His Majesty's government was prepared to accept. Therefore the London government had decided it would be preferable to approach the Amir with proposals for renewing the previous engagement. The home government sent an *aide-mémoire* with specific instructions to Louis W. Dane, head of the Kabul mission, to use as a guide in his talks with the Amir.²² According to this document, the reason for the deputation of a special envoy to Kabul was to close the rift that existed between the two governments and to arrive at a renewal of the previous agreement. Dane was to proceed on the assumption that the objects, the interests, and the enemies of the two countries were identical, and that their policy was one of harmonious cooperation.

First of all Habibullah should be assured that he would not be pressed to make any concession that would be injurious to his dignity and contrary to his policy. Dane, therefore, did not have to mention the question of railroads but to impress on the Amir the importance of the telegraph and point out to him some of the benefits he would derive from such an innovation. Britain was prepared to construct a telegraph line and then hand it over to the Afghans who would operate it. But in this matter, too, the Amir should not be pressed.²³

The document further stated that the deputation of British officers to Afghanistan (i.e., McMahon to Sistan, Dobbs to Herat, and Donald to Kurram) had recently been successful and not accompanied by any unfortunate consequences; therefore, the sending of other officers to settle problems that undoubtedly arise "from a state of ignorance about important matters" was desirable. But the Secretary of State felt that the idea of the loan of British officers on a more systematic and permanent basis was one that should only be pursued with the absolute concurrence of the Amir. The *aide-mémoire* also stated that it should be unnecessary, but it might be wise, to repeat the assurance to the Amir that no interference in the internal administration of Afghanistan was either contemplated or desired.

THE DANE MISSION   47

The home government felt that the written assurance given to Abdur Rahman in 1880 was deemed sufficient and there was no need for Dane to press for a more formal instrument. The important thing was that this agreement, just as the one before, was a personal one concluded between the British government and the Amir, not the ruling dynasty or the State of Afghanistan. The absolute control by Britain of Afghanistan's foreign relations was the cardinal point of the agreement. Dane was to examine the Amir's contention that it was impossible to stop communications with Russia in matters of commerce. In what sense were commercial communications required on the Russo-Afghan frontier which were not wanted on the Indian frontier? Dane was also instructed to seek an explanation on the status of the Afghan commercial agent at Samarkand.

The *aide-mémoire* reminded Dane that the British obligations under the assurances of 1880 should be frankly discussed. Under these assurances, the British government was made the sole judge of the manner and degree of the assistance in repelling unprovoked aggression which it would give.[24]

In regard to the military preparedness of Afghanistan, the Amir was to be made aware of the fact that his forces were incapable of making a prolonged stand against a European foe. The example of Japan, to which the Amir was in the habit of alluding, presented no analogy whatever to the condition of Afghanistan. Habibullah could not expect to be successful if he found himself engaged in a war with Russia. Dane was to sound out the Amir to determine if he wished reports made by British officers on the military features of the country between Herat and Kabul to facilitate British assistance to Afghanistan in case of war with Russia.

Subsidies were to be continued. The British Envoy was reminded that Britain's object was to bind the Amir to her by the tie of self-interest. As long as his conduct was satisfactory, the Amir should receive the subsidy and facilities for the import of arms. The *quid pro quo* from him should be: (1) control of his foreign relations, (2) abandonment of his "intrigues" with the frontier tribes, (3) maintenance of a power friendly to Great Britain as a barrier to Russian advance, and (4) commercial facilities.[25]

The Defence Committee of the home government had come to the conclusion that it would be dangerous to assume the training of the Amir's troops, even if he would permit it. Since the amount of subsidy limited Habibullah in his purchases of arms, it was considered not desirable to increase his subsidy. The *aide-mémoire* further contained a list of "misunderstandings" that had to be cleared up before a new agreement could be concluded:

1. The Mohmand border question must be settled, and the entire line from the Nawa Peak to the Sisubi Pass had to be defined. It was necessary for India to build a railroad in the neighborhood of the Khyber Pass and another one up the Kurram valley. The Amir must not adopt a hostile attitude toward these projects.

2. The status, treatment, and position of the British Agent at Kabul must be discussed and a promise for improvements obtained from the Amir.

3. Incidents on the Anglo-Afghan border, such as Afghan conduct at Shinpukh, Smatzai, and Darband, as well as the imprisonment of Colonel Yate, should not happen between allied countries and must not occur in the future.

4. Afghan relations with transborder tribes must cease. The Amir should stop his attempts to enlist transborder tribes into his army. (British enlistment of Afghan Hazarah into frontier forces need not be mentioned.)

5. Facilities would be given by the government of India for the import of arms into Afghanistan, but it was preferable not to include a stipulation to this effect in the agreement.

6. The question of a more liberal "commercial policy" toward India should be discussed with the Amir. After all, "Afghanistan is the sole civilized country in the world ... with which we do not possess a commercial agreement. It has been found desirable even by uncivilized countries" like Tibet.[26] Since the conclusion of a commercial convention would almost inevitably lead to a similar demand by Russia, it was preferable merely to obtain assurances for the free passage of trade caravans across the Anglo-Afghan frontier. As to the form of the new agreement, the home government invited the advice of the Foreign Department in India.

The Viceroy's government acknowledged this communication and asked for a general provision that would secure India the right to enter the country with military force when it became necessary to repel aggression.[27] If the home government was unwilling to press for the appointment of British officers on the northern frontier, attempts were to be made to obtain the Amir's consent to the deputation of native newswriters or commercial agents to Maymana, Mazar-i-Sharif, and Faizabad.

The government of India submitted a two-part draft treaty consisting of a treaty of friendship and union between India and Afghanistan with a more qualified reiteration of guarantees for protection in exchange for control of Afghan foreign affairs, and a subsidiary agreement defining in ten articles the responsibilities of both countries.[28] The draft treaty was essentially a compromise between the versions suggested by India and Britain, and London finally approved it, on the condition that the treaty was made with the Amir personally and not with the State of Afghanistan. The home government also wanted certain passages changed to prevent the commercial provision from developing into a commercial convention.[29]

The stage was now set for negotiations. The proposed treaty was quite similar to the previous arrangement, except that it permitted British troops to enter Afghanistan in defense of foreign aggression. The subsidiary treaty also permitted British involvement by institutionalizing the delegation of British officers to assist the Amir in matters of defense. Although the treaty gave the British much less than the government of India has desired, it provided for an increase of British influence in Afghanistan and could have led to a tightening of British control which might have proved fatal to the Amir's independence.

NEGOTIATIONS

Foreign Secretary Dane arrived in Kabul on December 12, 1904, and received a most cordial welcome. He proceeded to the Mehman Khana while five regiments were drawn up with presented arms, the British national anthem played, and a salute of twenty-one guns fired. A *diyafat* (present of hospitality) of 30,000 Kabuli rupees was presented to Dane.[30] Two days later, Habibullah received the mission in formal durbar where friendly greetings were exchanged, and the Amir agreed that he was most anxious to renew the agreements made between his father and the British government, "since their mutual friendship was a boon for both countries."[31] On December

15, 1904, the Amir received Dane, Dobbs, and Grant and their interpreters in a private interview at his palace. The Amir was surrounded by his council, and the attitude of the Afghans was most cordial.[32]

Thus the discussions began, destined to last for many weary weeks, until the end of March, 1905. It became apparent very soon that the major issue was the question of the nature of the Anglo-Afghan Agreement of 1880. The Amir and his council saw the disadvantage of a treaty with Britain which would be subject to renewal at the death of every Afghan ruler. (Nasrullah, the Amir's brother and principal adviser, expected to accede to the throne one day and, therefore, had a stake in this issue.) The Amir had managed to hold off the British for three years until he had to acquiesce in permitting a mission to Afghanistan. If Habibullah finally was successful in obtaining a renewal of the previous agreement, it was not assured that all future Afghan rulers would be equally astute and succeed in maintaining Afghanistan's precarious independence.

Britain's major objective was both to obtain the renewal of the Agreement of 1880 with favorable modifications and to solve the vexing question of Russo-Afghan relations. Since Russia would not be drawn into a definition of how she would limit her relations with Afghanistan to local matters of a nonpolitical nature, it was necessary that the Afghan ruler advance a plan for this purpose. By getting the Amir to endorse an acceptable scheme, Britain's position vis-à-vis Russia would be strengthened, for Russia could not have any relations in the face of an Afghan refusal.

The discussions began with expressions of mutual goodwill and hopes for a speedy settlement of the affair. Dane stated that he was instructed to speak with candor and freedom and in a spirit of true friendship, and the Amir told him to "lay aside all purda" since he would also speak what was in his innermost heart. Dane began by attempting to show that the analogy between Japan and Afghanistan was not a correct one, and he denied that the British assisted Japan with money and ships before she became involved in the war with Russia. Next he asked the Amir whether he wished to receive "active military assistance in such time and in such manner as this could be effectively rendered"; and he warned that if the Amir relied on the admitted bravery of the Afghans alone, even though these were fully armed and equipped, he must fail. Dane cautioned that the British government could not acquiesce in the conquest by any foreign power of Afghanistan, the gate of India, and that she must in any case safeguard her own vital interests. He concluded by mentioning some of the subsidiary questions that had to be settled before the new treaty could come into effect.[33]

The Amir reiterated his willingness to conduct all political relations with foreign powers through British mediation and said he would ask from his friend such help as he could receive without damaging his honor and religious prestige. The Amir saw the danger from Russia as being much greater now than during the time of his father, and he promised to give a written expression of his views on Dane's suggestions.

Dane declared himself generally satisfied with his first interview, but in India his tactical error was quickly noticed. Clarke, the Assistant Secretary to the Foreign Department, deplored this premature emphasis of the military question.[34] Indeed, asking the Amir whether he would accept British assistance under certain conditions was contrary to the British government's desire to concede no veto on that proposal.

Lord Curzon, who had just returned to India, warned Dane in a private and confidential letter, dated December 9, 1904, that it had required a good deal of effort to get the home government to permit the conclusion of a new treaty at all. He said that the cabinet wanted to keep things quiet and therefore felt no sympathy with the "bold military programme put before them."[35] According to Curzon, London believed that the Amir was not likely to agree to organize his tribes on a British plan of defense, and, even if he did agree, there was no guarantee that he could adhere to it. The Amir's main objective was to remain independent, not to serve as a "mere pawn on the chessboard of Indian military defence." The presence of British officers along the northern border of Afghanistan constituted a violent departure from the status quo and a challenge to Russia, and Britain's close association with the country's defense would bring her the odium of failure as it did at the Panjdeh defeat. Arthur Balfour and his cabinet also held little regard for the value of the Afghan forces. They thought that a powerful army, equipped with

British arms, would be almost as likely to use its arms against Britain as against Russia. The treaty with Afghanistan was desired solely as a warning to Russia that an attack on Afghanistan would be considered a *casus belli* by Britain.[36]

Dane was quite optimistic in his reply to Lord Curzon. He defended his approach, saying that the Amir "is almost going too fast in the negotiations, and it was partly to prevent his rushing me before I could consult Your Excellency fully that I at last agreed . . . to give him a brief *pro memoria* note, and to accept a written note in reply." The Amir would not talk of anything but the question of the defense of Afghanistan, and Dane felt it was impossible to broach the questions of his "intrigues" with the tribes and his treatment of the British Agent and other British officials. Dane had learned from the Afghan Envoy that the Amir was prepared to agree to British examination of the country beyond Kabul, and he wanted to "strike while the iron is hot"; he only waited for an opening from the Amir to touch the question of British defense of the Sistan area by direct military assistance. Dane was impressed by the cordiality of the Amir who held his hand for long periods of time and repeatedly thanked him for being so frank. It was mainly the clever and quick Abdul Kuddus Khan who promised to be difficult.[37]

From the beginning the Amir had insisted on written communications during the negotiations and on December 20 he submitted a long memorandum in which he gave his position on the subjects mentioned by Dane. The Amir protested Dane's contention that his nation could not be counted equal to Japan, and he cited in his advantage the crores (1 crore = 10 million) of his coreligionists in Russia, who would rise and attack the Russians in the rear if summoned to jihad by the Amir. To Dane's question of whether the Amir was willing to accept immediate active military assistance from the British, the Amir replied that he required not troops but arms and money. On the deputation of British officers, the Amir wanted to give his opinion "after the strengthening and increase" of the treaty; and he promised he would not tolerate a friendly word being uttered in friendship for Russia "after I have seen what increase has been made in the promises" of Britain. The Amir continued to maintain that the Agreements of 1880 and 1893 were made with the Afghan nation, and proceeded to outline a plan which he thought would end the danger of Russian attack. This was best done, according to the Amir, by a concerted Anglo-Afghan attack upon Russia: Afghan troops armed by Britain would invade Central Asia after a declaration of jihad against Russia, and, while Afghan troops advanced, British soldiers would besiege the few Russian forts in the area.[38]

This memorandum caused the government of India a great deal of anxiety. Lord Curzon hoped that it represented merely a blowing off of steam, but he deplored these rather unexpected developments which he somehow related to Dane's tactical error in bringing up the question of military support.[39] In India the Amir's stand was seen as especially objectionable since he reserved his decisions on such questions as the acceptance of British officers to survey parts of his territory, the status of Abdur Rahman's treaty, and his position on British rail terminals in their own territory, until he had seen the new treaty and knew what increase in assistance it would provide.[40] Furthermore, Habibullah's success in getting Dane to agree to an exchange of written memoranda, thereby providing a written record of his stand as "depending on circumstances," was an unexpected departure from procedure. Thus the Amir got his remarks recorded and Dane was put on the defensive in his replies. Before Dane could expound his point of view, the conversation seemed to get diverted into new and unforeseen channels.

Dane quickly discounted the Amir's proposals. He said he was not authorized to discuss a scheme of military attack upon Russia and declared himself convinced that his government would not sanction such a step since Russia had not provoked an attack. The British Envoy also refused to give any specific information regarding the extent and manner of aid promised by his government and only declared that Britain would fully and loyally carry out her obligations.[41]

The Amir then suggested that it would simplify the discussions if Dane gave him a copy of the British draft treaty that he was authorized to conclude. Dane acquiesced and gave orally the substance of the treaty.[42] An argument followed when the Amir objected to the word *"siyasi"* as a translation for "political" regarding his foreign relations (*dar bab-i-munasibat wa ta'alluqat-i-biruni-ye-khud*). The Amir demanded a definition of what relations were considered political. For example, if a sheep were stolen by Afghans from Russian subjects and the Russians asked for compensation, was this a political procedure? Dane took this opportunity to ask why such relations between border officials were not permitted at the British frontier. The Amir replied he could not leave such matters to his subjects because they were not sufficiently civilized to know how to act. Dane concluded the December 22 meeting by raising some of the subsidiary questions. He also inquired about the Amir's wishes regarding the subsidy, which "form of help, unusual between civilized and allied states," might have been expected to be no longer necessary.[43] Habibullah promised to consider these questions in detail. As to the alleged ill-treatment of British newswriters, the Amir informed Dane that he had recalled the Governors of both Herat and Kandahar. Habibullah also wanted to know what Dane meant by saying that Afghanistan would not be prevented from importing "reasonable quantities" (*meqdar-i-munasib*) of arms. Dane assured the Amir that the British government would certainly raise no objection to the importation of any arms and munitions of war required by the Amir.

The government of India saw an undesirable trend reflected in this second memorandum, and Lord Curzon remarked pessimistically that "there is nothing to be done except prepare ourselves for a possible failure in the negotiations."[44]

In a memorandum of December 26, Habibullah said he had agreed to meet Dane since he understood that the subject of their discussions would be how to deal with a Russian advance and "not with the advance of border outlaws" or the renewal of a treaty which had existed for many years and under which Britain was still advising him in his dealings with Russia. The Amir said he was holding the Russians off because, although they spoke of restoring Afghan territories then held by the British, their objective of seeking passage through Afghanistan for an attack on India would also lead to the destruction of his own country. Another reason the Amir cited was that he considered himself bound to Britain in the alliance concluded by his father.[45]

Dane's position was made difficult by the fact that, regarding the Amir's foreign relations, he was instructed not to "whittle away" at the cardinal feature of absolute British control while at the same time His Majesty's government had virtually conceded Russia the right to nonpolitical relations with Afghanistan.[46] It was hoped that Habibullah would formulate a device to guarantee that contacts with Russia would remain of a nonpolitical nature. Since the Amir did not volunteer any suggestions, Dane found it difficult to bring up the question of appointing British consular officials to Afghanistan's northern boundary. Furthermore, Dane hoped to obtain some kind of concession from the Amir in exchange for the grant of a subsidy and the payment of arrears in subsidy.

Finally Habibullah sent Dane an undated and unsigned memorandum on January 1, 1905, which also included a "petition" by his State Council (*Ahali-ye-Shura*) with an Afghan version of a draft treaty. The Amir brought pressure to bear on Dane by declaring that if Britain insisted on concluding a new treaty he would be compelled to consult his nation and would be unable to say anything until the representatives (*wakilha*) of the whole nation were assembled.[47] On the other hand he declared himself ready to agree to the treaty proposed by his council.

The document of the Amir's council first denied that the 1880 treaty was personal and insisted that the subsidy was paid in return for lands ceded by Afghanistan. Since Afghanistan had gained nothing by her friendship with Britain except the enmity of Russia, Britain must contribute to Afghanistan's defenses by agreeing to a plan of military action. The document gave the text of a treaty which confirmed the one concluded with Abdur Rahman,[48] and spelled out the details of the type of British assistance expected:

British aid in arms was to be rendered in a predetermined quantity and with a definite schedule of delivery. For the defense of Turkestan, British military assistance should proceed by way of Chitral, to which place the Government of India was to build a railroad. The Afghan Government would agree to construct, with British assistance, a connecting road which would lead into Afghanistan. Britain should agree to furnish Afghanistan with ships for the Oxus River and assist in the training of Afghan sailors, "so that the English can work on their own ships." At each port on the Oxus there should be constructed a fort (*mahkama*) which would be garrisoned by Afghans.

In the Herat area, the Afghan government would agree to build with British help, a strong fortification at Hashtadan. This fort would be held and defended by Afghan troops until a British railroad was constructed to this point; then it would be handed over to the Government of India. If Herat were attacked by the Russians, British troops were to come to the city's defense, whereas the Afghan troops at Herat would assist the British against an attack at Hashtadan.

For the defense of Farah, the Afghans were prepared to build, with British assistance, a fort in the Sistan area, near the Indian boundary, and hand it over to Britain. In case of a Russian attack, the British should fight in the south from the direction of Nushki and Chaghai, while the Afghans would fight from the north. If the enemy arrived at Kandahar, the British should assist from the direction of Chaman, while the Afghans would fight within the limits of Qalat, Muqur, and Ghazni. Afghan troops would further hold the mountain passes, assisted by the Afghan tribes, and British troops would attack by way of Paiwar and the eastern tracts of Afghanistan.

The Afghan Government would permit the government of India to construct a railroad which would start at the Indian border and travel along the Perso-Afghan boundary northward to Hashtadan. The land for the railroad would be ceded by Afghanistan, but the entire area was to remain under Afghan jurisdiction. Fortifications should also be built in various places in the Hindu Kush. Afghanistan would accept British assistance under the following conditions: (1) as the Afghans gave their lives, the British should give their arms; (2) if the Afghans gave territory, the British should give territory in exchange; (3) Britain should provide the funds for the construction of forts and roads; and (4) if Britain wanted Afghanistan to increase her troops, she should increase her monetary assistance in proportion to the increase desired.

The initial reaction in India was conjecture whether the council had been set up to assist the Amir in his negotiations. Clarke was inclined to think that the council was ruling the Amir, that it was averse to conclusion of a new treaty, and that the threat to call all the tribes of Afghanistan if new agreements had to be made was a mere bluff. After all, the British treaty was a triviality compared to the one the Amir wanted to conclude without consulting his people. Clarke also thought that the fear of losing the arrears in subsidy might be behind the Afghan's refusal to admit the personal character of the previous agreements. Therefore, he recommended that Dane be authorized to drop a hint that the payment of arrears depended on no more than the Amir's cooperation in reaching a speedy settlement.[49] Clarke thought one could not be sure that the proposals for military cooperation were not put forward in the hope that Britain would reject them. The railroad project was, according to Clarke, "as impossible as it was undesirable," and the result of building it as well as fortifications on the Oxus "would be soon followed by war with Russia." The plan for the defense of Sistan was worthy of careful consideration, but India could hardly wait until Russia reached Kandahar and Kabul before she was permitted to come to the defense of these cities.

The memorandum also showed India that the Afghans did not desire active British cooperation in the defense of central Afghanistan, except as a last resort. Clarke thought it remarkable that the Secretary of State should have rejected Lord Kitchener's proposal for a secret military convention on the grounds that it was more than doubtful that the Amir would consent. In the end, Clarke held, India would stand on safer ground in adhering to the program of the home government.

Lord Curzon pointed to the "absurdity" of the fact that Afghanistan, rather than rejoicing at the British proposals, should be frightened of them. He saw the cause of this "strange phenomenon" in the fact that Dane failed to "dangle before the Amir the rewards," namely the payment of the arrears in subsidy. Curzon thought that if Dane let Habibullah know that he would receive both the subsidy and the arrears, the Amir's irritation and misunderstanding "could be removed in five minutes."[50] This assumption was, however, proven wrong.

Dane's interview with Habibullah on January 5, 1905, ended in deadlock when the Amir declined to consider any subsidiary questions until the decision of the government of India on the Amir's draft treaty was communicated.[51] The Amir admitted that the proposals of his council need not be discussed *en bloc,* and he also indicated his willingness to make concessions on his railroad proposal.

The government of India now decided to make a concession on

the question of arms imports. In view of the opinion held by the home government that Dane's return without a treaty would be a serious misfortune, it was decided to go as far as to allow the Amir to import, free of duty, sufficient munitions of war for the full equipment of his army, reserving the right of controlling imports only under "special and exceptional circumstances." The Secretary of State had favored "a reasonable concession" in the question of arms which did not involve (1) complete abandonment of power to control the import of arms in special and exceptional circumstances, and (2) an admission that any claim hitherto denied by Britain can be made as a right.[52]

The Viceroy deplored Dane's tactical error of starting his negotiations by bringing up the military question. He saw that Dane was now in the position of the supplicant for information, giving the Amir options on questions in which he ought not to have had any. Lord Curzon considered the question of arms control irretrievably lost when Durand gave his assurances in 1893, and he thought the only check that could be imposed on the import of arms was the amount of money given to the Amir in subsidy and the threat of breaking with him if his imports reached a point where he became either a menace to India or forced Britain into a war with Russia. Dane was, therefore, instructed to give way in the matter of arms imports as he did in the question of the arrears in subsidy.[53]

Habibullah's demand for the old Martini rifles that were being discarded in the Indian army were met by a British refusal; the question of arms gifts was referred for discussion at a separate meeting after the signing of the British treaty.[54]

The Secretary of State finally cautioned the government of India that the publication of a blue book on the Anglo-Afghan treaty was planned and that the Amir should be told in a form that could be made public that (1) there was no intention of treating for an attack on Russia, and (2) that the views attributed to Edward VII by the Amir (namely, that the King favored an offensive alliance against Russia) were without foundation.[55]

On January 20, 1905, the home government again urged India to agree to the arrangement as it existed before. As to the matter of direct communication with foreign powers, Dane was advised to tell the Amir that "except as to purely local matters of non-political complexion" such relations are not permitted.[56] Lord Curzon remarked to this that the home government was beginning to "wobble badly," but he agreed to demanding from Afghanistan the immediate forwarding of only political correspondence, whereas letters of a nonpolitical character were to be forwarded in copy at a later time.[57]

Habibullah's intransigent stand finally led Dane to recommend confronting the Amir with the ultimatum of either agreeing to the British draft treaty or coming to a break in the negotiations.[58] On February 2, 1905, the government of India reported to London that a deadlock had been reached.[59] The Amir's position was given as follows (1) the engagements were permanent, and he had a right to the full subsidy, complete arrears, and unrestricted import of arms; (2) he wanted to strengthen the original agreement, by which he meant that his draft treaty should be accepted, the subsidy increased, free gifts of arms be given, and the treaty be considered dynastic; (3) after these concessions were granted, the Amir would be willing to discuss Britain's subsidiary questions.

The Indian government was of the opinion that a yielding to Habibullah's position would mean a surrender of the sole lever Britain had over Afghan affairs and would leave the Amir as the permanent master of the situation. India had offered the Amir a renewal of the personal engagements with his father in identical terms, but in the more binding form of a treaty, the sole *quid pro quo* being that the Amir should meet them on a number of subsidiary points.[60] India saw itself unable to discover any more concessions that could be made, and thought "future relations with an ally who had thus successfully trifled with us could not be satisfactory." The Viceroy's council, therefore, unanimously recommended that, after one more attempt at negotiations with the Amir, the mission should leave on a specified date.

The Secretary of State responded to this recommendation in a telegram of February 3, 1905, declaring that the breaking off of negotiations was most undesirable, and suggesting that the only alternative left was to accept the Amir's settlement along the lines of the Amir's draft treaty, which should, however, include an explicit recital of engagements set forth in the British draft.[61] London warned that a break in negotiations "cannot fail to have [a] disturbing effect; and, if Russian preparations in Tashkent mean anything, may precipitate their action."

Dane had already given his opinion that an indefinite stay of the mission at Kabul was "neither very dignified nor very safe for a representative of the Government of India," and he reported rumors to the effect that a plot on the life of British members of his mission had been discovered. On January 31, Habibullah announced the withdrawal of the proposal for military cooperation which was offered by his council. He informed his "dear and beloved friend, Louis W. Dane [that] from the expressions and statements used by you yesterday, it has become thoroughly apparent and clear that your Government has no intentions whatever to deal with Afghanistan with equity and justice, and that whatever is said or stated is all by way of high-handedness and force." [62]

It was clear that the Amir realized what it would mean to come to a break in the negotiations. In an informal note he warned Dane of the results of a dismemberment of Afghanistan, saying that if Britain took Kabul and Kandahar, the Russians would take Herat and Turkestan, and then he asked, "What will be the state of affairs of your Government at the front and in the interior?" [63]

In the meantime, Reuter's reported on February 15 from London that Balfour hoped Afghan negotiations would terminate successfully. He denied that Britain was pursuing a provocation policy and said "it was a cardinal element of sound policy that the Indian Government should be on good terms with a neighbor between them and a more powerful military Empire." [64] It was, therefore, not surprising that the Secretary of State "recommended" on February 16 that the Amir's treaty was acceptable and Dane should sign it.[65] The main point to the home government was that the Amir's draft treaty accepted the obligations undertaken by his father, and "if control of the Amir's relations is secured, we do not think any question of form should stand in the way."

Alarm over "warlike preparations on a large scale" by Russia in Turkestan and the threat of a revival of the dispute over Yangi Kila, an island in the Oxus River, seemed to make the Amir more receptive to coming to terms with the British. Also the return of his son Inayatullah from India, where he had been hospitably received, seemed to have strengthened pro-British feelings.

On March 14, Dane informed Habibullah of his government's willingness to accept the Amir's treaty and also showed him Abdur Rahman's letter of 1880, in which the former Amir bound himself to follow British advice in the conduct of his foreign relations. The Amir promised a prompt reply.

But the battle was not yet over. The Amir was still trying to obtain concessions from Britain by adding to the preamble of his own treaty a clause that would have made it national rather than personal. This Dane would not permit. Habibullah then sought to discuss certain points which were not clear to him, especially Clause VII of the Durand Agreement, which covered the import of arms to Afghanistan. He said that the treaty would be useless to him without such clarification.

But finally Afghan opposition ceased, and the treaty was signed on March 21, 1905. Sir Percy Sykes tells the following anecdote about the signing of the treaty: As the Amir was affixing his signature, he shook some ink from his pen over the English copy of the parchment and exclaimed: "It is spoilt; we must write out other treaties." Dane, a notable Persian scholar, replied "This is only a mole on the fair face of the treaty," and quoted from Hafiz: "If this Shiraz beauty will accept my heart, for her Hindu-dark mole I will give Samarkand and Bukhara." This apt quotation eased the situation, but Abdul Kuddus Khan exclaimed: "See, Your Majesty, Mr. Dane gives you Samarkand and Bukhara." But Dane's prompt reply was: "Nay, the mole is on the face of the British treaty and for this the Amir abandons Samarkand and Bukhara."

Two days after the signing of the treaty, the Amir sent Dane an official letter in which he set forth his views on various minor matters he was willing to consider. They were (1) that the Amir would guard and preserve the British cemetery at Sherpur, (2) that a British arbitrator should be appointed to settle the Perso-Afghan frontier at Musabad, (3) that the undemarcated portion of the Indo-Afghan frontier should be demarcated after the next harvest, (4) that, with regard to the frontier tribes, the Amir would "not go beyond his father's principles" (a promise Dane optimistically construed to mean that Habibullah would strictly adhere to his father's engagements), and (5) that he would appoint a committee of seven officers to deal with frontier crime in accordance with the *Sharia* and his code. On March 27, the mission made a final appearance before the Amir and then set out on its return to India.

In Parliament comments on the success of the mission were contradictory;[66] foreign observers, especially the Berlin *Neue Preussische Zeitung,* saw it as a diplomatic triumph for India, owing to the reverses of Russia in the Far East;[67] and His Majesty's government, unlike India, was satisfied with the result. The Secretary of State expressed his general satisfaction and said that an ultimatum to the Amir, as suggested by India, "might have led to a war with Afghanistan which would have been a calamity to both India and the British Empire."[68]

The government of India expressed its dissatisfaction with the treaty and London's retreat all along the line. India pointed out that the relations with Abdur Rahman were anything but satisfactory, and that it had been established policy that on the death of the Amir a new treaty would be concluded which was to be founded on a more satisfactory basis. The home government was at times more demanding than India in stressing that new agreements were indispensable.[69]

It is quite apparent that the home government was not willing to upset the status quo and risk military action that might involve the Russian empire. Lord Curzon's independence and his disputes with London over strategic and political requirements had been a continuous source of friction. Curzon was personally acquainted with Habibullah and his father, having been to Afghanistan in 1894, and now he expected that this would help him gain the confidence of the new ruler and tie him and his country closer to India. Looking at the history of Anglo-Afghan relations, it is difficult to understand the optimism prevailing in India and the expectation held that an Afghan ruler would ever voluntarily agree to subordinate his independence and personal sovereignty to British strategic considerations. Most of the grievances held by the government of India, such as the status of the British Agent in Kabul and the newswriters in Herat and Kandahar, the resistance by Afghanistan to better communications with India, and the refusal of the Amir to sever his communications with the transborder Afghans, showed clearly the isolationist character of the Amirs' foreign policy and should have been conclusive proof of their desire not to permit peaceful penetration by India under the auspices of a defensive alliance.

It is impossible to say whether the Amir was really willing to agree to the military plan of his council; but even this plan did not provide for the presence of a British force in his country.

The result of the Dane mission was a complete victory for the Amir. On the question of the character of the Anglo-Afghan treaty, the Amir had never abandoned his contention that it was permanent; and both sides accepted the treaty but interpreted it differently, without making specific statements to this effect.

Britain's control of Afghan foreign relations was continued; Britain was willing to permit some local communications of a nonpolitical character on the Russo-Afghan frontier, but the Amir was expected to submit a proposal as to how he would conduct and control such relations. On the matter of British assistance to repel unprovoked aggression against Afghanistan, there had long existed a disagreement between Afghanistan and India. Beginning with the 1890's, Abdur Rahman insisted that British aid should not be in troops, which he had himself in great numbers, but in money and arms. The Dane mission brought this difference of opinion no closer to a solution since all matters of a military character were expediently deferred for future discussions.

The arrears in subsidy were granted without a *quid pro quo* from the Amir. But India's attempt to make London responsible for this is unjustified, for during the negotiations both Clarke and Curzon deplored the fact that Dane had waited so long to hint to the Amir that he might, indeed, receive both the subsidy and the arrears.[70]

The question of arms imports to Afghanistan also remained where it was, and no limitations were imposed on the Amir in the new treaty. The Amir consented to the demarcation of the Mohmand boundary, but he appointed for this task the Sarhang of Dakka, whom the British considered notoriously unfriendly.

The position of the British Agent at Kabul was "improved" insofar as he was now permitted to be seated in durbar among officials of higher rank. Also the Afghan guards were removed from his residence. The Amir promised that, regarding his relations with the Afridis and other tribes across his frontiers, he "would not in future go beyond the principles of his father." And if one looks at the principles held by his father and the many complaints of British officials about his "intrigues" with those tribes, this could only mean that the same unsatisfactory situation would continue.

Habibullah did not permit the appointment of British newswriters at Maymana, Mazar-i-Sharif, and Faizabad; and such questions as the admission of British officers to reconnoiter various areas in Afghanistan, or the granting of land for a railhead at Dakka were postponed for future discussions.

As far as India was concerned, the Dane mission left Anglo-Afghan relations in the same unsatisfactory state as before. It was small consolation to India to have left the Amir in a "friendly and favourable frame of mind." The question was whether this attitude would be lasting.[71]

4. Anglo-Russian Convention and Relations as Usual

HABIBULLAH'S VISIT TO INDIA

After the British mission had left, the Amir thought it advisable to tour parts of his country and announce in public durbar that nothing had happened, except that the old engagements with Britain were reconfirmed and relations were to continue as before.

There was, however, the question remaining from the Dane negotiations whether or not military matters should now be discussed. Habibullah was approached to determine his feelings about making a visit to India, and in February, 1906, the government of India first received an intimation that the Amir might be inclined to come to India.[1] There was some opposition in Afghanistan to the Amir's visit to India, because it was feared that Britain would force a reopening of the Dane negotiations or at least hold the Amir to his promise to discuss matters of military cooperation with the government of India.[2] Rumors were current in Afghanistan that the British wanted to detain the Amir in India, and there was talk of a prophecy warning that the Amir would die if he went to India.

India was not interested in discussing a military alliance but wanted the visit mainly for its effect on the frontier tribes who relied on the Amir's support in their opposition to British forward moves. An invitation was finally issued, requesting the Amir to come for a friendly visit of "sight-seeing and shooting" and Habibullah accepted, arriving in India in early January, 1907. The Amir requested that Dane be his official host, but Sir Henry McMahon was appointed for this function instead, in order to avoid the assumption that the previous negotiations were to be resumed. Lord Minto, who had become Viceroy after Curzon's resignation, cordially received the Afghan ruler. The reluctance of some members of the government of India to acknowledge the Amir's title of "Padshah" was overcome when King Edward VII in a message of welcome addressed Habibullah as "Your Majesty." A thirty-one gun salute was grudgingly presented, and the Amir was feted and generally treated with friendship and cordiality.

Kitchener and McMahon took it upon themselves to initiate the Amir in the freemasonic fraternity without consulting the Foreign Department of the government of India.[3] This act was to have great repercussions in Afghanistan and was causing the Amir the loss of some popular support. Habibullah proved that this trip was solely for pleasure by taking great interest in hunting, socializing, and English ladies. So greatly did he like what he saw that he failed to adhere to the itinerary to which he had pledged himself and lingered in Calcutta and Bombay. The Amir ignored and ridiculed the sirdars in his retinue,[4] and he scandalized many by refusing to take off his shoes in the Delhi mosque.[5] It was with considerable difficulty and amid rumors of plots for his assassination that he was induced to move on from Calcutta.[6] Dane discreetly arranged for an interview with the Amir, but only the subject of arms purchases was brought up.

After Habibullah had returned to Afghanistan, the government of India nervously began to assess the results of his visit. Impressed by what he had seen in India, the Amir had become convinced that his country needed reforms. He engaged a number of technicians and experts in various fields, and he ordered the construction of roads from the Indian border to Kabul and even proposed the construction of a railroad within Afghanistan. So eager was the Amir in his reforms that the Foreign Secretary wondered whether the Amir "is not going too fast in opening up his country." And Clarke remarked that "if the coming summer passes without trouble in Afghanistan, then we may admit the complete success of the visit."[7]

Religious elements, especially certain mullahs of the Laghman district, publicly accused the Amir of having secretly embraced Christianity and of being now ready to "hand over his country bound hand and foot." The Afghan Agent in India reported similar sentiments reaching him from Kabul, and he complained "I have come to grief all around. The Sardars who came to India with the Amir hate me because they say I made money out of the feeding arrangements. Sardar Nasrullah Khan curses me for being the originator of the visit to India, and for making the Amir change his views and religion."[8] The agitation subsided only when, upon his return, the Amir had four mullahs hanged. Habibullah then went on a tour of his country to explain to his people that his policy was identical to the one of his father, and that no concessions were given to Britain.[9] The Amir's enthusiasm for the more obnoxious of his innovations disappeared as rapidly as it was aroused, and the situation returned to normal. It was the conclusion of the Anglo-Russian Convention which finally brought the Amir again to share his people's distrust and hatred for Britain.

AFGHAN REACTION TO THE CONVENTION

The Anglo-Russian Convention of 1907 was an attempt to prevent conflict between the two powers, and, as far as Afghanistan was concerned, to obtain a treaty that would formally confirm what the Granville-Gorchakov agreements and the discussions subsequent to the Russian Memorandum of 1900 attempted. Renewed negotiations received an impetus when the Marquess of Lansdowne wrote to Sir C. Hardinge on October 3, 1905, about a conversation with the Russian Ambassador in which the question of coming to an understanding over the Persian situation was brought up.[10] In subsequent letters, Lord Lansdowne reported that the Russian Ambassador discussed the possibility of an amicable arrangement between Great Britain and Russia. The Ambassador declared that the Anglo-Japanese agreement had come as a shock to the Russian people, but his government was willing to come to an understanding over Afghanistan, Persia, and the Near East, provided it was understood that such an arrangement was not directed against Germany.[11] Sir Edward Grey, the Foreign Secretary, and Sir C. Hardinge reported conversations along similar lines. A message from Count Lamsdorff, delivered through Count Benckendorff, stated that the Russian government noted with much satisfaction, how, without any anterior agreement, England had gradually shown a tendency to cooperate with Russia.[12]

The London *Times* correspondent in St. Petersburg quoted the "generally Anglo-phobe" *Novoe Vremya* of April 1, 1906, as seeing in a rapprochement between the two powers a natural development.[13] The newspaper saw a rapprochement or even an alliance with England as merely a return to the cordial relations that existed before the era of Lords Palmerston and Beaconsfield. For Russia the advantages would be to obtain a breathing spell after her defeat in the Japanese war; and an agreement with England was seen as inevitable for the future settlement of the unavoidable difficulties that would accompany the breakup of the Ottoman Empire. Furthermore such important points as the joining of the Russian and Indian railroad systems could be achieved. The *Habl al-Matin* of Calcutta also favored an alliance between England and Russia.[14]

While the Amir was visiting India, Benckendorff asked Grey whether he might assure A. Isvolsky, the Russian Foreign Minister, that the visit of the Amir to India did not imply any changes that would affect the conditions of negotiations with Russia, and the Foreign Secretary assured him that the visit was merely "to confirm our friendly relations with the Amir, and not to change his political status."[15] The India Office agreed with the Foreign Office, in a letter of March 1, 1907, to instruct Sir A. Nicholson (the British Ambassador to St. Petersburg) that, although at a later stage of the negotiations it would become necessary to make certain recommendations to the Amir, it was premature to raise the question of communications between Russian and Afghan frontier officials. It was desirable that the British government first know the Russian proposals regarding Persia to ascertain whether they were likely to be acceptable and to know exactly what Russia proposed in regard to direct Russo-Afghan relations, before the Amir was to be contacted on the subject.[16] Drafts were prepared by both parties and the negotiations continued.

The government of India, which was informed of the negotiations but not really consulted, was suspicious and did not at all share the views of the home government.[17] Dane wrote in a semiofficial letter of March 3, 1907, that the Amir might wink at informal communications between his frontier officials and the Russians, but he would not readily agree to authorize these formally. Commenting on British and Russian drafts of certain articles of the Convention,

Clarke remarked that there was no information available on commercial dues levied in Afghanistan which would prove or disprove the Russian contention that Britain enjoyed a preferential position. Article VII of the Convention would give both Russia and Britain the same facilities and place their subjects on the same footing when trading in Afghanistan. Clarke declared Article VII unsatisfactory and denounced Article III as impossible. In the latter article Britain agreed not to annex or occupy any portion of Afghanistan. Britain was to exercise her influence in Afghanistan in a pacific sense and take it upon herself to abstain from any military action which might be considered a menace to Russia. Reading both articles together, Clarke felt that Russia was aiming at the perfect equality of Britain and Russia in Afghanistan, and if Britain agreed to such equality she could not hope to obtain exclusive railroad concessions in Afghanistan.[18]

Lord Kitchener held that any arrangement which would disturb in any manner India's fundamental relations with Afghanistan should be resisted to the "last extremity." The Commander-in-Chief believed that Britain was bound by treaty to come to the aid of the Amir in case of unprovoked Russian aggression and that it was not feasible to distinguish between what were offensive and what were defensive measures threatening the Russian frontiers. Kitchener foresaw the possibility of a situation arising whereby Britain might either be compelled to prevent the Amir from strengthening his defenses or, being unwilling to coerce the Amir, be forced to permit Russia to undertake such a measure.[19] He also felt that if the Amir or his successor were to ally himself with Russia, "we should be unable to enter the country and enforce our undoubted rights of intervention without a breach of the Treaty and a consequent risk of war with Russia." And as serious as war with Russia might be, a war with the combined forces of Russia and Afghanistan would be infinitely more so. Lord Kitchener, therefore, recommended that an entente with Russia be indefinitely postponed.

London was informed of the opinion of the government of India, but the negotiations continued, and all that India could do was to suggest modifications in the British counterdraft to Russian proposals. In the Anglo-Russian Convention, which was signed on August 31, 1907, Russia's definition of Afghanistan as a buffer state was eliminated, and the Russian government declared Afghanistan outside her sphere of influence. Britain on her part declared that she had no intention of changing the political status of Afghanistan. She would further exercise her influence only in a pacific sense, and, recognizing her Treaty of 1905, she had no intention of interfering with the internal government of Afghanistan. No territory would be annexed, provided that the Amir also fulfilled his obligations. Russian and Afghan authorities were permitted to establish direct nonpolitical relations. Equal facilities were to be granted to both powers, and the Convention was to be considered in force with the consent of the Amir.[20]

While in Europe there seemed to be general satisfaction with the Convention, the government of India was faced with the question of "how to tell it to the Amir?" During the negotiations with Russia, the home government did not want to inform the Amir until it was certain that there would be a treaty, and it was not until September 10, 1907, that the government of India officially contacted the Amir about the Convention. Habibullah was informed that for some time past "negotiations of a most delicate character" had been in progress between Russia and Britain, "largely, if not mainly, with a view to secure the integrity of Afghanistan and removal of causes of jealousy between the British and Russian Governments." Lord Minto's letter then gave the text of the Afghan portion of the Convention and the Viceroy expressed his feelings, saying with somewhat exaggerated optimism, "I cannot but think that Your Majesty will regard the conclusion of this Convention with lively satisfaction." By way of explanation, he pointed to Article I in which Britain stated that she had no intention of changing the political status of Afghanistan, while Russia declared her neighbor outside her sphere of influence. Minto defined Article II as a repetition of British pledges given in the Treaty of 1905. Article III was explained as a concession in the interests of peace in Asia and of the prosperity of Afghanistan and India, and the Amir was advised "that the earnest wish of the Russian Government should be conceded," and direct contact between frontier officials be permitted in matters of a nonpolitical nature. It was left to the Amir to seek the advice of the government of India even in these nonpolitical relations. With regard to the equality of treatment of Russian trade with that of British subjects, the Viceroy thought that the Amir would not object, since "British and Russian trade with Afghanistan is already accorded equal treatment." The Viceroy then pointed to Article V, according to which the approval of the Amir was required before the Convention would come into force, and asked Habibullah to give his formal concurrence with the least possible delay, because "his prerogatives and interests had been jealously safeguarded." Since the Advantages of the Convention were so self-evident, the government of India thought it unnecessary to add anything more in explanation, but it was prepared, if the Amir desired, to send one British officer, accompanied by only one assistant, to explain matters more fully.[21]

Habibullah answered on September 29, 1907, saying that he was at the time making a tour of Afghanistan and could not respond immediately, but, God willing, he would do so upon his return to Kabul in the middle of the following month.[22] It became apparent that God was not willing, for many months passed before the Amir took a stand on the Convention.

Now began a period of anxious waiting. There was uncertainty as to the validity of the agreement between the two empires, and the fact that the Afghan ruler seemed to have a veto in it caused no little embarrassment in several capitals. The government of India carefully studied every lead from the Afghan capital which might indicate the reaction of the Amir. The British Agent at Kabul was sounding out Afghan officials; British Military Intelligence, frontier officers, and British consular officers consulted their agents to precipitate an answer and to find out what it might be.

In the beginning of March, 1908, the Afghan Envoy in India told Clarke confidentially that the Amir had directed him to send a detailed report with all the clauses of the Anglo-Afghan Convention. The Envoy also said that he had advised the Amir to sign the Convention. From the Afghan agent in Meshed the British military attaché learned that the Amir was determined not to allow any closer intercourse either with India or Russia. The Afghan Agent also quoted the Amir as saying that he opposed the Convention even before he had received any official communication on the subject from India.[23]

In Parliament the question was frequently raised whether the Amir had finally given his assent to the Convention, but embarrassed government officials could merely reply in the negative. Lord Curzon, who was at that time again a member of Parliament, severely attacked the Convention.[24] According to the military attaché at Meshed, Russian public opinion gave little importance to the fact that the Amir had not accepted the terms of the Convention. The Russians considered it most important that Britain had come to terms with them; and if the Amir refused to receive Russian commercial agents and to open his country to trade, they expected that Britain and Russia would jointly force him to do so.[25]

The hospital assistant with the Kabul agency reported on May 23, 1908, that the Amir's council had met frequently during the past week and decided that the Amir should not sign the Convention. Another, more ominous, report from the Kabul agency stated that in durbar the Amir declared himself opposed to the Convention, adding that he now had enough ammunition to last him for ten years of war, and enough rifles to arm all adults in Afghanistan. A British newswriter reported in April, 1908, from Samarkand that, according to a trustworthy source, the Mohmands from the Khyber area had sent a deputation to the Amir offering their allegiance and asking for help against the British. The Amir purportedly sold them eight thousand rifles and promised them other help if they fought the British.[26]

The Russian *Novoe Vremya* of June 9, 1908, saw in the meeting of the British and Russian monarchs at Reval a fresh security for the peace of Europe and held that, thanks to the rapprochement, "England can treat the Mohmand rising, and Russia the events in Persia, as local incidents, deprived of international character, and can extinguish at leisure a spark which two years ago might have threatened a conflagration." [27] The paper further urged that "the buffer state can now become a linking state, and the material for strategic railways collected on both frontiers of Afghanistan in ten years of mutual distrust can become the potent means of economic union." The field open for the joint political activity of England and Russia was wide and profitable and, according to the newspaper, "not by any means limited by the points mentioned in the agreement." [28]

On June 23, 1908, Lord Minto sent a wary letter regarding the Convention to London in which he said, "the fog is very thick, and I cannot see my way out of it." He stressed the immense value to

India of a friendly Afghanistan and urged that, in whatever Britain might do, the necessity of the Amir's friendship should be an axiom. He warned that the hostility of Afghanistan would mean the certainty of war in which all the tribes on the frontier from Waziristan to Kashmir would join, while India would be faced with serious internal difficulties. The Viceroy saw the Amir's refusal as certain, and he warned that the Convention might have been a Russian trick to involve England and Afghanistan in hostilities. Habibullah was reported to have received letters from Persia and Russia asking him not to sign the Convention. But the Viceroy was unable to suggest much in the way of a remedy. A polite letter might be sent reminding the Amir to give his reply; a mission might be dispatched possibly under McMahon, but it would be surrounded by so many dangers that one could scarcely be justified in sending it. A bribe would only lead to a demand for more money. There had been large-scale Mahsud raids into British territory and there were the usual rumors of Afghan connivance. Minto confessed that the "Waziristan position has haunted me," and he deprecated the sending of a punitive expedition since it was tantamount to "throwing lives and money away."[29]

On July 30, 1908, His Majesty's government urged that, in view of both the situation of the Russian government and of considerations of British prestige, it was necessary that another letter be sent to the Amir. The Russian government, it was held, could not be expected to allow the situation to drift indefinitely, and it would regard the refusal of the Amir to send a reply as a formal refusal to the conditions of the Convention. London felt that "we should thus in any case be confronted with [the] necessity of discussing with Russia arrangements to be made in consequence of [the] Amir's direct or indirect refusal to accept [the] Convention and the danger you point out of [the] political situation in India consequent on [the] Amir's failure to consent becoming known, [the] seriousness of which we fully recognize, would arise." The London government approved the draft of a letter to the Amir and suggested alternative action depending on the Amir's reply or lack of it.[30]

Finally, after a delay of over a year, Habibullah responded on August 14, 1908, to the British announcement of the Convention.[31] The Amir wrote a friendly letter to which he added the opinion of his council, contained in a fifty-four-page document. Without stating any opinion of his own, the Amir invited Lord Minto's reaction and recommendations as to the steps necessary for the "good of the Governments of Great Britain and Afghanistan."

The Afghan council's views were as follows: The Convention destroyed the independence of Afghanistan; it had no advantages and was equally harmful to Britain as it was to Afghanistan. The Indian government had sent to the Amir only a translation of the Convention relating to Afghanistan, whereas three conventions were drawn up simultaneously. The council, therefore, cited the three conventions as telegraphed by Reuter's correspondent from St. Petersburg (which was not identical with the one actually signed). Referring first to the Persian Convention, the council contended that since Persia had been divided into four parts of which two were allotted to Russia, one to Britain, and only one part was left to Persia, the words of "freedom and independence" as applied to Persia were meaningless. Since these words were not mentioned in the Convention regarding Afghanistan, the council contended that this implied that the position of Afghanistan would be subordinate only. Further, since the Persian Convention provided for the construction of railways, while the Tibet Convention provided that neither England nor Russia should make railways or telegraph lines in Tibet, the council suspected that the two powers reserved for themselves the right to build railways and telegraph lines in Afghanistan.

Referring next to the British treaty with Japan, the council held that it provided for the protection of the Indian frontier, while the Afghan Convention provided for the extension of influence by way of trade. But without railroads and telegraphs, such commerce would not be possible, and troops to protect the railroads and to operate them would follow. Russian commercial agents would be imposed on the Afghan government, and, since trade was not confined to the capital, these agents would spread into other areas. This would surely lead to conflict because they would be attacked by the Afghans.

Next the council argued that, since there was a clause in the Tibet Convention prohibiting the grant of land to either Russia or Britain, the omission of such a clause in the Afghan Convention entitled

Russia to buy lands in Afghanistan from fugitives from Herat. The council pointed to the great responsibility that would be imposed by this on the Afghan government; it cited the murders of L. Cavagnari and G. Fleischer as examples, and said that the Afghans would have to be disarmed like the people of India.[32] These, the council represented, were the transparent disadvantages, but what was hidden should also be mentioned: "Afghanistan is the gate of India, and Herat is the gate of Afghanistan. Russia is in close connection with Herat by three routes, while Britain, seeing only one route open to Herat, has relinquished the idea of defending it. And the leaving open of this gate is the ruin of the house."

The council then proceeded to outline a plan by which both Afghanistan and India could be protected; it had some resemblance to the one proposed to the Dane mission. In conclusion the council stated

> . . . [it could] never disregard the written and verbal advice of our late King to the effect that the necessity for our friendship with the British Government and our enmity with the Russian Government is proved by the fact that one is aiming at the protection of India and the other at seizing it. In the course of our discussions with the Dane Mission it was repeatedly explained by us that, in the interests of our nation and Government, we consider this incumbent on us. We will not act contrary to our principle. If they [the British] act in contravention of the principle laid down by them in the past, they will have to show a better principle to their own Government and to ours.[33]

Although the comparisons and deductions made by the council were at times not quite logical, they were not so absurd as some members of the government of India asserted. It is clear that, by granting Russia concessions in the north of Afghanistan which India did not enjoy in the south and for the sake of equity now demanded, Britain in fact attempted to solve the Afghanistan question over the head of the Amir. The division of Persia, arranged in the same document, seemed to show to the Afghan council what might be in store for them.

The Kabul agent reported on September 16, 1908, that Sirdar Nasrullah and Abdul Kuddus Khan were responsible for the reply to the Viceroy, and that they thought their reply was most reasonable and at the same time polite and hoped that this was the last they would hear of the Convention. Nasrullah was further quoted as saying that, according to Islamic law, the Amir had no power "to part with or alienate the rights of his subjects on his own personal opinion," and the Afghan people and the council, which is their representative, were authorized to "guard their rights and interests by using force."[34] Lord Minto thereupon suggested that the best solution of the difficulty would be an attempt by His Majesty's government to persuade Russia to agree to cancel Articles III and IV of the Convention.[35] Sir Roos-Keppel, Chief Commissioner in the North-West Frontier, reported the Amir's "real attitude and feelings" to S. H. Butler, Secretary to the Foreign Department. He said that Habibullah was convinced that the British were determined upon his destruction, that Britain had a secret understanding with Russia for the partition of Afghanistan, and that Britain would within a short time declare war. Having been disappointed by Britain, the Amir was said to have gone to the other extreme of distrust. He did not believe that he could stand alone against India, but he knew the strength of the frontier tribes and had, according to Roos-Keppel, an exaggerated idea of the power of the Indian Nationalists, with whom he was in constant communication, and who assured him that they welcomed him as the ruler of India. The Amir did not want war, but he believed it would be forced upon him and he saw his only chance in taking the offensive.[36]

The London government had in the meantime agreed with Russia that the consent of the Amir was not needed, and, since Habibullah neither raised any objections to Article III nor prohibited frontier communications, his apparent tacit approval was enough until such time as he signed the Convention.[37] Thus, once again, a crisis in Afghanistan's foreign relations was permitted to pass.

AFGHAN RELATIONS AS USUAL

In view of the Anglo-Russian pressures on the Amir, it was not surprising that the old issues, which the Dane mission had hoped to resolve, remained and Afghan foreign relations continued as before

The isolation of British agents in Afghanistan was not ended. Since 1894, Abdur Rahman had made it a custom to reject almost invariably the first British nominee for the position of agent in Kabul, and it appears probable that he did so in order to remind Britain of the fact that the agent was at Kabul with the express permission of the Afghan ruler.[38] The reasons given for rejection of the British candidates was often that they were Shiah or suspected of having such sympathies, or that they were persons of dubious character. Habibullah made an innovation of sorts in November, 1907, when he vetoed the appointment of Malik Umar Hayat Khan on the grounds that he was young and unexperienced.[39] Lord Minto resented this evaluation of the qualifications of a man he had appointed, but he was reluctant to force his choice on Habibullah because without the goodwill of the Amir the agent's mission would be condemned to failure from the start.

Afghan policy was similar with regard to the newswriters in Kandahar and Herat, only that these officials did not have the status of the representative in Kabul and were therefore subject to greater harassment and supervision.[40] A serious challenge to the effectiveness of the British agent in Kabul and his personnel was the Amir's insistence that, with the exception of the agent, all be subject to Islamic law. Although it at times surrendered native employees to Afghan jurisdiction, the government of India insisted that its employees enjoy consular immunity.[41] But India did not want to press this matter because it would have had to reciprocate in the case of Afghan officials in India, and this would have been tantamount to a recognition of Afghan independence. Subsequent to the Dane mission, the government of India repeatedly addressed the Amir in this matter and attempted to induce him to accept the system prevailing in the Ottoman Empire, according to which foreign embassies had jurisdiction over their nationals. The Amir declined to accept a system calculated to "lead to much dishonour" to him and his country. There was nothing that could be done, and Britain was put in the odious position of having to surrender her Afghan employees. This was rationalized in India by agreeing that an Afghan subject "must take his chance of the punishments customary in his own country."[42]

That this state of affairs prevented the efficient collection of intelligence is obvious; and the fact that reporters and informants for Britain were at times executed as spies was sufficient deterrent to

Afghans to prevent them from seeking British employment in large numbers.[43] The dispensary of the British agency in Kabul was open to Afghans and could have been a means of access to British officials for spies and informants; but the Amir kept an Afghan guard at the gate of the agency and thus also closed this channel for British intelligence.

The problem of the tribes was another perennial issue which affected Anglo-Afghan relations. Afghan rulers had customarily exercised a suzerainty over the independent tribes lying between Afghanistan and British India. Habibullah continued this policy, subsidizing tribes and inviting tribal deputations to Kabul where they would receive khilats (robes of honor) and various presents. The Afghan rulers were interested in having a buffer zone of independent tribes between Afghanistan and India, and no Afghan ruler could see with equanimity that Britain was slowly trying to penetrate this security belt to push forward her railroad toward the Afghan border. Since there was a reservoir of fighting men which could be utilized against Britain if she should attempt to invade Afghanistan, it was in the interest of Afghanistan that British penetration be foiled and the tribes protected and armed.

For this reason the Amir could not be expected to cut off the illicit arms trade with the frontier, and he could not make common cause with the government of India in curbing frontier violence. Raids were conducted with some impartiality into both India and Afghanistan, and neither of the two governments was able to effectively guard the frontier. On occasion, both countries arranged a settlement of accounts by setting off cases against each other; the party with the larger amounts of offenses paid blood money and fines according to established rates.[44]

The Afghan love of firearms made it inevitable that much raiding into British India was conducted for the purpose of capturing guns. There was even some specialization in these offenses. The Ut Khels, a tribe of some three hundred Ghilzays from the Laghman valley in Afghanistan, specialized in the stealing of rifles. They roamed far into India and became such a threat that the government of India contemplated the restricting of the free influx of Afghans. This was, however, not feasible because some half a million seasonal immigrants went yearly to India.[45] Arms were also smuggled via

Muscat and other Persian Gulf areas and found their way into the hands of the Afridis and other transborder tribes.[46] In Afghanistan arms were freely sold and bought "by every class and creed who could afford to buy them."[47] And it was a common boast of the Afghans that the price for a good rifle was the same in Kabul as in Calcutta.[48]

The question of demarcation of the Indo-Afghan boundary also did not find its solution under Habibullah. The Durand Agreement of 1893 laid down the border, but when demarcation was taken up in 1895 Abdur Rahman claimed that he was to receive the entire Mohmand territory and not merely a section of it. In 1896 the Amir protested discrepancies on the map attached to the Durand Agreement, but Lord Elgin told him that the frontier drawn on the map must be followed. The Viceroy made some minor concessions to the Amir, coupled with an ultimatum that these concessions would be withdrawn if the Amir failed to begin demarcation of the boundary. Abdur Rahman permitted British and Afghan commissions to be set up for demarcation of the boundaries, but demarcation was never accomplished because the Amir failed to arrange for the protection of the British commissioners (protection from tribes on the British side of the border). During the frontier disturbances of 1897, British troops overran the Mohmand territory including Bohai Dag which was previously given to the Amir in exchange for an early demarcation. Habibullah defended his full rights to Bohai Dag, and the government of India began to regret having permitted this valley to remain in the possession of the Amir.[49] Habibullah asserted his right to Smatzai in 1905; a request from Lord Curzon for demarcation of parts of the boundary did not lead to any solution.

In 1908 Lord Minto suggested to London the sending of a punitive expedition into the Bazar valley against the Zakka Khel Afridis who had conducted a series of raids into Indian territory and seemed to be encouraged in their anti-British activities by Afghan support, especially from Nasrullah Khan. The government of India assured London that it did not contemplate the dispatch of a punitive expedition on the old lines, which included the burning of villages, blowing up of houses, cutting down or ringing of fruit trees, and other acts of destruction. What was wanted was merely the recovery of a fine and the disarmament of the section, the capture and trial of ringleaders, and the construction of a road that would contain this section in the future.[50]

The expedition was approved, and, for the sake of convenience, the Mohmands were punished at the same time, although they seemed to have taken up arms only in response to British moves into their territory. As happened before, the punitive expedition aroused the surrounding tribes, and Afghans from Nangrahar prepared for jihad and moved large lashkars (tribal armies) to the border.[51] The years 1908 and 1909 were consequently marked by unrest on the North-West Frontier.

Russo-Afghan relations under Habibullah were not materially affected by Russian pressure either. The Russian Memorandum of 1900 was a notice of intentions on the part of Russia to Britain, but without the concurrence of the Amir relations could not be established. The case of the "lost" boundary pillars did not force any relations, nor did the Russian occupation of Yangi Kila, an island in the Oxus. In 1908 about fifteen hundred Jamshidis from Afghanistan crossed the border into Russia to flee from what they claimed was oppression from the Amir's officials. This wholesale emigration led to some correspondence between Russia and Afghanistan, but Russia carefully avoided making any reference to the Anglo-Russian Convention.[52]

In 1912 Russia asked for the good offices of the British government in helping to bring about an arrangement between the Russian and Afghan governments for the regulation of irrigation rights on the Murghab and Hari Rud rivers.[53] In further exchanges of notes between the Russian and British governments, the former complained of a lack of Afghan cooperation in fighting the locust menace and also brought up the question of Russo-Afghan trade. Britain saw in these steps Russian attempts to force the Amir to act in the sense of the Convention.[54]

The actions of Russia in northern Persia, the Turco-Italian War, and the Balkan War had affected feelings of Muslim solidarity even in Afghanistan, and the government of India did not feel that this was a good time to address the Amir in connection with the Convention.

During the reign of Habibullah, Turkish influence began to spread in Afghanistan. As sunni Muslims they were better suited for work in Afghanistan than Christians. They were subject to Islamic law, at least in theory, and they were more acceptable for these and other reasons to the people of Afghanistan. The spreading of Turkish influence in Afghanistan was due, at least in part, to the activities of Mahmud Tarzi, an Afghan who was forced into exile by Abdur Rahman and lived many years in Damascus and Constantinople and other areas in the Ottoman Empire. Tarzi witnessed Ottoman attempts at reform and saw the vulnerability of a Muslim state in relations with Western powers. Tarzi's later activities proved that he held Pan-Islamic sentiments, and after he and his family were established in Kabul in 1905, Tarzi became the nucleus of a nationalist party. Nasrullah and other members of the Amir's court gravitated into the Tarzi camp. Mahmud Tarzi's influence was consolidated when he gave two of his daughters in marriage to sons of the Amir and he assumed the position of editor of the *Sirāj al-Akhbār*, a most influential Kabuli newspaper.[55]

The British Consul at Damascus learned as early as the beginning of 1904 that Habibullah had developed pro-Turkish tendencies: the Amir introduced the fez in Kabul, supported the Hejaz Railway, and hired Turkish teachers and mullahs.[56]

In 1904 the Ottoman government considered sending Habibullah the Mejidi Order and refrained from doing so only when discouraged by Britain.[57] In 1907 a group of seven Turks arrived in Kabul among whom were a physician, a military officer, and an engineer. They were brought to Afghanistan through the agency of the nephew of the Naqib of Baghdad.[58] The British military attaché in Constantinople claimed that the Turks in Afghanistan had Pan-Islamic tendencies and were in continuous contact with the Pan-Islamic League through the Naqib's relations.[59]

In 1911 Count Benckendorff, the Russian Ambassador, informed Britain that a high Turkish officer, presumably Shukri Pasha, was at Kabul for the purpose of inducing the Amir to conclude a treaty of alliance with Turkey.[60] Whatever the connections and secret objectives of these Turkish nationals may have been, there was no doubt that their presence in Afghanistan served to remind the Afghan people of their community of interest with other Islamic peoples such as the Turks.[61] The Turco-Italian War and the Balkan wars were factors in dramatizing the common plight of the Muslim world in the face of Western imperialism. Events in these wars were widely reported in the *Sirāj-al-Akhbār*, and much was made of atrocities claimed to have been committed by Turkey's antagonists in the Balkan wars. Habibullah publicly criticized Britain for her neutrality in the wars threatening Turkey and said that this would alienate the hearts of a large number of Muslims. He added that this neutrality was against Britain's national interests since she had more Muslim subjects than any others. The Amir warned that Britain's Muslim subjects were no longer passive, and declared that "the eyes and ears of all have become open and sentiments of freedom and self-government have kindled their brains." [62]

In early 1912, Russian activities precipitated a war scare in Afghanistan when it was reported that attempts were made to build a bridge across the Oxus. The Amir warned the Afghan tribes not to raid British territory, and he was said to have consulted the mullahs on the advisability of asking for British aid in case of a Russian attack. [63]

The military attaché in Meshed reported in April, 1912, that the Russians were greatly frustrated at the paucity of beneficial results they got from the Anglo-Afghan Convention. The Russians blamed the British for maintaining their suspicions of Russian motives and for failing to persuade the Amir to accept their "moderate" wishes. [64] Russia also requested the extradition of Russians kept in Afghan prisons, basing her request for British assistance in this case on Article III of the Convention. But Britain was not willing to admonish Habibullah to have more cordial relations with Russia and thus risk the worsening of her own relations with the Amir. Secret negotiations between Russia and Britain continued in which Russia was willing to make concessions in Tibet for a *quid pro quo* in Afghanistan. Russia demanded more influence in northern Afghanistan; spheres of influence were to be drawn which would have opened Herat to Russian penetration. Negotiations continued until the imminence of World War I relegated this question to the background. [65]

5. World War I and Neutrality

THE NIEDERMAYER EXPEDITION

The outbreak of World War I again brought Afghanistan into the picture of international politics. And this time, the situation was drastically changed: gone were the pressures that had been exerted on Afghanistan by her two neighbors; no contributions to the war effort were demanded; and the two powers were satisfied to see the Amir neutral in the international dispute. While the consequences of a major war with Afghanistan were quite unpredictable in ordinary times, during a period of danger in Europe they could easily be catastrophic. Both Russia and Britain were, therefore, prepared to go to some lengths to appease Afghanistan, although this was made difficult by such events as the arrival of the Niedermayer expedition in Afghanistan, which ended the isolation of that country and presaged danger to the war effort of the two empires.

The Niedermayer-Hentig expedition was Germany's answer to a proposal of Enver Pasha. Even before becoming a party in the war, the Turkish Minister of War had suggested that Germany should participate in a Turkish mission to Afghanistan for the purpose of aligning that country on the side of the Central Powers.[1] Enver Pasha was thinking in terms of a few men who would represent these European powers and thus give greater importance to his mission without detracting from its essentially Pan-Islamic nature. After Turkey had become a participant in the war, Enver Pasha reported receipt of a message from the Afghan ruler, according to which Habibullah had asked whether he should attack Russia or Britain.[2] The War Minister saw in this more than a mere gesture of Islamic solidarity and believed that the Amir was eager to begin hostilities against India and was only waiting for support and encouragement from the Central Powers.[3]

The approval of the project by such Orientalists and world

travelers as Dr. Max von Oppenheim and Sven Hedin carried great weight in the considerations of the German Foreign Office.[4] The Auswaertige Amt accepted the suggestion and decided to set up a group of suitable people. It is clear that the mission was not a long-planned and carefully thought-out enterprise, for most of its members had been serving in various European battlefields and were collected only gradually from all points of the compass. Some of the members suggested other suitable persons and thus the group began to grow.

In early September, 1914, the first contingent of twenty-three Germans set out for Constantinople under the leadership of Wilhelm Wassmuss, the only one of this group with a personal acquaintance with the Middle East.[5] Niedermayer soon followed with another group of Germans. After the groups had moved on to Baghdad in mid-January, 1915, the expedition was thoroughly reorganized, new members were added, and those unqualified for the task were eliminated. Niedermayer had by that time worked himself into a leading position. The German group was to be integrated into a Turkish force under the command of Colonel Rauf Bey, a hero of the Turco-Italian War; but German preparations had gathered momentum and dimensions that no longer permitted the Germans to be integrated into a Turkish-led project. Germany paid the cost of the expedition, and both Wassmuss and Niedermayer felt that they should not become the "tools of Turkish policy"; they wanted to take orders only from the German Foreign Office and the German General Staff.[6]

These developments, as well as personality clashes between the Germans and the Turks, resulted in much friction and mutual suspicion. The Turks especially resented German initiatives in Islamic propaganda and such independent action as the procurement of fetwas calling for jihad. Captain F. Klein, a former military attaché at the German Legation in Teheran, had gone to Karbala and obtained fetwas from the Shaykh Ali al-Iraqayn and the Great Mujtahids favoring a holy war against the Allies.[7] Rauf Bey blamed German indiscretion for publicizing the existence and purpose of the expedition and, in view of the changed character of the mission, he became reluctant to continue the project.[8] In the meantime, members of the Indian Committee in Berlin suggested to the German

Foreign Office that another mission be sent to Afghanistan for the purpose of establishing contact with the Indian revolutionaries and carrying anti-British propaganda into India.[9]

Germany agreed to this project, and a group under the joint leadership of the Indian Prince Mahendra Pratap [10] and the German Lieutenant Werner Otto von Hentig set out for the Middle East. A Turkish officer, Kazim Bey, joined the group one day before its departure from Baghdad.[11] Mahendra Pratap had a series of interviews with German and Turkish government officials and audiences with Kaiser Wilhelm II, Sultan Muhammad Ghazi V, the ex-Khedive Abbas Hilmi, and the Shaykh al-Islam. Pratap's mission was to seek the advice of the Amir of Afghanistan "whose heroic armies had so often destroyed British and Russian forces" regarding the steps needed to liberate India. Mahendra Pratap was to report on the situation in Europe and to express his conviction that the Central Powers would soon win the war. Hentig was to initiate diplomatic relations between Germany and Afghanistan and assist the Indian Prince in establishing contact with revolutionaries in India.[12]

Niedermayer insisted from the beginning that the expedition be organized along military lines of command, subject to martial law, and urged integration of the Hentig group under his orders. Disagreements as to who would command the expedition had already led to the resignation of Wassmuss and others, but the disputes were finally resolved when both groups met in Persia and traveled under joint leadership from Tabbas via Bushruye to the Afghan border.[13]

The Turco-German plans did not remain secret for long. Already in September, 1914, the Viceroy had informed London of information received from the political officer in the Persian Gulf, according to which thirty-two secret emissaries had set out for the Middle East with the object of agitating for jihad in Afghanistan and India.[14] And on July 3, 1915, Lord Hardinge informed the Secretary of State for India of the measures he had authorized to counter the activities of the Germans in Persia and to prevent their entrance into Afghanistan. Money was to be spent freely to get information on the movements of the Germans, and local militia and Russian troops were to be organized to capture and annihilate the expedition. The British Ambassador in Teheran deprecated the use of British troops in Persia since this "would antagonize Persia and give the German cause a great impetus." Therefore the British Consul at Kerman was instructed to secretly employ Afghan camelmen for this purpose, so that if they were defeated by the Germans there would be no loss of British prestige.[15]

On November 5, 1914, the Viceroy informed Habibullah that Turkey had joined the war on the side of the Central Powers.[16] Lord Hardinge emphasized that there could be no talk of a religious war since Turkey had allied herself with two Christian powers against Britain, "the greatest and most sympathetic Muhammadan Power in the world." He also cited the declaration of the British government according to which the Islamic holy places would be immune from British attack, and he called the Turks the dupes of the Germans, tricked into the war by a small minority. The Viceroy claimed widespread support for Britain among the Muslim ruling chiefs in India and the Arabs in Aden and the Persian Gulf and urged that "in view of these facts and of the friendship and alliance of our Governments, I feel sure that Your Majesty will not waver from the attitude of neutrality which, under my advice, you have already guaranteed." Habibullah had declared his neutrality at the outbreak of the war and he reconfirmed it on October 3, 1914.[17] While he merely regretted the war in Europe, he was seriously concerned when Turkey became a participant.

On March 3, 1915, the Viceroy informed the Amir of Russian concern over "alarming reports" from frontier officers in Turkestan of "unusual military preparations on the Afghan border." Hardinge said he personally discounted these rumors, stating he had not the least reason to believe that the Amir had ordered any military movements beyond what was necessary for the maintenance of peace and order. He said he was absolutely certain of the Amir's intention to maintain his neutrality.[18] But the Viceroy expressed his astonishment that the preposterous German propaganda, according to which the Emperor of Germany and his people had embraced Islam, should find such widespread credence on the Afghan frontier.

To London, the Viceroy reported that the Afghan people were generally pro-Turkish, but that the Amir was sincere in his declaration of neutrality. He warned, however, that the presence of German agents with armed parties in Afghanistan would make it doubtful whether or not the Amir could maintain his neutrality.[19]

On July 6, 1915, the government of India warned the Amir of the passage of groups of Germans, Austrians, Turks, Armenians, and Indians through Iran with the intention of entering Afghanistan and asked the Amir to treat such groups as they would be treated in any other neutral country, namely, to arrest them, disarm them, and intern them until the end of the war.[20] In further communications the Viceroy requested Habibullah to contradict the stories current in Afghanistan and on the frontier, which announced that a Turco-German army was on the march to India via Afghanistan.[21]

In his reply, the Amir promised that he would deal with foreign parties entering his country in the manner requested by the Viceroy. He said he had given instructions to that effect to the Governor of Herat, and, in a postscript in his own handwriting, the Amir assured the Viceroy to "have no anxiety about the movements of those parties, for firstly they will not enter Afghan territory. Should they do so, please God, they can in no way interfere with the neutrality of Afghanistan."[22]

In spite of Anglo-Russian measures it was impossible to prevent the Niedermayer-Hentig contingent from crossing the border, but it was possible to close the gap and prevent a group under Seiler from following with the radio equipment and much of the baggage of the expedition.[23] In an intercepted message to the German Ambassador in Teheran it was optimistically stated that "the Afghan frontier which is guarded by the British has been happily crossed by the southern party. Their welcome locally was very hearty, so that we can depend on receiving gratifying news from K[abul]."[24] The British Consul General at Meshed reported on August 24, 1915, that the remainder of the expedition of about sixty men had arrived in Herat and were staying in the Bagh-i-Shah. The Governor visited them in full dress and gave them the freedom of the town. Lieutenant General T. W. Haig had further learned that "some foolish people are kissing the hands of the party and otherwise behaving in a foolish manner, but public opinion in favour of the visitors is by no means unanimous, Kadahari and Kabuli sepoys are at present pro-German, but the Herati sepoys are unanimously inclined for quietness and peace and it may be hoped that wiser counsels prevail among all."[25]

On September 12, the Consul General reported that the Germans were received in durbar by the Governor where they exhibited a proclamation of jihad from the Sultan of Turkey. The Germans were also reported to have promised military assistance to Afghanistan and declared that Germany was prepared to help them gain Turkestan, as far as Samarkand, and India, as far as Bombay.[26]

It quickly became apparent that the foreign emissaries enjoyed considerable freedom in Herat and were being treated by Muhammad Sarwar Khan, the Governor, with great consideration. The Governor permitted some members of the expedition to return to the Persian border and allowed others who had arrived at the border to proceed to Herat. There was some friction between the Governor and the commander of the Afghan troops. The Afghan Commander objected to the appointment of a colonel as head of the guard over German officers no higher in rank than captain, and he warned the Governor that he would have to stand guard, should a German general succeed in escaping to Afghanistan.[27] The Germans did little to gain the goodwill of the Commander and openly criticized the Afghan arms as antiquated and many Afghan officers as "old and past work." [28]

C. Nabokoff, the Russian Consul at Simla, complained to Foreign Secretary Sir A. H. Grant about the Amir's permissive attitude toward the Germans, and Grant admitted that it was casting doubts on the sincerity of the Amir's declarations.[29] The government of India, therefore, suggested to the home government that the Amir be reminded of his obligations to Britain. The Viceroy wanted this accomplished by sending a personally signed letter from the British King to Habibullah, commending him on the "scrupulous and honourable way" in which the Amir had maintained the strict attitude of neutrality which he had guaranteed at the beginning of the war.[30] In another communication the Viceroy suggested giving some material benefit, and it was finally decided to grant the Amir an increase in subsidy amounting to 2 lakhs.[31]

Meanwhile, the Niedermayer-Hentig expedition left Herat on September 7, and, traveling by the Hazarajat route, arrived in Kabul on September 26, 1915. The mission was well received: the Turkish employees of the Amir were gathered to give them a rousing salute, and Khayri Bey, who trained the Afghan troops, took it upon himself to give the foreigners a parade and a military salute.

(Khayri was temporarily dismissed by the Amir when he heard of this event.)[32] The whole group was accommodated in the Bagh-i-Baber on the outskirts of Kabul where they were supplied with provisions and other necessities at government expense.

The expedition was not at all the dignified affair which its members hoped it would be. For greater mobility, the group had crossed into Afghanistan without much of their equipment: a wireless transmitter, ten boxes of money, the letters to the Indian princes, and some of their credentials were lost in Persia. The Governor of Herat had uniforms made for the leaders of the mission so that they would appear more presentable.[33] The mission was kept strictly isolated from the population: upon their arrival in Herat and Kabul, the foreigners were kept in confinement, and when they were finally permitted to move about, they were constantly escorted by Afghan guides. After their promising reception at Kabul, the members of the mission were kept confined to the Bagh-i-Baber, and only by the threat of a hunger strike did they succeed in obtaining an interview with the Amir.[34]

Habibullah had remained longer than usual in his summer quarters, staying in Paghman until November 4. Some attributed this to a desire on the part of the Amir to put off his encounter with the foreign mission, but it appears more likely that he preferred to interview the foreign emissaries in the privacy of his mountain retreat where the proceedings could be protected better from the curious eyes of the British Agent in Kabul. Finally, in the middle of October, 1915, the Amir received the group in Paghman, telling them that he looked upon them as merchants and they should spread out their wares before him so that he could choose whatever he liked and leave whatever he did not need.[35] As it turned out, the expedition had not much to sell but fiery speeches. They offered some of the presents that they had not lost in Iran, and then revealed the nature of their mission. Letters from the German Reichskanzler, Enver Pasha, and, according to one source, from the German Kaiser were presented to the Amir.[36] Hentig, Niedermayer, Mahendra Pratap, Barakatullah, and Kazim Bey (who was upgraded to be the official representative of the Ottoman Empire) gave their individual presentations and the negotiations began.

In two interviews with the Amir at Paghman during October,

and in subsequent meetings at Kabul, the mission attempted to encourage the Amir to follow the call of jihad and ally himself with the Central Powers against his traditional enemies. The letter from Enver Pasha was reported to have covered the following points:

1. Announcement that jihad had been declared by the Ottoman Sultan. The Amir was asked whether he would follow the call.

2. Would the Amir permit the passage of Turkish troops through Afghanistan to India?

3. Afghanistan was called upon to break her relations with Britain.

4. The Amir's permission should be given for influential mullahs to follow the call for jihad.[37]

Habibullah was reported to have stated in reply that the Afghans were devot Muslims but did not have the means to fight. They were always ready for war but could not make a sustained effort. The Amir said Afghans would be a formidable opponent and the whole nation would willingly join the battle in defense of their own country. He explained away the poverty of his country as the price of independence and said that Afghanistan had no national debt and was not dependent on any foreign country.[38]

Members of the mission declared that the nonexistence of arms factories was a matter of regret, but they promised, if an understanding could be reached, that the Central Powers would give Afghanistan every kind of military assistance required. These powers would also pay a 12-lakh subsidy so that British help would no longer be needed. The main objective of the mission was presented to be the desire to prevent a fratricidal war among Muslims when Turkish troops reached the Indian subcontinent.[39] The Amir did not give any definite answer and referred the matter for study to his Majlis-i-Shura.

As the negotiations continued it became apparent that the Amir's advisers, personalities at court, and members of his family were generally divided into two camps. The so-called war party included Nasrullah, the Amir's brother, and Inayatullah and Amanullah, the Amir's sons, who also had the support of General Nadir Khan and Mahmud Tarzi Khan. These personalities were supported by most of the members of the religious establishment, the pro-Turkish element, and a majority of the Afghan tribesmen. The pro-British group appeared to center around the person of Abdul Kuddus Khan, the Chief Minister, and the group allied with Bibi Halima, the stepmother of the Amir, who never ceased intriguing and hoping that her son Umar Khan would one day succeed to the throne of Afghanistan.[40] Some groups in Herat as well as many merchants trading with India were also interested in peace with British India.

The Amir seemed to be playing off the two groups against each other, cautiously supporting the pro-British forces. Some of the members of the "war party" were in frequent contact with the foreign mission, and public opinion in Kabul expected that the Amir would soon proclaim jihad. Hafiz Sayfullah Khan, the British Agent at Kabul, was secretly warned that "some mischief-makers may want to attack the British Agency to precipitate military action with Britain."[41]

On December 12, 1915, Sir A. H. Grant expressed his grave concern at the lack of any reply from Habibullah to the letter of the British King and the Viceroy's announcement of the increase in the Amir's subsidy. He expected a momentous pronouncement shortly, since the Amir had summoned a Loe Jirga, an assembly of tribal leaders and delegates from all over the country, a step which is taken only in case of national emergency.[42] But a report by the British Agent at Kabul of an interview with the Amir brought some relief to the government of India.

Habibullah acknowledged receipt of the British Sovereign's letter, but he complained to the Agent about the "trifling" amount of the increase in his subsidy.[43] He warned the British Agent to make no mistakes in his reports to India about the Amir's attitude, saying:

> You . . . are required by your position and call of duty to judge all what happens here, not from what is current as rumours or the Bazar gossips, but from what actually occurs as an event resulting from my deeds or utterances. As a Muslim and Afghan [44] no one can better know than you the gravity of the situation caused by the existing war since a year or two, and the strenuous efforts on my part to discourage the agitating frontier minds, and it is a fact, no doubt that a slight deviation on my part from what I have held laboriously as my ideal, at great pain and anxiety, would have thrown me either in the pit of doubt in the British Government, a pledged friend of old, or have secured for me a verdict of infidelity and heresy at the hands of both of my Muslim subjects or the frontier Muslim tribes. . . . You may

rest assured and can convey my assurances to your Government in plain and repeated terms that I am a true friend of the British Government, keeping up neutrality to the last so long as the internal interests of Afghanistan are not exposed to danger or self-defence, for were this to happen it would become an unavoidable necessity to appeal to arms, or set aside the neutrality.[45]

Sayfullah also reported intelligence according to which the Amir had told the German mission that he could not give them a definite answer until certain noblemen had perused the old records and documents relating to political correspondence and discussions between the late Amir and the British and Russian governments. These might furnish precedents on which the Amir could then base his answer.[46]

On December 22, 1915, the British Agent reported that it was common talk in Kabul that the mission had failed and the Amir had refused their demands. The frontier tribesmen both inside and outside the Afghan boundary were scoffing, and calling the Amir a kafir (infidel). But the British Agent also heard conflicting reports indicating that secret preparations for mobilization were under way and war was imminent.[47]

The government of India wanted to strengthen the Amir and sought ways of expressing its appreciation. Relying on what in India was proverbially called "Afghan greed" the Viceroy's council expected that a gift of money to Habibullah would be all that was needed to keep Afghanistan out of the war. The question was only how much should be offered. A gift of 15 lakhs was suggested, but there were doubts whether this amount would be sufficiently impressive, considering the fact that the Amir had a balance of over 50 lakhs of funds from his subsidy with the Indian government.[48] A decision was finally postponed, and India preferred to wait until the Amir himself would bring up the question. In that event it was expected to be easier to limit the Amir in his demands.

Finally on January 16, 1916, the Amir answered the letters of the British King and the Viceroy of India and said he considered such small compensation an insult to the honor of Afghanistan. Habibullah held that his policy of neutrality had to be strengthened by internal measures costing much more money than Britain was willing to give.⁴⁹ To George V, the Amir wrote that he was grateful for the King's letter and reiterated that "in future also, provided no injury or loss occurs to Afghanistan, the sublime God-granted Government of Afghanistan will remain neutral and will always view with satisfaction and honour the friendship of Your Majesty's Government." ⁵⁰

As the negotiations with the foreign mission continued, the Amir seemed to be temporizing by misrepresenting the state of affairs in Afghanistan. The Afghans reportedly claimed that the treasury was empty, they asserted that the British subsidy was 36 lakhs of rupees, and they demanded enough war material to arm the entire population, all of them being fighting men.⁵¹ Wilhelm Paschen, a member of the Niedermayer expedition who remained in Herat and was on his return to Persia captured by Allied forces, declared in his Tiflis prison in October, 1916, that the German officers wanted to leave Kabul in early 1916, "as one day the Amir says he is for us and the next against us. Twice before this Niedermayer had made up his mind to leave, but each time the Amir detained him by giving positive assurances, but again backed out of them." Paschen further said that "Niedermayer also stated in his letter to me that the Amir was unwilling to let them go in case circumstances should change and Afghanistan should declare war, in which case they—the German officers—would be necessary to him." ⁵²

On January 24, 1916, Habibullah finally initialed the draft of a treaty which gave the mission a face-saving document and at the same time appeased the war party and provided a breathing spell in order to determine what actions might be required in response to subsequent events.

In a message to the German Foreign Office, Niedermayer and Hentig summarized the events leading up to signature of the draft:

> Up till now Amir harping on declared neutrality and traditional friendship with England; undecided; leaning (doubtful) on English party alone. By November our work so far successful that, in spite of complete isolation, tide took a perceptible turn in our favour. On our side came in Prime Minister, brother and successor, and his father-in-law [Tarzi]. When towards the end of December we tried to force on a decision, we were asked by Nasrullah whether we had full powers to conclude a treaty. Said no; declared myself [Hentig] ready

to draft if he wished. He received promise of German help in money and material so far as actually possible, as also of claims to a subvention proportionate to achievements at the conclusion of peace, provided Afghanistan made preparations for war forthwith. The foregoing has been made by the Amir, after and in spite of every conceivable objection each more impossible than the last, [into] the following Treaty draft: [The text of the treaty followed.] [53]

The treaty had ten articles and began with a declaration of friendship between Germany and Afghanistan and their rulers. Germany and the Central Powers would recognize the independence of Afghanistan, while the latter agreed to "perfect" her military resources and administration. Afghanistan was to establish political relations with the "peoples" of Persia, India, and Russian Turkestan. Germany would supply, with no obligations to Afghanistan, 100,000 modern rifles, 300 guns, and other equipment, and the sum of 10 million sterling. Germany was required to open the way through Persia so that she could help Afghanistan effectively. Diplomatic relations were established, Hentig being recognized as the German representative in Afghanistan, and an Afghan official was to be sent to Persia to negotiate there with representatives of the Central Powers. Next followed clauses defining in detail various questions of consular relations and the establishment of an embassy in Kabul.[54]

In the same telegram to the German Foreign Office, both Hentig and Niedermayer offered their opinions. Hentig noted that "the draft may be taken as successful in so far as it affords the basis for immediately getting to work, [and] the arrival of Germans [in the sense of Niedermayer's proposal] means war."[55] Niedermayer added an estimate of the military requirements. He urgently requested a wireless station, large quantities of arms, and at least 1 million pounds in funds. Niedermayer optimistically judged that the best time for war to begin would be at the end of April. In a postscript he added that according to the Amir's statement "war begins at once as soon as 20,000 to 100,000 German or Turkish soldiers arrive in Afghanistan. On these would fall the task of covering Afghanistan's rear against Russia."

With this lesson in *Realpolitik* Habibullah could leave the matter up to the Germans; for if they could spare a force of a hundred thousand men to come to the aid of Afghanistan, they must surely be winning the war. The Russian offensive in the Caucasus and the lack of Turkish success against Egypt seemed to make victory quite unlikely, however.

On January 25, 1916, the day following signature of the German-Afghan treaty, the Amir summoned Hafiz Sayfullah Khan, the British Agent, to a private interview and reiterated his determination to remain neutral. He further declared that he intended to hold a full durbar in which he would make an announcement of neutrality in the presence of tribal chiefs and representatives from all areas of Afghanistan. The Amir thought that such a durbar was necessary because of the general excitement aroused by the presence of the Turco-German mission. Habibullah told Sayfullah that his announcement would be couched in terms calculated to assuage popular feeling, but the British should not misunderstand his words. Pamphlets explaining the *real* meaning of jihad would be distributed after his announcement.[56]

Durbar was held on January 29, 1916, and, in a dramatic performance in which Habibullah appealed to the self-interest of the Afghans, he told the people of Kabul and the leaders of the country that he could not deviate from Afghanistan's traditional policy toward her neighbors and must continue to remain neutral in the war.[57] The people of Kabul and the Afghans from the frontier, who expected a declaration of jihad, were generally disappointed. The Germans, whose hopes had somewhat risen again, at first saw in this appeal merely a tactical step by the Amir, but soon the Amir ceased to cooperate with them and they realized that "the game was up."[58] Although he had just agreed to a treaty with the Germans, the Amir increased his demands for joining the war and declared that he would only act if *all* of India would rise against Britain.[59]

Shortly before the Germans left in May, 1916, Nasrullah made a final attempt to keep them in Afghanistan by offering to act against Habibullah and take over the leadership of the frontier tribes in a war against Britain, but it was too late. The Germans had become convinced that the Afghans would not act on mere promises and without any guarantees and tangible help; tired of the prolonged negotiations in which they had nothing to offer, they wanted to leave and turn to more fruitful activities.[60]

The German expedition to Afghanistan was successful insofar as it accomplished some of its objectives: it disturbed Russia and Britain greatly with its activities, and it carried hostile propaganda into an area hitherto the exclusive concern of those two European powers. The expedition came with no more than a message and it nearly succeeded in involving Afghanistan in the war.

In their personal evaluations some members of the expedition blamed each other for its ultimate failure, or accused the German Auswaertige Amt for lack of support, or felt British gold (the Germans did not have an adequate supply of it) responsible for swaying the mind of the Amir. It seems safe to say that the expedition was not successful because the Central Powers did not win the war. The Amir and his advisers closely watched the events in the war. He was willing to conclude a treaty with Germany and her allies, for he could not predict the fortunes of war and he wanted his independence recognized also by these powers. As long as the Central Powers could not defeat Russia and Britain it was folly for the Amir of Afghanistan to attack one of them single-handed. Abdur Rahman's advice had not been forgotten; it was merely obscured by the appeal of Islamic ideology influencing the minds of some of Habibullah's advisers. With the German treaty the Amir wanted to buy time to see what the future might bring.[61]

The claims of German members of the expedition to having participated in general-staff planning, to having contributed to the construction of fortifications, and to the mobilization of Afghanistan were greatly exaggerated. The Germans did participate in various activities and contributed to some minor reforms, but only in the capacity of advisers and without any authority or veto over Afghans.[62] Of greater practical effect, and therefore much more dangerous to the interests of Britain, were the non-European members of the expedition. The Muslim members could appeal to the Afhans on the basis of Islamic solidarity and incite them to action by warning that both the Caliphat and Islam were in danger. They also knew local languages and could have a more intimate contact with the people and be much more effective with the frontier tribes.

INCITEMENT OF THE TRIBES

Although raids into India had never completely stopped, the Amir was successful in keeping the tribes relatively quiet. The government of India for its part chose to play down the importance of occasional raids. Major Prideaux, the British Consul in Sistan, suggested in early 1916 that British troops be allowed to pursue raiders into Afghanistan, but the government of India strongly opposed any such action. Denys Bray, of the Political Department, remarked on this subject that "these are not the halcyon days of 1901 and 1905 when we could afford to tread on Afghan corns. Afghan susceptibilities are now factors in world politics, and a violation of Afghan territory by regular troops might set the country in a blaze." [63] Sir A. H. Grant warned that "if things went bad in Kabul, this could be made a *casus belli* at once."

Turkish nationals continued where the Germans left off and also began to be active on the frontier. The British Agent at Kabul reported in January, 1916, that four members of the Turkish mission had obtained permission to see Jelalabad in order to inspect the border area of Eastern Army Headquarters.[64] A week later he reported that some of the mission had been deputed to see tribal areas of the Mohmands, Afridis, and Waziris.[65]

In January, 1916, an apparently forged letter purportedly signed by the Amir, Nasrullah, and others and addressed to the "mullahs and maliks and kazis of the Tirah Ilaka" was circulated on the frontier. It read:

> We are much pleased with you and you should prepare yourselves for holy war which will, if God pleases, take place in summer next. You should completely prepare yourselves. We will supply you with rifles, as many as you require. You should make each and every man firm to take up this enterprise and fortify each and every place. This is not fictitious. We have informed you of the occasion. On arrival of the German ships in your country you will be put to trouble.[66]

An instance of the Amir's intervention to curb raiding activities is given in a telegram to the Chief of General Staff, Simla, dated June 20, 1916:

> Amir on receiving news of British conquest of Arhad sent orders at once forbidding men to enlist under Germans and ordered Germans to proceed to Kabul. . . . When Germans were preparing Kalahikang [Qala-i-kang] Fort, Afghan Sardars of Helmand district were preparing to attack and raid British posts and line of communications west of Quetta. This news reached Amir who immediately ordered the Governor, Kandahar, to arrest those Sardars and sent them to Kabul.

... British occupation of Sarhad has had great effect on southwest Afghanistan and ... Afghans are afraid to loot in this direction.[67]

Activities by members of the foreign mission in Russian Turkestan were also reported to India in January, 1916. The report stated:

> ... having lost hope of carrying out their original objects in Afghanistan, and with the object of employing profitably their enforced sojourn there, the German party are occupying themselves in fomenting sedition among Turkestan Musalmans, especially Turkomans. They sent agents to Bokhara, Charjui, Merv, Samarkand, Tashkent and Katta Kurgan. The Russian agent at Herat recently recognized two individuals who had returned from Bokhara, Charjui, Merv, and Tashkent, whither whey had been sent by Wagner. Both Kazim Bey and Barkatulla are assisting in this activity.[68]

Roos-Keppel, the British Commissioner on the North-West Frontier, reported in July, 1916, that "besides the parties sent to Tirah and Bajaur, other parties [of Turks] with escorts of Afridi deserters have gone to the Mahsud border and to the neighbourhood of Chaman." The Commissioner thought it impossible that the Amir lacked any knowledge of this. Roos-Keppel said that these Turks offered the Afridis Ottoman suzerainty and a share in the loot of India, but the Afridis pleaded poverty and asked for something on account.[69]

Sir A. H. Grant came close to describing Afghanistan's tribal policy when he discussed Afghan "cognizance if not connivance" in Turkish activities at the frontier. He saw this in accordance with Nasrullah's traditional policy of "keeping the frontier sore open." He remarked that Nasrullah:

> ... has always aimed at preventing, so far as possible, the establishment of really good relations between us and our transborder tribes. A belt of disturbed territory is a safeguard to Aghanistan, so Nasrullah thinks. This does not, however, mean that Nasrullah wants war between Afghanistan and India—at present anyway. All he wants at present is to detach the Afridis from their allegiance to us in case circumstances later make war between Afghanistan and India inevitable. I do not believe that the Amir is a definite party to this business, though he probably gives Nasrullah a free hand to intrigue as he thinks fit up to a certain point.[70]

In August, 1916, Roos-Keppel noted:

> ... the Turks seemed to have gotten over their first fright and are now more active. ... They have gone for a tour amongst the

Orakzais and the smaller tribes on the Kurram border. Had they started this campaign at the beginning of the summer they might have caused us considerable embarrassment, but the time is unfavorable for them as the cold weather is approaching and the Tribesmen are looking forward to coming to British territory as usual.[71]

The Commissioner thought that the Afridis should be rewarded for not having joined the Turks. He further proved the collaboration between the Turks and Nasrullah by pointing to the fact that the *daks* (mail caravans) carrying messages between them were proceeding quite openly.[72]

In August, 1917, Roos-Keppel reported that some Mahsuds and Waziris had come to Matun to ask the Afghan Governor whether the Turks who had come to them and exhorted them to jihad were there in the name of the Amir.[73] A month later he reported that "the Afridis who were sent by the Turks to Kabul have returned, having all been granted allowances by Nasrullah. The allowances were not large, but their grant has set at rest the doubts of the Afridis as to whether the Turks came with authority from Kabul or were merely adventurers."[74] The British Agent at Kabul reported an interview with the Amir in September, 1916, in which the latter asserted that these people were dismissed employees of his who could not leave because of the war and were now occupying themselves with these kinds of activities.[75]

In 1917 isolated acts of raiding erupted into a general uprising in Mahsud country; Roos-Keppel blamed public pronouncements for this. The Lords Hardinge and Chelmsford had demanded punishment of the Mahsuds, and when the Mahsuds heard of this they feared they "might [as well] be hung for a sheep as a lamb" and decided to make the best of it.[76] What complicated the matter was that Habibullah sent a letter to the Viceroy, pleading that the British should punish the Mahsuds only mildly so as not to embarrass him and to prevent the outbreak of a general border conflagration that might draw both countries into war.[77] The Mahsuds on their part received messages from Kabul telling them that the government of India was pledged not to take any offensive measures against them.[78] India took all measures it deemed necessary to contain the frontier tribes. An electric barbed-wire fencing to bar the Mohmands' access to India seemed to have been used with some success according to accounts by Shinwari and Mohmand tribesmen.[79] The tribal situation was finally permitted to remain quiet and both Afghanistan and India endeavored to keep it that way.

Another potential danger to peace appeared with the announcement of the Arab revolt in the Hejaz. The British Agent in Kabul, Hafiz Sayfullah Khan, reported:

> ... much excitement is being felt here in favour of the Turks and against the improvident Arabs, who are, at the instigation of the pro-Turks here, being cursed on account of their lack of sense of nationality and co-religion with the Turks.... The question of the Khalifate is also arising from the discussions and receiving attention of those who are better informed. His Majesty the Amir is said to have called the secret meeting of the Shura to meet the case of the future fate of the Khalifate.[80]

Again on July 12, 1916, Sayfullah reported that the Afghan ruling class was spreading the word that talk of the Arab revolt was merely British propaganda; thus they hoped to pacify the people and prevent trouble caused by popular excitement.[81] But in the *Sirāj al-Akhbār* of July 16, 1916, an article appeared under the heading "When Infidelism Rises from the Ka'ba, Where Will Islam Go?" (*Chū kufr az ka'ba bar khīzad kojā mānad musalmānī*) which strongly condemned the treason of the Sharif of Makka.[82] The British newswriter at Kandahar reported on August 15, 1916, that during the Id durbar in that city the mullahs demanded that since the holy places were besieged the time had come to declare jihad. The mullahs met for a four-day conference with the Governor and drafted a memorial to the Amir.[83]

Habibullah finally permitted a show of solidarity with Turkey and caused some release of pent-up excitement when he held a durbar in August, 1916. Mahmud Tarzi made the opening speech condemning the Sharif, and Barakatuallah and Mahendra Pratap were also permitted to speak along similar lines. But no action was requested by any of the speakers since it was expected that the revolt would soon be crushed by the Turks anyway.[84]

THE *Sirāj al-Akhbār*

With the establishment in Kabul in 1911 of the *Sirāj al-Akhbār*, a bimonthly newspaper, a powerful means for the education of the

Afghan people and for the propagation of Islamic modernism and Afghan nationalism had been created.[85] The *Sirāj al-Akhbār* soon became a forum for the expression of Pan-Islamic policies and tended to influence Afghan foreign policy along the lines of Islamic solidarity.

Mahmud Tarzi (1866–1935), founder and editor of this newspaper, was a member of the ruling Muhammadzay clan and a descendant of Payanda Khan, one of its leaders. Tarzi was forced by Abdur Rahman to live in Ottoman exile for about twenty years. Upon his return to Afghanistan, he became a tireless worker for reforms and progress. He advised Habibullah about the need for education and was the originator of many reforms. Tarzi has been called the "father of Afghan prose" because of his prolific writings, with some fifteen books to his credit, including translations of four books by Jules Verne and one book on the Russo-Japanese War, in addition to about five hundred articles published in his newspaper.[86]

The *Sirāj al-Akhbār* first became involved in international politics as a partisan of the Ottoman Empire at the time of the Turco-Italian War. It analyzed the policies of the European powers and reported on such subjects as the "European methods of grasping the lands of the world" or the "Western intentions of destroying Islam." Appeals to Muslim unity were issued from time to time, and in May, 1916, an article by Mahendra Pratap of the Niedermayer expedition appeared in this newspaper.[87]

Initially the *Sirāj al-Akhbār* was not hostile to Britain but, with the approach of World War I, its tone became increasingly critical. The most offensive attacks on Britain and Russia often appeared in the form of "letters to the editor." Excerpts of Allied as well as Central Powers newspaper articles were given, but a pro-Ottoman bias quickly became apparent. Because of the high rate of illiteracy in Afghanistan and the fact that it was written in Persian with only an occasional poem or article in Pashtu, the *Sirāj al-Akhbār* was somewhat limited in its impact.[88] Copies of this newspaper were, however, read publicly in the bazaars of Afghan towns and in the area of the Pashtu-speaking frontier tribes. Furthermore, the paper was read and quoted in India, Persia, and the Ottoman Empire.

In September W. M. Hailey, Chief Commissioner of Delhi, complained to Sir Charles Cleveland, Director of Criminal Intelligence, about the hostile tone of the *Sirāj al-Akhbār*, and recommended that the newspaper be banned in India.[89] Hailey especially objected to an article stating that the unrest in Persia was attributable to the Anglo-Russian Convention, which put the Persian government against its people. The article further held that in Afghanistan the same was tried, but "the infidels were confounded." The Viceroy requested the Amir in December, 1914, to forbid the publication of such articles, and the Amir promised to do so. But the Pan-Islamic tone of the newspaper could not be suppressed, and other articles appeared whose authors gloatingly reported that the infidels had fallen out with each other and hoped that they might all be ruined.[90]

After the government of India repeatedly protested about various articles, the June, 1915, issues were somewhat improved. Mr. A. H. Grant, of the Foreign and Political Department, remarked optimistically:

> We cannot expect this paper suddenly to become pro-British. That would not only destroy its sale, but would bring the Amir into definite odium with his subjects. A Kabul paper must inevitably be pan-Islamic in its tendencies and also anti-foreign. If future issues are as temperate as this, we may, I think, congratulate the Amir on the faithful manner in which he has carried out his undertaking in this matter.

The Viceroy agreed with this assessment.[91]

In subsequent months, however, the newspaper again appeared objectionable to the government of India and discussions began as to the best way to suppress it. Grant feared that any action taken against the *Sirāj al-Akhbār* would result in strengthening the war party in Kabul. He favored a "policy of drift" since "every day that the Amir is able to maintain his neutrality is a day gained."

The government of India began nevertheless to intercept all copies of the *Sirāj al-Akhbār* which were sent into India. On August 24, 1916, a new policy was set up which directed that (1) the system of interception should be continued, but as *quietly and unostentatiously as possible;* (2) no overt action should be taken against the *Sirāj al-Akhbār;* (3) nothing should be said to the Amir regarding these measures unless the Amir inquired about them; and (4) Afghan officials, if they inquired, should be told that the government of India had no information to give them.[92]

The British measures did not escape the attention of the Afghans. In the *Sirāj al-Akhbār* of August 15, 1916, Mahmud Tarzi discussed the history of his newspaper and stated that it was forbidden in Russia in 1913 and a year later in India. He stated that the newspaper was in no way an official organ of the Afghan government. He was proud of its influence far beyond Afghanistan's borders and he maintained that the newspaper's moderation was often criticised by its readers.[93]

THE AFTERMATH

The German Auswaertige Amt attempted once more to conclude a treaty with the Amir, but not along the lines of the previous draft; it wanted merely a treaty of friendship and the establishment of diplomatic relations.[94] When the German mission left Kabul on May 21, 1916, Nasrullah gave Hentig a letter to the German Reichskanzler which Hentig had transmitted to Berlin. In this letter Nasrullah requested that Germany conclude a treaty with Afghanistan on the lines approved by the Amir in January, 1916.[95] A representative of the Amir, Sirdar Abdul Majid Khan, the Governor of Shibirghan, had come to Kermanshah in December, 1916, to conduct discussions with Turkish and German officials. Niedermayer, who had by this time also arrived in Kermanshah, took part in some of the discussions; it became apparent, however, that Abdul Majid had no authority to sign any agreement. The Afghan representative told the Germans that they needed a big bomb—namely, Afghanistan. He urged them to continue the war and they would surely pass through the "gate of India." If they came with a big army to Isfahan and Yazd, Abdul Majid promised that the Afghans would meet them at Kirman. But in case the Germans wanted to make peace, they would have to guarantee Afghanistan's independence and must help her gain access to the sea.[96] The Afghan representative moved on to Constantinople, where he was received with pomp and great honors, and finally he returned to Afghanistan with the German draft treaty.[97]

Secret channels of communications between Kermanshah and Kabul remained open and were maintained by Germans in Herat and Austrians in Kabul. Habibullah had insisted that all the Germans must either stay in Kabul or leave Kabul at the same time. Therefore the Germans delegated their authority to Captain Schreiner, one of the many Austrian prisoners of war who resided in Kabul after they had escaped from camps in Russian Turkestan. The last member of the German expedition left Herat in October, 1917, after he had given up hope of receiving any communication from the Amir concerning the German treaty of friendship.[98]

Turkish defeats in Mesopotamia finally put an end to the hopes of the pro-Turkish party for united action against India. The Revolution in Russia and the defeat of the Central Powers in 1918 again changed the international picture. There was some relief in Kabul at remaining out of the struggle and not following the Ottoman Empire into defeat, but there was also much soul-searching among Afghans, who wondered whether they had not betrayed Islam in its most crucial hour. There appeared to be widespread resentment against the Afghan Amir.[99]

The Indian and London governments were discussing what they could do to reward the Amir for his loyalty. It was clear that the Afghans expected a reward. The British Agent in Kabul reported in August, 1917, that Abdul Kuddus Khan asked him how long he intended to remain in Afghanistan. On hearing that the Agent intended to leave at the end of the war, Abdul Kuddus said he must remain longer in the interests of the Afghan government, which would never permit him to leave "unless their hopes and aspirations in connection with the sincere services rendered by the Afghan Government in keeping its neutrality during the war . . . are not satisfactorily re-adjusted between both Governments."[100]

Denys Bray wondered what Habibullah had in mind. He believed that the Amir wanted direct representation in London and suggested permitting this "since the Amir does not trust his Envoy in Simla a yard; he is not likely to trust an Envoy in far-off England an inch." He further thought that the Amir wanted territorial concessions, and perhaps representation at the Peace Conference after the war.[101]

On December 22, 1918, the British Agent at Kabul reported that the Amir and members of the Shura had expressed in council the "ardent wish" for Afghan participation at the Peace Conference, and they were disappointed at not having secured this concession from

Britain. The Amir wanted his independence recognized by Britain, and this was to include the freedom of having political relations with any foreign country in the world. But London was remarkably unwilling to make any concessions. The Secretary of State for India consulted with Lord Chelmsford, the Viceroy, asking if he should recommend that the King give Habibullah the "Garter," something he really wanted, or if an autographed letter was sufficient reward for the Amir.[102]

The Viceroy replied to London, saying that "the services of the Amir have been immense, and when the time comes to reward them we must be generous." Chelmsford apparently thought that the time had not yet come and he wanted to wait until the Amir started asking. But it was clear to the Viceroy that the Amir seemed to "hanker after" the following concessions from the British: (1) complete political freedom, (2) territorial aggrandizement, (3) money, and (4) representation in England.[103]

On February 2, 1919, Habibullah wrote to the Viceroy demanding that Afghanistan be represented at the Peace Conference because his country was independent and had remained neutral during the war. He said if the Viceroy could bring a signed certificate of Afghan independence from the conference he would be satisfied; otherwise an Afghan representative must be permitted to go there to obtain one.[104]

Lord Chelmsford's council was prepared to offer some concessions to the Amir, but it was not certain how far it should go. Denys Bray remarked on Habibullah's demands that:

> . . . our control of Afghanistan's foreign relations has been so long a fundamental principle of our Afghan policy that it requires an effort of mind to conceive of our willingly consenting to any diminution of it. Possibly it may prove essential that it should continue to dominate our policy. But the present is so different from the past, and the future seems likely to be so much more different still, that the time has come for us to scrutinize our traditional policy anew.[105]

Bray thought that Afghan neutrality during the war was attributable to "the Amir's shrewd perception that Afghanistan until the Russian Revolution lay between the 'upper and nether grindstone' or to the bias in our favour given him on his visit to India. . . ." Denys Bray recalled that "great pressure was put on us from home at so late a stage as June 1918 to make some departure (not precisely defined) from our traditional policy by an offensive alliance with Afghanistan. And secondly that it was only by winking at flagrant breaches of the Amir's fundamental Engagement regarding our control of his foreign relations" that the government of India was enabled to carry its policy to a triumphant conclusion. He accepted the draft treaty between Habibullah and the Niedermayer expedition as forced by the circumstances, compelling the Amir to break the letter of his agreement with Britain in order to maintain what was important to England—namely, Afghanistan's de facto neutrality.

Therefore Bray suggested that the Amir be bound to Britain and that this could best be accomplished by concluding a definite treaty between Afghanistan and the government of India. The 1905 engagements with the Amir, prohibiting him from having foreign relations with other powers, should now not be enforced. If Russia was Bolshevist, Bray reasoned, Habibullah would not make an alliance with her; and if she were a peace-loving republic, relations could not be prohibited. Or if the Central Asian states created a federation of Muslim states "with the Amir of course as Sultan or even as Khalif," how could Britain prevent relations between Muslim states. Bray concluded that, since Britain wanted only two things, Afghan independence and her friendship, Britain's political position as the most favored nation should continue to be maintained. Bray wanted the subsidy continued even after Afghan independence.[106]

The mood of generosity prevailing in India, however, was not shared by His Majesty's government. London suggested greater frankness in the reply to Habibullah to "avoid leading him to make embarrassing demands." The Viceroy was advised to stave off the Amir, telling him that participation at the Peace Conference was open only to belligerents, and that international guarantees would be no good to Afghanistan, even if they could be secured, since they might lead to interference by other nations.[107]

This difference of opinion between England and India over vital matters of policy was, of course, not a new phenomenon, but it is a matter of regret that at this stage no satisfying solution to future Anglo-Afghan relations was found. During the war, when the military situation seemed to require such a step, London was ready to conclude an alliance with Afghanistan in exchange for which the latter would have obtained a measure of independence. In India such an alliance seemed an obstacle to a return to the prewar status quo, the British suzerainty over Afghanistan, and therefore it was opposed by the government of India.

For Habibullah any reward that might have strengthened his internal position came too late. On January 1, 1919, he left Kabul for his winter quarters in Jalalabad, leaving his third son Amanullah in charge of the capital, and, on the night of February 19-20, Habibullah was assassinated in Kalla Gush in the Laghman district.

6. Amanullah

THE THIRD ANGLO-AFGHAN WAR

Amanullah's accession to power over the claims of Nasrullah and Inayatullah, his uncle and his brother, came as a surprise to many, although there were reports as far back as early 1917 indicating that Amanullah enjoyed great popularity in Kabul, and it was assumed by some courtiers that he would succeed to the throne.[1]

Some British observers at the time saw the plot against Habibullah as the act of an ambitious and vengeful woman, Ulya Hazrat, mother of Amanullah Khan.[2] According to their view, Ulya Hazrat and her son had fallen from royal favor when Amanullah began his campaign to win popularity among the people of Afghanistan.[3] He helped men of importance and they were later helpful to him. When the royal family moved to Jalalabad, Amanullah had to stay behind as a form of punishment.[4] According to other sources, the plot against Habibullah was initiated by members of the so-called war party (to which Amanullah also belonged) who wanted to put Nasrullah on the throne.[5]

On the day following the assassination of Habibullah, Nasrullah was proclaimed Amir in Jalalabad. Two days of durbar followed after which Amir Nasrullah Khan addressed the army and appointed Inayatullah as Naeb al-Saltana. On the same day Amanullah addressed the Kabul garrison and vowed not to rest until the death of his father had been avenged. Amanullah was in possession of the Kabuli treasury and the arsenal and was therefore in a position of strength. The Kabuli troops then announced their support of Amanullah who was proclaimed King. On February 27, Nasrullah, Inayatullah, and members of the Musahiban family (descendants of the Peshawar sirdars, also called Yahya Khel) were arrested by the troops of Jalalabad; the following day Nasrullah abdicated and joined Inayatullah in offering *bay'a* (allegiance) to

Amanullah. The British Agent who had accompanied Habibullah to Jalalabad was asked to return to Kabul, and on March 11, the European employees of the Afghan government were permitted to depart for India under Afghan escort.

According to eyewitness accounts, Amanullah held durbar at the Qanuni Bagh at Kabul on Sunday, April 13, 1919, and presided at the trial of the suspected assassins. Colonel Shah Ali Reza Khan was indicted for the murder amid rumors of Nasrullah's complicity. The colonel was sentenced to death and immediately executed. Nasrullah was sentenced to prison for life, and Inayatullah was condemned to live in retirement. Nadir Khan and twenty-one other prisoners were declared innocent.[6]

The British Agent at Kabul reported that the Musahiban family had been greatly compensated for the indignities suffered from the suspicion of murder held against some of its members. Amanullah gave two of his sisters in marriage to Ahmad Shah and Muhammad Ali who belonged to the Musahiban family. The Agent further reported that the Jalalabad troops were incensed at the release of members of the Musahiban family since they feared retaliation for having arrested them.[7] The subsequent developments in Anglo-Afghan relations and the Anglo-Afghan War of 1919 are described by some British observers as the direct result of the assassination of Habibullah which compelled the young Amir to consolidate his power and unite the people behind him in the face of unrest and popular suspicion that Amanullah might have been involved in the plot. Thus the Third Afghan War would have been no more than an attempt to divert the popular anger from the Amir and set it against the British, the traditional enemy.[8] While this may have been a factor, there was a still more important one: the fear that, having overcome her temporary weakness, Britain might return to her former forward policy or even aim at the conquest and division of the entire Islamic world.

On March 3, 1919, Amanullah informed Lord Chelmsford of the murder of his father. He said: "I have no doubt that Your Excellency, my friend, will be much touched by the news of this painful event, for the observance of all the conditions of neutrality and the upright conduct and friendly relations displayed during the past and present by His Majesty, my late father . . . require no mention." He further informed the Viceroy that he was made Amir and that the "usurpers" had abdicated, and he added pointedly:

> ... nor let this remain unknown to that friend that our independent and free Government of Afghanistan considers itself ready and prepared at every time and season to conclude, with due regard to every consideration of the requirements of friendship and the like, such arrangements and treaties with the mighty Government of England as may be useful and serviceable in the way of commercial gains and advantages to our Government and yours.[9]

The British Agent reported that, during durbar on April 13, 1919, Amanullah announced:

> ... I have declared myself and my country entirely free, autonomous and independent both internally and externally. My country will hereafter be as independent a state as the other states and powers of the world are. No foreign power will be allowed to have a hairsbreadth of right to interfere internally and externally with the affairs of Afghanistan, and if any ever does I am ready to cut its throat with this sword.

He ended his speech and then gently calling out the British Agent said, "O Safir, have you understood what I have said?" The British Agent answered, "Yes, I have."[10] The British Agent also reported that the Amir had appointed Muhammad Wali Khan to be the Afghan representative at Bukhara, and that the latter was about to set out for that city. Amanullah intended to continue his show of independence and initiated discussions in his council for the selection of a safir for Persia.[11]

The government of India was at a loss to decide whether it should accept this *fait accompli* or not. After maintaining for so long that Anglo-Afghan agreements were made personally with the amirs, it was difficult to deny that Amanullah had a right to demand a new treaty for Afghanistan. Therefore, Lord Chelmsford was quite noncommittal in his reply. He decried the loss of the great ruler who "by his wise statesmanship preserved it [Afghanistan] from the horrors which the war, just ended, has brought upon so many nations." He merely thanked Amanullah for the information that he was acknowledged as Amir "by the populace of Kabul and its surroundings" but referred to the mourning over the former Amir as an excuse for not discussing the agreements mentioned by Amanullah.[12]

The new Amir lost no time in initiating administrative reforms and established a cabinet in which Mahmud Tarzi was Minster of Foreign Affairs and Abdul Kuddus Khan was Prime Minister. The fact that the Amir had ambitions for his country was clear. On March 11, he announced to the Afghan Envoy in India that "the Government of Afghanistan hopes by the grace of God, within a short time, to have itself counted as one of the most well-known and honourable Governments of the world."[13] A firman was issued which stated that Amanullah was proclaimed King by the people and that he accepted on condition that (1) Afghanistan should be internally and externally free, (2) the people should unite with him to avenge the assassination of Habibullah, and (3) the people should be free and no one be oppressed, and government should be by law.[14] It was soon apparent that these pronouncements would be followed by action.

On May 1, 1919, Saleh Muhammad Khan, the Commander-in-Chief, moved to the Indian border, arriving at Dakka with two companies of infantry and two guns, for the ostensible purpose of inspecting the border. At about the same time Muhammad Nadir Khan moved to Khost and Abdul Kuddus Khan proceeded to Kandahar.[15]

On May 3, an escort of Khaibar Rifles accompanied a caravan to the border and was stopped by Afghan pickets in the disputed area between Landi Khana and Torkham. The leader of the Afghans, Zar Shah, a Shinwari from Nangrahar with a reputation for daring raids across the frontier, declared he was acting under the orders of the Afghan Commander-in-Chief and produced a firman from the Amir.[16] The British force then withdrew.

The Amir's firman, which began to circulate on the frontier, called the tribesmen to be ready for uprisings in India. It stated in part:

> I send this order to all subjects of the Eastern circles who are Sayyids, Shaikhs, Mullahs, Khans and Motabars and tell you that there is great unrest in India. Hindus and Muhammedans have almost all remained

faithful . . . but it is a pity that they have been rewarded by cruelty [zulm] and all kinds of injustice in connection with their religion, their honour [izzat] and their modesty [sharm].

The firman stated further that risings had occurred in India which also affected Afghanistan; therefore Saleh Muhammad was deputized with full power for the protection of Afghanistan's boundaries.[17]

During durbar in the beginning of May, the Amir read letters he had received from India and then told his people: "See what tyranny has been practiced on our brethren in India! Not only this but Baghdad and the Holy Places have been seized by tyranny!" He then addressed them: "I ask you if you are prepared for holy war. If so, gird up your loins! The time has come!" The reply of those present was in the affirmative, and Amanullah then said: "I will take no more revenue, but all of you should collect grain for the holy war and rich men should buy from the arsenal rifles and ammunition, while the poor will have them issued on security."[18] On the following day, leaflets were circulated along the border, claiming that Germany had resumed the war, that Egypt and India had successfully risen. The leaflets ended with the slogan "cursed be the English and cursed be the tyrants."[19]

The Viceroy reported to England on May 4 that, although the wording of the Amir's firman was about as bad as it could be, it still left a loophole and the Amir had not definitely committed himself. Lord Chelmsford said that his government was impressing on Roos-Keppel the capital importance of avoiding all frontier incidents at Torkham or elsewhere and asked him to consider the advisability of having Abdul Kayyum, the Political Agent at Khyber, try to arrange a meeting on the frontier with Saleh Muhammad Khan.[20]

The Viceroy also addressed a letter to the Amir and informed him of the firman shown by Zar Shah and of his action against the British escort of the Khyber caravan. Giving the Amir an opportunity to disclaim any knowledge of it, the Viceroy said that this firman could only be the work of an enemy of the Amir, and he asked the Amir to denounce it as a forgery and to have Zar Shah arrested.[21]

On May 4, Afghan uniformed troops occupied Bagh, a Shinwari hamlet above Landi Khana and Kafiri Kot on the British side of the frontier, and began to cut the water supply to Landi Kotal. The British reacted by closing the Khyber Pass. Two days later the Afghan forces at Bagh were increased to three regiments with two guns and Afghans occupied Tor Trappar and Spinatsuka. The Afghans then moved three regiments from Jalalabad to Mohmand country, and Nadir Khan arrived at Khost with troops and several thousand tribesmen, most of them Ghilzays.[22]

The British countered on May 7 by dispatching a column to Landi Kotal and another to Parachinar in support of their Kurram forces. The first battalion of the first brigade reached Landi Kotal on May 7, and the remainder was to reach it on May 8. The second brigade was ordered to Jamrud for support, and the third was concentrated at Peshawar. A cavalry brigade was sent on May 7 to Shahgai on the Malagori Road.[23]

On May 5 the government of India had decided to stop demobilization of all combatant forces in India, as well as the frontier force, and to recall all British officers of the Indian Army. India intended to confront the Afghans with an overwhelming force in the Khyber to induce them to withdraw quietly without fighting. But during May 8 the Afghans received large reinforcements and advanced their positions to Ashraf Khel, commanding Landi Kotal. The next day British forces at Landi Kotal drove back the Afghans from the vicinity, and the Afghans moved to positions near Khar Gali. The British then began bombing Loe Dakka.[24]

In Peshawar the situation deteriorated rapidly. The center of anti-British activity and propaganda was the office of the Afghan postmaster. Roos-Keppel wanted to arrest the postmaster and a number of Indian revolutionaries who were in the city, but they were in a quarter of the city which was inaccessible and difficult to attack without arousing a general riot. On May 7 Roos-Keppel reported that the feeling was distinctly bad in the city and that there was much talk of an attack by a mob of seven thousand to eight thousand on the cantonments. The British Commissioner acted swiftly and on May 8, at 2 P.M., he had the city surrounded and demanded the surrender of the postmaster and some of the Indian agitators. The city depended on outside water, electricity, and food supplies and could not have hoped to resist for a long time. Therefore, the postmaster and the Indians, Milap Singh, Abdul Jalil, and

Dr. Ghosh, were forced to surrender without any resistance to the British. The messenger sent into the city by the British was the only casualty in this action.[25]

Amanullah replied to the Viceroy's letter of May 5, refusing to arrest Zar Shah in view of the "tyrannical law" (Rowlatt Bill) enforced by the government of India against its Hindu and Muslim subjects. The Amir called the firman mentioned by the Viceroy an "expression of my Islamic sympathy and human feeling towards mankind, and the abhorrence of my Royal mind of things affecting the faith and religion, and freedom and liberty of human beings." He said he meant to unite the tribes for the protection of the independence of their country and for the maintenance of peace on the frontier, which was being threatened by quickly approaching revolutions. The Amir further complained that the Viceroy did not reply to his letter within a reasonable time, and that when he did so he answered in an offensive spirit. Another grievance of the Amir was that Chelmsford refused to accept the appointment of the new Afghan Agent; Amanullah considered this a hostile act indicating that India did not recognize the new Amir. He further stated that he was still willing to conclude a treaty of friendship with India, and he asked the Viceroy to avert the dangers "by abolishing the tyrannical laws recognizing the absolute independence, equal rights and freedom in all respects of the Government of Afghanistan, which is ready to conclude treaties and engagements in every way beneficial to each other, so that the doors of calamity may not be opened upon the world, for it is right to demand right and it is not right to shed blood without right in the path of right."[26]

The government of India was not prepared to meet the Amir in his demands, so hostilities took their course. On May 15, the Viceroy reported to London that British troops had occupied Dakka, which is a few miles within Afghan territory, and suggested that Jalalabad should be taken since this would demonstrate the British military superiority to the tribes and induce them to stay out of the war. Jalalabad would also be a good base for a march on Kabul. The Viceroy further reported that the attitude of the troops was excellent and that they were ready for such a move. The occupation of Kandahar should also be considered.[27]

London was reluctant to sanction these steps. The Secretary of

State for India commented on the seriousness of the Indian proposal which would constitute an act of war. He feared that such action would involve a long commitment of war with Afghanistan, in which British troops would be surrounded by hostile tribes. The Secretary said he lacked enough information to determine if this was really a war or merely a border clash; he also wanted to know what kind of armistice the Afghans wanted. The London government warned that an attack on one of the few remaining independent Muslim states might have serious consequences elsewhere. The Paris peace negotiations would surely be affected, and London wanted to know whether peace could be made with a return to the previous status quo.[28]

The government of India felt that an offensive was better than a static defense and therefore wanted to move, although no one was certain whether a formal declaration of war had been issued by the Amir. Amanullah's combination of jihad with agitation against the Rowlatt Bill threatened an anti-British conflagration which, the government of India feared, would engulf Afghanistan, the frontier, and India.[29]

The tribal situation proved to be especially serious for Britain. The practice in India of controlling the frontier with local tribal militia now received a severe setback. The great number of desertions from the Khaiber Rifles made it necessary to ask the men individually whether they wanted to remain in British service or be discharged from their units. Out of seven hundred men, six hundred elected to be discharged, and the government of India thought it safer to disband the entire force.[30]

But peace feelers were quickly extended. On May 21 the Chief Commissioner at Peshawar reported receipt of a telegram from Sirdar Abdur Rahman, the Afghan Envoy in India, in which the latter informed the commander of the British troops at Dakka that he had talked to the Amir and now wanted to meet the British party with a view to making peace.[31]

The government of India had previously permitted the Envoy to cross into Afghanistan to persuade the Amir to end his hostile activities. The Commissioner, however, did not trust the Afghan overtures and suggested to Simla (the Indian summer capital) that this was merely a tactical move on the part of Afghanistan to gain time for winning over the tribes. But the Viceroy considered the situation so critical all along the frontier and the time of such vital importance that he authorized the commanding officer to meet with the Afghan Envoy.[32]

The London government had in the meantime informed Simla that it agreed with the measures proposed by Lord Chelmsford and urged resolute action. Nevertheless, London deplored the fact that an advance on and occupation of Jalalabad was necessary at such an unhealthy time of the year and warned India "that you will not have forgotten [the] lessons of history, that we have not so much to fear from [the] Afghan regular Army as from the irregular tribesmen and their constant attacks on our isolated camps and lines of communications."[33]

The government of India soon learned that the Amir's diplomatic initiative had included talks with Soviet Russia. There were reports of Bolshevist emissaries en route to Kabul.[34] Major General W. Malleson reported to India that both Amanullah and Mahmud Tarzi had written messages to Lenin and the Commissar of Foreign Affairs. Amanullah announced his accession to the throne and his intention of adhering to the principle of equality of all men and peaceful union of all people, and Tarzi expressed his hopes that permanent and friendly relations would soon be established between Russia and Afghanistan.[35]

The government of India began to search for means to counter Afghan propaganda. It obtained a letter from the Aga Khan for distribution in India and on the frontier in which he condemned the "wanton and foolish" attack on India and exhorted his followers to remain loyal to the British and "open the eyes of others."[36] The so-called Hindustani Fanatics, who had long conducted a verbal war against the British, did not show themselves as "fanatic" as expected, and their Amir discouraged talk of jihad in exchange for a personal pardon and some land in India.[37]

It was also suggested in India that the Sultan of Turkey be approached to obtain his pronouncement for prohibiting jihad and "disowning those by whom it may be proclaimed."[38] Nothing came of this, nor were other moves very successful. The Naqib of Baghdad, who had two brothers in the area, one in Kabul and the other in Chaman, also declined to issue any declarations. He held that he could give a fetwa only in answer to a question by members of the Indian ulema.[39]

Finally a letter from Amanullah, dated May 24, 1919, gave official sanction to previous peace feelers. He stated that Afghanistan was induced by fear of disorder in India to take steps to protect the Afghan border. This led to mistakes on both sides. Afghan soil was invaded and the Afghans had to fight. When Abdur Rahman learned in India that war was not wanted by the government of India, the Amir revoked his call to jihad and his National Council decided that the Envoy should be deputized to explain matters and to stop the bloodshed. Amanullah bitterly attacked British aerial bombings of Jalalabad and Kabul in which among other targets, the tombs of Abdur Rahman and Habibullah were destroyed; he expressed his regret that Britain was copying in these bombings the example of the Germans. But the Amir did not want the old friendship between the two states to be broken and enmity grow through further bloodshed and therefore suggested the establishment of an honorable and dignified peace that would be useful to both parties.[40]

The events in the war now took a new turn. While the frontier around Dakka had become stabilized, Britain's favorable military situation was seriously upset when Nadir Khan advanced into the Waziristan area and British troops were forced to withdraw. The Chief Commissioner of the North-West Frontier reported on May 31 that he had ordered the withdrawal of all frontier constabulary posts in Shirani country. He reported the Thal post in danger and the situation in Idak acute. The Khoedad Khel Zaimukhts were said to have joined the Afghans, and all the Kurram border tribes seemed likely to rise "unless we have success against Nadir Khan shortly."[41] In addition, rumors appeared that the Afghans were strengthening the garrisons at Jalalabad and Kahi and that airplanes from Russia had arrived.

Roos-Keppel, the Chief Commissioner at Peshawar, reported on June 1, 1919, that the Jandola and Manji posts were surrounded by a large number of Mahsuds and a Mahsud lashkar was approaching the Zarkani post. The Kajuri and Shinkai posts were abandoned and the Isha post taken by the Afghans. As for the tribes, the "Orakzai were still quiet, the attitude of the Kohat Pass Afridis was good, and the Mohmands were quiet and in a good mood." [42] To check the tribes it was suggested that leaflets be distributed over the area to announce receipt of the Amir's letter and to express the hope that peace negotiations would soon begin. India hoped that this would prove that it did not want to destroy Afghanistan.[43]

British strategy was greatly affected by this new move. John Maffey, the chief political officer with the field force, indicated in an unofficial letter to Simla that the "threat to Thal has delayed the Jalalabad move, as the motor transport available does not admit of two simultaneous offensives." Maffey thought that this delay "serves the purpose of giving the Amir a breathing space to consider some further diplomatic overture. It will also prevent the Afridis and Mohmands from rushing into the dangerous half-held belief that we are pledged to a swift war of extermination." He addressed Simla, saying, "You will appreciate the danger of steam roller tactics. As it is, these tribes will think that negotiations may still be going on and that they had better keep on their fence." Maffey also feared a revolt in Kabul and said he was "desperately afraid of our having to push so far that there will be nobody to settle up with." [44] When Amanullah's letter of peace arrived, Maffey welcomed it with great satisfaction, saying, "Having seen the trials the troops are undergoing, and knowing from experience up and down the line what little keenness there is among the troops to face the Kabul River Valley at this season of appalling heat, I can assure you Amanullah's communication has been a great relief to me!" This move by the Amir would put the Afridis and Mohmands permanently out of the hostilities, and Maffey thought it advantageous to "carry things on through the rozha and to give all the tribal organizations time to break up for lack of work." Meanwhile, Maffey suggested, "we can pack the healthy Kurram Valley with troops and our peace terms can then be presented as an ultimatum with a short time limit. Let us avoid too much chat! . . . This time we shall have got the Afghan really cold, I hope." Maffey continued: "The tribal mess still wants clearing up, but the defection of the Afghan will rob the position of any real danger and we can put off dealing with the Mahsud till weather permits. A squadron of good aeroplanes next autumn will soon finish the job." [45]

A week later, Maffey suggested that no forward move be made in

Dakka, saying, "I see a great rock of offence in a British Dakka and a whole fabric of hate and distrust built thereon to our danger and discredit." He reported that the loyal Shinwari chiefs had cautioned him not to seek any territorial surrender. Maffey thought they showed a good deal of sympathy with Amanullah, who, they felt, was grossly misled and deceived. The Shinwari chieftains expected Britain to show generosity.[46]

In fact, the Amir was impressed by reports from the Afghan postmaster in Peshawar which indicated that India was on the verge of revolt and that it required only the spark of an Afghan invasion to destroy the British in India. In an intercepted letter to the Amir, the postmaster reported that he was ready to begin holy war in Peshawar City. He claimed that about eight thousand of the people came to his assistance who were to be strengthened by two thousand more men from the surrounding villages. The Sikhs, according to the postmaster, assured the Muslims that they would not shoot at them, and both Muslim and Hindus would be "much displeased" if the Amir did not attack.[47]

The government of India was quite willing to accept the advice from London to seek a return to the previous status quo, and it was searching for ways to end this situation which was so fraught with danger and uncertain consequences. Denys Bray, of the Foreign Department, noted that magnanimity was the best policy in making peace with Amanullah because Afghanistan was needed as a buffer. Also, Muslim opinion, already aroused by the treatment of Turkey, would be alienated. Furthermore, without Afghan cooperation it was difficult to establish peace on the frontier. Therefore, Bray wanted the old days back—only more so. He wanted Afghanistan to be "still more conservative, shutting her doors to all foreigners, especially Russians, and while just as passive as ever in so far as opening the closed door to ourselves is concerned, to be more actively friendly as regards the frontier tribes." He recalled that Britain was prepared to "consider releasing Afghanistan from our tutelage over her foreign affairs as a reward for Habibullah. We were even prepared to consider accepting with as good grace as might be the *fait accompli* when presented to us by a not openly unfriendly Amanullah." But Bray thought it out of the question to accept it under the threat of war. Since Britain wanted so little from the Amir, "the solution will probably have to be found more in the stern wording of the terms than in the terms themselves." [48]

As to the terms with the Amir, Bray suggested the following:

1. Control of Afghan foreign affairs.
2. Improvement of the status of the British agent at Kabul and the representative at Kandahar.
3. Instant dismissal of all foreigners.
4. Nonadmission of delegates from foreign powers to Afghanistan.
5. Acceptance of the old border, except where Britain defines adjustments.
6. Surrender or expulsion of Indian "seditionists."
7. Surrender or dismissal of Mahmud Tarzi and Abdul Kuddus Khan.
8. Abolition of the Afghan post office.
9. The right of Britain to regulate the import of arms.
10. Arming of the tribes by Afghans to be prohibited.
11. Permission of direct relations between frontier officers.
12. Removal of restrictions such as the Chaman boycott.[49]
13. Permanent removal of outlaws and raiders from the border.
14. Payment of a reduced subsidy, conditional on friendly relations.[50]

Lord Chelmsford finally replied to Amanullah's proposals for peace of June 3, 1919, and transmitted the following conditions for a cease-fire: The Afghans would have to withdraw 20 miles from the British positions, whereas British troops would remain where they were and keep their freedom of action, but without advancing any further. British planes would also be free to reconnoiter and must not be attacked by the Afghans. If a British pilot was forced to land in Afghan territory he must be safely returned. Finally, the tribes on both sides of the border must be restrained; they were to be informed of the cease-fire and warned that they would not receive any help from the Afghans if they attacked the British forces. The Viceroy suggested that the peace conference be held at Rawalpindi.[51]

On June 11 the Amir replied that he was glad about the success of their mutual peace efforts. But he defiantly recalled that Afghans had previously defeated intruders, getting strength from their religion, which makes death a cause of revival, and from their nature, which makes Afghans "prefer visible death to subordination to a foreign power and to consider it perpetual life." Regarding the withdrawal of Afghan troops, the Amir said that the Afghan people could not be moved—all of them being soldiers. He wanted the troops to remain where they were and objected to British reconnaissance by air since "there are guns in every house" and even if he wanted to he could not restrain the people from firing at the planes. Thus peace could easily be endangered by "someone with an evil mind." The Amir agreed to the selection of Rawalpindi as the site for negotiations and announced the composition of the Afghan delegation which was to be headed by Ali Ahman Khan, his Minister of Home Affairs.[52]

The home government was somewhat surprised at the "unexpected clemency" shown by the government of India, but India said in defense of its stand that, having demonstrated British strength and punished the Afghan troops, resulting in Afghan prayers for peace, the termination of hostilities was consistent with the maintenance of British prestige. India expected that if Afghanistan would "quit now, humiliated, the tribal situation would at once cool." India pleaded that the entire frontier was in a condition of acute tension, British troops were exposed to intolerable heat and most unhealthy conditions, and, as a most effective warning, the government of India held that the continuance of the war would involve large and constant demands on England for technical troops and material of all kinds. The government of India feared that, if its reply to Amanullah had been delayed, the Amir would have concluded that Britain was implacably determined on war and would not agree to any peace. This would have forced an indefinite prolongation of the war. So long as Amanullah remained de facto ruler, there was no alternative to accepting him and treating with him. The fall of Amanullah would mean chaos and anarchy. Lord Chelmsford thought this a good opportunity to show the Muslim community that Britain had no wish to wipe out or trample her Muslim neighbor. He held that there was really no halfway house between a policy of complete subjugation of Afghanistan and a policy of attempting to establish mutual trust and really friendly relations.[53] The home government, although skeptical about the favorable interpretation by India of the Amir's letter which it found questionable and in parts defiant, approved the proceedings with the hope that India's belief would be justified.[54]

In further correspondence with the Amir, the Viceroy named the composition of the British delegation to the peace conference. He chose to ignore the Amir's defiant attitude since it was clear that only a resumption of hostilities could force the Amir to change it.[55] The Third Afghan War was started by Afghanistan to wrest from a weakened India what it was unwilling to concede—Afghan independence and territorial concessions.

Amanullah had an exaggerated view of the events in India, and he overestimated his resources and capability for offensive action. The war was to be a concerted attack on Britain from three Afghan bases: Dakka, under the command of Saleh Muhammad, the Commander-in-Chief; Khost, under General Nadir Khan; and Kandahar, under Abdul Kuddus Khan. The Afghan forces were to be supported by tribal lashkars. An uprising in Peshawar was to coincide with an Afghan offensive.

But these activities were not properly coordinated. The revolt in Peshawar was nipped in the bud on May 8, 1919, and premature action on the Khyber front led to British capture of Dakka before Nadir Khan had started his march on Spinwam on May 23 and attacked Thal on May 28. On the Kandahar front no major moves occurred until May 27-28, when British forces attacked the Spin Boldak Fort and finally captured it in the face of brave Afghan resistance.

Nadir Khan's success prevented British offensive moves against Jalalabad and aroused tribal attacks against the British lines of communications. British aerial bombings caused some panic in Jalalabad and led to looting of arms and material by Afghan tribes from the surrounding area. In Kabul the King's palace and other targets were bombed on May 24; cease-fire was declared on June 3, and an Afghan delegation arrived in Rawalpindi on July 25 to begin peace negotiations.

The Third Afghan War was not won by the British. Both the Afghans and the British held enemy territory, and no decisive battles were fought and no one was definitely defeated. But this war did result in an end to Britain's suzerainty over Afghanistan and for this reason is justly called a victorious war by the Afghans—even though the victory was finally won in the field of diplomacy rather than the field of military action.

PEACE NEGOTIATIONS

The government of India now began to consider the terms it should offer the Afghans. Lieutenant General Kirkpatrick recommended a "rectification" of the border by annexing Dakka and the surrounding area, Khost, Lat Poti, and Shurawak, and the area north of Chaman. Others also thought of territorial changes: (1) the Wakhis had petitioned the British to take them under their protection; (2) the Mehtar of Chitral wanted Nasrat, and the Kafirs wanted the British to take over at least part of Kafiristan; and (3) the British agents of Sistan and Baluchistan wanted to take over Gaud-i-Zirreh and the headwaters of the Helmand.[56]

Henry Dobbs, the Foreign Secretary, did not favor any drastic territorial changes, but he thought that minor border "corrections" would not seriously embitter the Afghans or arouse general Islamic sentiment. After the "benevolent" tone in the Viceroy's message to the Amir it was difficult to make territorial demands without being accused of trickery by the Afghans.[57]

The government of India submitted for approval by the home government the terms it wanted to see in a peace treaty with Afghanistan. The following terms were drafted:

1. From the day of signing there should be peace.

2. Because of Afghan aggression, the importation of arms through India would be prohibited.

3. No subsidies would be granted, and the arrears were forfeited.

4. If the Amir were contrite, after six months, new negotiations might establish new friendly relations.

5. Until that friendship was established, British troops would remain in Afghan territory in the Khyber area. Other positions would be withdrawn.

In order to obtain a treaty of friendship from Britain, the Amir must show his condition by:

1. dismissing all hostile foreigners from his country;

2. having foreign relations with no country other than Britain;

3. expelling Obeidullah and other Indian "seditionists";

4. cooperating in keeping the borders safe from outlaws;

5. improving the position of the British agent and other British representatives. The position of the Afghan envoy would be correspondingly upgraded.[58]

The government of India held that the attitude of the Amir would decide what kind of final arrangement he would get. The Viceroy was, however, wary about Article V, which he adopted only at the insistence of his military advisers. He felt that British occupation of Dakka was an irritant not only to the Afghans but also to the Afridis and Mohmands. Therefore, he recommended that British troops should withdraw after the undemarcated parts of the border had been defined by the British.[59]

His Majesty's government expressed approval of the suggested probationary period, but objected at first to two-stage negotiations.[60] The Secretary of State maintained that the treaty seemed to contain only penalties and offered the Amir no inducement to sign. And after the probationary period, he thought, there would be fruitless discussions and arguments as to whether the Amir had fulfilled the conditions for renewed friendship. London wanted a provision for obtaining a rail terminal at Kam Dakka, and suggested that Amanullah should forfeit all arrears of his subsidy and that the practice of maintaining an Afghan postmaster in Peshawar be discontinued. The Amir would get a subsidy if after six months the British government was satisfied that he had faithfully observed the terms of the treaty.

The Viceroy was impressed by the need for establishing an immediate peace and wanted to leave the more difficult task of obtaining an acceptable treaty for future negotiations. Lord Chelmsford saw the crux of the matter in the problem of British control over Afghanistan's foreign relations. He recognized that there were profound changes in the political outlook of the Middle East which were caused by "general unrest, awakened national aspirations, the pronouncements of President Wilson, and Bolshevik catchwords." Afghanistan could no longer be forced into isolation, and the Amir would not accept British protection from unprovoked aggression as a *quid pro quo* for their control of his foreign relations. The Viceroy thought that Amanullah would soon be convinced of the impossibility of conducting his affairs single-handed and expected that, "if we regain the confidence of Afghanistan and get them to turn voluntarily to us in their difficulties, we shall have secured more than we can do by any 'scrap of paper.'" The hands of the British negotiators should not be tied to any rigid preconceived draft treaty to avoid the example of the Dane mission, but matters should be referred for orders before committing the British government.[61]

The Secretary of State finally agreed to Lord Chelmsford's suggestions but warned that negotiations with Afghans had a tendency to take a different course from the one anticipated. As a whole he did not contemplate any substantial change in the political relations with Afghanistan, and he impressed on the Viceroy to leave no doubt in his actions that British troops had been victorious.[62]

Although Afghan and British regular forces stopped all offensive military action, the position of British troops was endangered at several places by tribal snipers and raiding attacks. Tribesmen harassed the British supply lines and carried off whatever they could. Lieutenant General G. N. Molesworth tells of the successful theft by tribesmen of a tent from over the heads of the British soldiers sleeping in it.[63] The government of India hoped that the arrival of the Afghan peace delegation in India would have a sobering and calming effect on the tribes.[64]

The tribal situation was aggravated by the personal disappointment of Abdul Kuddus Khan. The Afghan Prime Minister felt greatly dishonored by his inability to prevent the loss of Spin Boldak Fort. With British troops within Afghan territory, he could not permit the withdrawal of his troops to 20 miles from the British position as demanded by the British. He therefore incited the tribes to attack British lines of communications and continued the war verbally, trying to win British concessions he could not win by military action.

In a number of messages to the British general commanding at Chaman, the Afghan minister warned the British not to set themselves against the Islamic world by "trifling with Afghanistan," and to give Russia her chance at gaining influence in Afghanistan.[65] He wanted the British to surrender Spin Boldak Fort, claiming that otherwise his tribesmen would not obey his orders for a cease-fire. He also wanted to have the British promise that they would not punish the tribes for supporting the Afghans. Abdul Kuddus feared that his position and power would be endangered if he as Prime Minister were not a participant at the peace negotiations. Therefore he wanted to conduct his own negotiations with the British at Chaman, and held back the news of the cease-fire and the signing of the peace treaty until the evacuation of Spin Boldak by the British.[66] He wanted to give the impression in Kandahar that peace was established only after he himself had induced the British to surrender Spin Boldak.

Sir A. H. Grant, head of the British delegation at the peace conference, suggested improving the deteriorating situation in Baluchistan by hitting those tribes that were within British territory. But Grant did not want to give Abdul Kuddus an ultimatum to withdraw since he feared that the Afghan would not comply, and "we have to eat our words" or start hostilities without having a chance to commence negotiations.[67]

When the Afghan peace delegation had arrived in India, the Amir issued a proclamation in which he acknowledged the proof of courage he had received from the Afghan people and the frontier tribes. He announced that an armistice existed at the time and said if honorable peace were retained with all respect and honor for Afghanistan, well and good, but if not he would carry on holy war until death.[68]

The Afghan peace delegation was headed by Ali Ahmad Khan and consisted mainly of men who had been in India before and who could generally be called "pro-British."[69] The Afghans met with the British for the first time on July 26, 1919, and the heads of both parties delivered their initial statements.

Grant began by warning the Afghans to keep the tribes under control. He said that in spite of his government's desire for peace it could not show infinite patience and ignore tribal aggression. He wanted the Afghans to realize how "near the breaking point had come during the armistice," and he warned that "any continuance of intrigues with the tribes must make negotiations between us impossible."[70] Grant then deplored the senselessness of the war, saying that all India mourned the death of Habibullah and claiming that the Viceroy was so astonished at the Afghan attack that he could not believe it had occurred with Amanullah's approval. Now believing the Amir contrite, Grant was ready to make peace.[71]

Ali Ahmad alluded in his opening address to recent legislation in India which he claimed was responsible for the war. He said that the government of India needed Afghan friendship more than vice versa, and he complained that Afghan friendship had not been rewarded. Ali Ahmad made no attempt to excuse Afghan actions. He maintained that Afghanistan did not sue for peace and that the first peace overtures came from the British when the Foreign Secretary sent a message to the Amir through Abdur Rahman, the Afghan Envoy in India. Ali Ahmad did not offer any concrete proposals. He merely talked about the awakening of national sentiment all over the world and the growth of "national requirements and aspirations." He suggested friendship and unity between Britain and Afghanistan in the face of the "Communist threat," and he deplored the fact that Britain broke with the Turks and was now faced with repercussions.[72]

At the second meeting on July 29, 1919, Ali Ahmad dwelt on Britain's difficulties with the tribes and asserted that they were caused by British hostility toward Afghanistan. He declared Britain responsible for the Anglo-Afghan war. The Viceroy withheld recognition of Amanullah by failing to reply to his letter, and Britain did not reward Afghanistan for her neutrality in the war and did not permit her to send representatives to the Paris peace conference. The Rowlatt Bill legislation in India and Afghan sympathy with Turkey were other factors in the deterioration of Afghanistan's relations with Britain.

Grant replied, calling British control of Afghanistan's foreign relations a partnership in which "wise rulers of the past" had delegated to the British a task which they, with their greater diplomatic experience and their efficient diplomatic agency, could perform better than the Afghans. Grant said there was great mutual advantage accruing from this arrangement and he urged that it should therefore be continued. Ali Ahmad made it quite clear, however, that the Afghans would not continue the previous arrangements and would insist on Afghanistan's complete internal and external independence.[73] Ali Ahmad again warned of the danger of Communism, expressing his "horror" of it and claiming that it was in their joint interest to keep the Communists out of Afghanistan. He also protested formally against the British bombings of Kabul and Jalalabad and deplored the damage caused to the graves of the two former amirs.

Grant reported to the Foreign Secretary about intelligence he had obtained which indicated that the Afghans were not prepared to agree under any circumstances to relinquish control of their foreign relations. The Afghans intended to propose an "astounding" readjustment of the border whereby they would receive Waziristan and other tribal areas. The Afghans further expected territorial concessions at Panjdeh and Kushk from the Bolsheviks. Grant also learned that the Afghan desire for complete independence seemed connected with hopes for the transfer of the Caliphate to Afghanistan.[74] Grant learned further that the Afghans would present the following demands:

1. freedom in foreign relations,
2. payment of the arrears in subsidy,
3. payment of a new subsidy,
4. payment of a war indemnity,
5. amnesty for the Afridis and Mohmands, and
6. cession of Waziristan.[75]

In view of these demands, Grant thought it better not to mention anything about the British desire for Dakka, leaving it for the subsequent friendship treaty when the Afghans would be "hungry and more compliant." Grant also obtained permission to present his treaty in the form of an ultimatum when he thought that the time was auspicious for such a step. He said he wanted to make use of this ultimatum only in connection with the terms of the treaty and not in response to local breaches of the armistice.[76]

On July 31 Grant finally submitted the British demands, as worked out between London and Simla, to the Afghan delegation and Ali Ahmad refused them *in toto*. It was not before August 4, during the fourth meeting of the delegates, that the Afghans acquiesced and accepted the treaty in principle, suggesting only some changes in its wording. They insisted, for example, on the substitution of "Afghan Government" for "Amir of Afghanistan," making the treaty between the two governments rather than with the person of the Amir; and they insisted on the elimination of passages that were derogative or fixed the blame for the war upon the Afghans. The Afghans also demanded the 1 crore of rupees which had been promised to the late amir and wanted the continuance of payment of the British subsidy and the arrears. They reasoned that the arrears were deposited in the British treasury and, being trust money, were not subject to confiscation. As they did during the Dane mission, the Afghans considered the subsidy a payment by India in exchange for the cession of territory. The Afghans suggested demarcation of the boundary to be made by a joint commission six months later.[77] Ali Ahmad next demanded that Britain withhold any action they might have planned against the tribes pending negotiation of the friendship treaty.

He gave the following conditions for a treaty: (1) Afghanistan and the British government should have the same enemies. (2) The British government should bolster the military strength of Afghanistan. (3) The entire tribal territory should be ceded to Afghanistan, who would run it along lines that would spare the British government all the trouble they had had in this matter. The Afghan government should be awarded half the amount of money spent by the British government on the control of the tribes.[78]

Grant found these demands unacceptable, but he permitted modifications in the wording of his treaty to make it more acceptable to the Amir. Grant was prepared to make important concessions, but was afraid to make them on his own authority. He complained to India about the lack of instructions regarding Afghanistan's foreign relations, and he expressed the rather novel view that "our policy throughout has been to give Afghanistan the liberty she now regards as essential, in the confident belief that money-hunger and need for guidance will before long bring her back to us for help and advice in practice, an infinitely better solution than the old arrangement." [79]

The Viceroy also felt that the time for concessions had come. He reported to London that the Afghans were adamant in their insistence on independence and were unwilling to go home without having it confirmed. For this reason Grant had not pursued the question of British control over Afghan foreign affairs and was willing to make the Amir's future conduct the test of his friendliness toward Britain. The Viceroy felt that "if we now surrender our hold on the shadow we may hereafter secure the substance of real control, such as we have never been able to exercise satisfactorily in the past." [80]

On August 5, 1919, His Majesty's government somewhat ambiguously sanctioned the treaty of the government of India, saying that "formal recognition of our control of foreign relations of Afghanistan has for [the] past forty years been [a] cardinal article of British policy, and you will appreciate reluctance of His Majesty's Government to abandon principle, to which great importance is still attached by them."[81] As to the subsidy, London deprecated the payment of a subsidy of any appreciable amount without control over Afghanistan's foreign relations.

During the fifth meeting of the conference on August 6, Grant submitted the text of his treaty to the Afghans, and two days later Ali Ahmad affixed his signature to it.

The treaty contained the following provisions:

1. establishment of peace;
2. prohibition of the import of arms through India;
3. confiscation of the arrears in subsidy and discontinuance of subsidy payments to the Amir;
4. acceptance by Britain of an Afghan mission after six months for the discussion of matters of common interest and the reestablishment of the old friendly relations, provided the Afghan government had shown by its acts and conduct that it was sincerely anxious to regain the friendship of Britain; and
5. acceptance of the Indo-Afghan frontier as it was previously recognized, subject to demarcation of undemarcated portions of the boundary by a British commission.[82] Not included in the treaty, and expressed in a separate letter to Ali Ahmad Khan, was an assurance by Grant that the treaty contained nothing that would interfere with Afghanistan's internal and external independence.

Asked whether Britain intended to publish the treaty, Grant answered in the affirmative, but stated that his letter would not be published with it since otherwise the entire correspondence and the record of the negotiations would also have to be published. He would, however, not object if the Afghans wanted to publish the letter in Afghanistan.[83] The home government was not entirely reconciled to the course of events, and it protested that Grant appeared to have underestimated the importance of his decision, "for his letter is either useless to Afghans or else involves permanently that substantial change in our political relations and that repudiation by Afghans of obligations hitherto acknowledged . . . [and] that they [the home government] would acquiesce in it, could not be taken for granted." [84]

But the government of India regarded the result of the peace negotiations as highly satisfactory, asserting that with few modifications, none of them essential, the Afghans had accepted their draft. India wanted to believe that this somewhat new experiment would prove in the end more satisfactory than the old arrangement, for the Afghans "are very sensitive on the outward shadows of their liberties, but . . . if due allowance is made for this, there is every chance that they will eventually seek our advice of their own accord in essential matters." [85]

The government of India did not have much space in which to maneuver. It could only make war or conclude a peace that was acceptable to the Afghans. Having reluctantly permitted Afghan independence, they had to stand by their decision and hope for future developments that might reestablish the former Anglo-Afghan relations. The fact that this decision was made without awaiting sanctions from London was excused in India by the need for swift action to avert the risk of a breakup in the negotiations.[86]

The home government could show its anger only by refusing to sanction the title of "Majesty" for the Amir, in spite of intimations by British delegates to the Afghans that such recognition would be given. London insisted to see first some evidence of goodwill on the part of the Amir before such recognition could be sanctioned, and it deprecated the tactics of the government of India "which are widely thought here to have involved us in the surrender of prestige." [87]

Before the British evacuated Spin Boldak on August 14, and Dakka on September 13, they completed the demarcation of the boundary. Demarcation was accomplished by John Maffey, who was actually on the spot defining the border as he went along. The Afghan General, Ghulam Nabi, accompanied the Englishman, but merely watched the proceedings without taking any part in them.

Britain was generous. It postponed the "rectification" in British favor of the Durand line, over and above assertions of previously disputed claims, for future discussions and negotiations when the treaty of friendship was concluded.[88] Demarcation was completed on August 29, and the British boundary commission attended a dinner given in their honor by Ghulam Nabi Khan. On the way back to their camp, the British officials were forced to a somewhat undignified retreat by Afghan snipers.[89]

Throughout the peace negotiations nothing had been heard of the British Agent in Kabul. On September 2, 1919, the chief political officer in Peshawar received the assurance of Ali Ahmad Khan that Hafiz Sayfullah Khan was safe and had permission to leave Afghanistan "as soon as the roads were safe." But it finally became known in India that the members of the British agency were kept in strict isolation and that all messages to India were suppressed. Sir A. H. Grant suggested that the Amir should be presented with an ultimatum to permit the return of the British agency personnel or face a renewal of hostilities. But Tarzi, in a letter to Lord Chelmsford, plausibly excused the Afghan measures as having been necessary for the protection of the British agency, and said that the Afghans did not interfere with Sayfullah's property and arms, and that he was again permitted to move about freely and would, after an interview with the Amir, return shortly to India.[90]

The Afghan peace delegation returned to Kabul, and at the Amir's durbar on August 14, Ali Ahmad gave his version of the peace negotiations, asserting that Britain had conceded every point they had demanded. He also stated that the tribes were included in the agreement with Britain.[91]

In a letter to Denys Bray, Grant attempted to justify his actions in the negotiations by saying that it was impossible to maintain control over Afghanistan's foreign relations except by subjugating the country. He believed that the old treaty served well with regard to Russia, but was not of much help against the German-Turkish mission. Grant thought that change was bound to come, and his solution fit in with the spirit of the time. He held that freedom in foreign affairs would not be worth much to the Afghans, for they would not ally themselves with the Bolsheviks and permit them to spread their influence in Afghanistan. Future relations with what was left of the Ottoman Empire also could not be very cordial because the Afghans had let them down. Because of their community of interest, Grant believed that the Afghans would side with Britain. The important thing was that the Afghan idiosyncracies be considered. Grant felt they responded to treatment, but were not cowed by words or threats: "They will accept the refusal of their most cherished desire, if it is put to them in temperate, friendly words and the reason for the refusal honestly explained. But any attempt to browbeat them, and still more any attempt to trick them, is doomed to instant failure." Grant compared the Afghans to the proverbial highlander whom harsh words will drive to harsh answers which they may afterward regret, but which they will never admit that they regret.[92]

It matters little whether the views of Grant, the government of India, or the home government were justified by the actual situation. What was important was that Britain had made a fundamental change in her relations with Afghanistan, and only the future could prove the wisdom or folly of the decision. It can be assumed with safety that in both England and India the hope persisted that all was not lost and that Afghanistan would in fact soon return to the fold, but it must have been clear that the international situation no longer permitted a return to the former Anglo-Afghan relations.

The Third Afghan War was attributable to the change in the international situation as much as it was to such factors as Afghan irredentism, Pan-Islamism, and fear of British aggression. The international picture had changed radically at the end of the war. The Russian Revolution had ended the pressure from the north. Internal divisions and agitation by the Muslim population for self-rule kept Russia busy at home. Afghanistan, no longer fearing an attack from the north, could risk military action against India. Britain seemed greatly weakened after the war, and her hold upon India was threatened by widespread strikes, open rebellion, and riots, culminating in the Amritsar Massacre.

Many Afghans felt that Habibullah had not taken advantage of a good opportunity to secure tangible rewards in the form of money and territorial concessions as a compensation for his neutrality in the great war. They did not want to let another, perhaps last, opportunity go by, so they convinced Amanullah that he must act at once. The defeat of the Ottoman Empire by the Allies and the occupation of and interference in places holy to Islam by the British aroused violent hatred among the Afghans who believed that the Christian powers were bent on the destruction of Islam.

Many Afghans, who had believed in the eventual victory of the

Central Powers and therefore obeyed the command of their Amir forbidding them to take an active part in the hostilities, felt that they had failed in their Islamic duty of rallying to the call for jihad. For a nation of warriors who were never at a loss in finding an excuse for attacking an enemy or avenging an insult, it was not an unusual thought to attempt to even the score.

No matter how cordial the friendship of Afghan amirs for Britain seemed at times, it cannot be denied that there was no love for Britain in Afghanistan. Afghan policy toward Britain was based on the fact that a community of interest existed between British India and Afghanistan. The differences of opinion between the pro-British party and the war party were not basic but merely concerned the manner in which Afghan interests would be served best. There was no doubt about the right and proper policy among the Afghan people. Two Anglo-Afghan wars had made Britain Afghanistan's national enemy, and the fact that the British troops always left the country after a more or less tenuous occupation did not impress the Afghans as acts of charity but rather of necessity.

Afghans could never believe in the sincerity of Britain, who, in the name of assisting Afghanistan, never failed to return to her forward policy. Hatred against Britain was kept alive as a result of periodic punitive expeditions by Indian troops into the territory of Afghan tribes along the North-West Frontier. The buffer zone of independent Afghan tribes between Afghanistan and the administrated borders of India, which Afghans considered as vital to their security from British aggression, was gradually penetrated by the British. While Russia merely loomed as a danger, Britain was actively aggressive. The Anglo-Russian Convention convinced many that sooner or later the two European powers would agree to divide Afghanistan between themselves. When Amanullah ascended the throne the political climate at Kabul had changed. Ideas of democracy, nationalism, Islamic solidarity, self-determination, and socialism had penetrated into the mountain fastnesses of Afghanistan. The *Sirāj-al-Akhbār* with its nationalistic tenor brought new ideas into the country and broke the intellectual isolation of Afghanistan. The Afghan people became involved in the issues of the day: the fate of the Caliphate, the fate of Islam, and the fate of their own nation.

As a newly appointed Amir, who did not personally benefit from the legitimizing power of having been a recognized ruler for many years, Amanullah could not flout the popular demands for an Islamic policy and, above all, for a policy of complete independence from Britain. The government of India could not help attempting to use its power of recognition of the new ruler as a lever to come to an advantageous arrangement with Afghanistan: but events moved too swiftly and the Afghans started the Third Afghan War. Although the course of this war did not go as the Afghans anticipated, it was destined to be a great victory, for as a result of it Afghanistan obtained her complete and permanent independence from Britain.

7. The Settlement

PRELIMINARIES TO MUSSOORIE

Peace had not long been concluded before Amanullah began testing the sincerity of the British recognition of Afghan independence. He sent a letter to the British King in which he expressed his thankfulness for British recognition of the independence of Afghanistan and conveyed his high esteem and due respects to "his great and kind friend."[1] The Amir sent similar friendly messages to Lord Chelmsford and Sir A. H. Grant. A letter from Mahmud Tarzi to Lord Curzon, his counterpart in London, conveyed the request that Amanullah's letter be transmitted to the King. Tarzi thanked God for the happy termination of the recent "unpleasantness" and rejoiced that direct channels for independent correspondence with the Secretary of State for Foreign Affairs had been opened.[2]

His Majesty's government, still not reconciled to this novel situation, thought it would be inappropriate for the King to correspond directly with the Amir, whom it considered not even technically a friendly potentate at the time. The home government, therefore, requested that the Viceroy acknowledge receipt of the Amir's letter, expressing once again his sorrow that the son of his loyal friend, the Amir Habibullah, should have without warning or provocation, waged war on him and his Indian people.[3] Lord Chelmsford should further state his hope that, at the subsequent meeting of their representatives, the relations between the two countries might be restored upon a "secure foundation." London wanted to see the Afghan Foreign Minister's letter answered by the Foreign Secretary to the government of India.

But the government of India was unwilling to accept London's suggestions, which implied a return to politics as before, and went counter to the promises and concessions made to the Afghans. The

Viceroy rightly felt that the Amir would see it as a refusal on the part of the King to regard him as a brother sovereign and to recognize his independence. Lord Chelmsford also deprecated the assumption that there would be a meeting with Afghan representatives in any event, for it ignored the fact that such a meeting was conditional on the Amir's fulfillment of Article V of the treaty. The Viceroy considered inadvisable the reiteration of reproaches for an unprovoked war, for it might revive a controversy that was by that time only of academic interest. In order to avoid any embarrassment, India recommended that no reply should be sent.[4]

It soon became apparent that the Amir was far from being contrite, making it difficult for the government of India to proceed with its plan for a treaty of friendship. Bolshevik missions arrived and stayed in Kabul, the Indian revolutionaries continued their activities, and the Amir continued to support the transborder tribes, keeping them agitated in case hostilities were to be resumed.

While he continued his policy of *fait accompli,* Amanullah maintained contact with the government of India. On November 5, 1919, he indicated in a letter that he desired to settle the frontier question with India and suggested border discussions between Grant and Nadir Khan. In the meantime the Amir wanted Britain to suspend all hostilities against the tribes. But the Amir left no doubt that to him a settlement required the cession of Waziristan and other tribal areas to Afghanistan.[5]

Grant suggested to Dobbs, the Foreign Secretary, that London be informed of continuing Afghan "intrigues" with Indian tribes which India must either ignore or use as a reason for the renewal of war. If London did not want war, Grant desired that they protect Indian actions from the criticism of the "Jingo" press and hostile politicians. He recognized that the tribes were the only real military asset of Afghanistan, and therefore the Amir could not afford to lose his hold over them, and he suggested that India fight the tribes piecemeal and thus weaken Afghanistan. But Dobbs deprecated such proceedings since it would show London that India's Afghanistan policy had failed. Dobbs held that Britain did not need the Afghans and could wait until they came for money and arms and were ready to sign a friendship treaty. He thought that Amanullah was merely trying to frighten the British by informing the tribes that the cease-fire would last only six months and would be resumed if Britain did not agree to the demands of the Afghans.[6]

The Amir continued his diplomatic offensive by sending a new Afghan envoy to India and by attempting to send a consul general to Peshawar. The government of India now began to fear that the Amir might send Afghan negotiators six months after the peace conference and confront the British with the decision of whether to accept them or not.

The value of a probationary term now became debatable. The government of India had insisted on the probationary term to facilitate a rapid conclusion of peace, and it had hoped that after six months things would have cooled down enough to obtain an advantageous treaty of friendship from the Afghans. But time was not on the side of Britain; in order to avoid a still further drift by Afghanistan, Dobbs suggested a meeting to "clear up suspicions and prepare the way for a permanent and friendly agreement."[7] The Viceroy agreed to the need for a preliminary meeting but wanted the overtures to come from Afghanistan.[8]

The Amir's letter to Grant was interpreted as such an overture, and the government of India replied that such important questions as frontier and commercial matters should be discussed only at the top level between the Viceroy and the Amir.[9] On January 5, 1920, Lord Chelmsford contacted London for approval of the text of a letter to Amanullah. The Viceroy wanted to let the Amir know that India would tolerate no interference in her relations with the frontier tribes on her side of the border. He also wanted to invite the Amir or his Foreign Minister to ascertain why Afghanistan had not complied with the stipulations of the peace treaty and to remove all the misunderstandings which might have arisen.

The Secretary of State for India thought that such a departure from the previous policy would be seen by the Amir as a sign of fear rather than magnanimity on the part of Britain, but he authorized the message to the Amir, provided that India made it clear beyond any doubt that the proposed discussion did not represent the second stage of the negotiations as provided by Article IV of the treaty.[10]

Lord Chelmsford obtained authorization from London by pointing out that Afghanistan possibly mistrusted British motives, suspecting an imperialist policy. He warned that the Amir's enemies might try to topple him by getting him embroiled with the British.[11] To dispel the hostile atmosphere, the Viceroy thought a personal meeting necessary. Another factor felt by the Viceroy was that Britain faced a period of weakness which would last until October, 1920, and this period could easily be bridged by preliminary discussions. If the Amir did not come to India, a mission could be sent to Afghanistan. As inducements for friendship, the Viceroy thought that the subsidy should be continued and the arrears be paid—including the 1 crore of rupees promised to Habibullah. Further inducements would be some kind of Afghan representation at the Court of St. James, recognition of the title of "Majesty" for the Amir, and technical and military aid to Afghanistan. The Viceroy thought that a tolerable friendship could be maintained with the Amir without forcing him to break with the Bolsheviks, with whom Britain herself considered concluding a commercial agreement.[12] The Viceroy wrote to the Amir on January 17, 1920, inviting him to the discussions and saying that talks were needed "for separation is the parent of misunderstanding and . . . the absent are always wrong." [13]

On February 10, Amanullah replied to the Viceroy's letter, justifying his relations with the frontier tribes and the Russian government. He said that the awakening of the tribes was motivated by the same feelings affecting the whole Islamic world; the tribes wanted the same liberties and freedom as others, and the British actions against them only fanned the fires of jihad. As to the proofs of friendship required by Britain, the Amir considered them irreconcilable with the national independence of Afghanistan. Amanullah wanted to be friends with all mankind and remain at peace with all. He could not expel the Indians from Afghanistan, and in giving them asylum he merely followed an internationally established practice. Reviewing Afghan foreign policy, the Amir said:

> When the Government of Afghanistan considered itself free in foreign affairs it looked in four directions. The first thing which attracted its attention was the Russian Government. . . . For long years Afghanistan was in distress between these two Governments, one of which is Russia and the other is the Government of my friend. Its fate was always decided between these two rival Governments with the

result that first the lands of Panjdeh and Kushk went out of our hands and were allowed to be swallowed by that sharp-toothed wolf; and in the same way, even more lands were taken out of our hands by your Government from our southern and eastern boundaries. Eventually when their friendship became stronger they intended to divide our country between themselves in a brotherly way. The friendship, however, turned into enmity. There was no occasion to carry out that division.[14]

The Amir declared that his relations with Russia were good for the protection of the rights of Muslims in that country and especially in Bukhara. Relations were first established with Russia because no other great power was able to carry out commerce and political relations in a free manner.[15] The Amir declared himself willing to help remove difficulties and misunderstandings between the two countries and invited suggestions from the Viceroy as to the time and place of negotiations.

Grant reported in a semiofficial letter of February 23 to the Viceroy that Afridi resistance to Britain was stiffening, and he made some suggestions for the coming negotiations. He recommended that Afghan relations with Russia and the Central Asian states be permitted, provided Afghanistan would not serve as a base for anti-Indian activities; and he thought that friction would soon cause this entente to die a natural death. Grant wanted Britain to make no territorial concessions to Afghanistan since every subsequent raid would constitute an international incident, threatening war between the two states.[16]

Amanullah continued to put India on the defensive. On February 23, 1920, he requested that the Viceroy render facilities and assistance to an Afghan deputation he wanted to send to England to ascertain the intentions of His Majesty's government regarding the question of the Caliphate and the custody of the holy places. The Amir claimed to speak on behalf of Turkestan, Bukhara, Khiva, and Ferghana in addition to Afghanistan, and he insisted that the Caliphate should have full and independent authority and rule over the Islamic holy places.[17]

The government of India was inclined to comply with the Amir's request, hoping that the difficulty of the trip would discourage the enterprise, or, if it succeeded, that it would offset the Afghan mission to Moscow and give Britain hostages during the Anglo-Indian negotiations. But the Indian government also feared that if the Afghans were going to London they would become aware of the Allied plans concerning the fate of the Ottoman Empire, and they would appear as the champions of Islam. Furthermore, the Amir's Central Asian ambitions, now coming to the fore, would cause trouble with Russia; and if Afghans were permitted to go to London, it might appear that Britain supported Afghan designs in that area.[18] The home government felt that the disadvantages far outweighed the benefits and it did not agree to receive the Afghan mission.[19]

On March 9, 1920, Lord Chelmsford invited the Amir to send his delegation to Mussoorie and asked for the names of the Afghan delegates.[20] A firman of the Amir, published in Nangrahar in the *Ittiḥād-i-Mashriqī*, a newly founded newspaper, called on all Afghans to unite under the banner of Islam. An article signed by Nadir Khan said that the six-month period with the British would expire in eight days and, turning to the question of the tribes, asked how the frontier tribes who had helped so much could be left in the hands of strangers. It was also reported that a conference on national union was held in response to the Amir's firman, and after speeches flags were distributed to the tribes.[21]

The *Times of India* of April 7, 1920, suggested that the Afghans, perturbed over Bolshevik absorption of the Turkoman states, desired friendship with Britain. The newspaper stressed that India wanted to see Afghanistan independent, free, and strong, but would not buy this friendliness at the cost of her self-respect. The newspaper suggested that India again pay a subsidy to the Amir, but that control over Afghan foreign relations would have to be maintained under such circumstances.[22]

The Afghan delegation finally arrived at the border, and, after being politely turned back for lack of proper credentials on April 7, the delegation, headed by Mahmud Tarzi, finally crossed the Indian frontier on April 12, and arrived in Mussoorie on April 14.[23] Britain was at the height of her power and in an unchallenged position throughout the Middle East at the time of the signing of the peace treaty, but since then a marked deterioration had affected Britain's international standing. In August, 1919, Mesopotamia was peaceful,

Persia had signed the Anglo-Persian Agreement, and the Bolsheviks were under constant attack by the forces of Kolchak and Denikin and the fall of Petrograd and Moscow appeared imminent. The Caspian province was controlled by counter-revolutionary forces, and the Bolsheviks in Turkestan, cut off from Russia, seemed on the verge of defeat. But by April great changes had occurred. Mustafa Kemal was in power in Anatolia, the Arab countries were in revolutionary ferment, British influence in Persia was waning, and the anti-Bolshevik forces had disintegrated, leaving the Bolsheviks in firm power in Turkestan and permitting them to support anti-British forces in Afghanistan.

RUSSO-AFGHAN RELATIONS

Russo-Afghan relations had received a sudden impetus when Amanullah ascended the throne of Afghanistan. On April 7, 1919, the Amir and his Foreign Minister sent messages to Lenin and Tchicherin in which they conveyed their greetings and expressed their desire to establish friendly relations with Soviet Russia. The Amir declared that hitherto Afghanistan had stood apart from all other nations, but, now that the standard of Bolshevism had been raised by Russia, he wanted to acknowledge that she had earned the gratitude of the entire world.[24]

General Wali Muhammad Khan was sent in April, 1919, on a mission to Russia and arrived in Moscow on October 10, 1919. The Afghan mission was accompanied by Kazim Bey and Barakatullah, who had previously come to Afghanistan with the Niedermayer expedition.[25] They were received by a guard of honor and accompanied by a band and the flags of the two states. Commissary N. N. Narimanov, director of the Musulman Near East Department, delivered the greetings, saying, "Welcome! In the name of the Soviet Authority and the Commissariat for Foreign Affairs, I greet in the person of Your Excellency, Afghanistan, and its first Embassy to the Capital of the Russian Workers' and Peasants' Government. This historic fact proves that Russian Imperialism striving to enslave and degrade small nationalities, has gone, never to return. . . ."[26] Sultan Galiev welcomed the Afghan Ambassador in the name of the Revolutionary Council of the Republic, saying, "Your small but heroic country is fighting for its emancipation from the age-long oppressors of the East—British Imperialism. We know that you need help and support, and that you expect this support from Soviet Russia. In the name of the Revolutionary Council, and in the name of the revolutionary organizations of the many million labouring Muhammadan masses of Soviet Russia, I declare to you that Soviet Russia will give you that assistance, as she herself is fighting against International Imperialism and for the rights of the oppressed nations of the whole world." [27] In reply Wali Muhammad said: "We know that the Muslim peoples of Russia are now free, and we strongly hope that, with the assistance of Soviet Russia, we shall succeed in emancipating our Afghanistan and the rest of the East." The Ambassador then inquired after the health of Lenin, Trotski, Tchicherin, and others.[28]

On October 18, Moscow Radio reported on Lenin's reception of the Afghan Ambassador. The meeting lasted over half an hour, and the Afghan Ambassador was quoted as again expressing his hope for Soviet assistance in emancipating the whole of Asia from European Imperialism. He presented Lenin a letter from the Afghan King which Lenin accepted "with great pleasure," promising an early reply.[29]

The Afghans seemed to have hoped for an offensive–defensive alliance with Russia. The Soviets were not prepared for such a step, but they were willing to give Afghanistan military and technical assistance.[30] Bogoyavlenski, the Turkestan Minister of Foreign Affairs, had already promised help, and he was authorized to permit the recruitment of Turkestan Muslims into the Afghan army. But the Russians did not want to sign any agreement as yet.

A Russian mission at Herat urged the governor to send a message to Kabul, pointing out the futility of fighting the British until the Afghans were properly equipped with airplanes and machine guns. The Russians wanted to impress the Afghans with the necessity of gaining time pending the arrival of aid from Russia.[31] The Bolsheviks further urged the construction of a railroad from Kushk to Herat, a request which the Afghans seemed unwilling to grant.

In another message to Tashkent, dated August 14, 1919, Moscow informed the Tashkent Soviet that military help to Afghanistan would be given free of charge as soon as railroad communications could be established with Tashkent. Airplanes would be dispatched in the near future. In the interest of a speedy liquidation of Kolchak's front, Moscow felt it desirable that a small detachment of Afghans should cooperate with the Red Army in fighting against the Cossacks. Moscow wanted to hear Afghan opinions regarding this proposal.[32]

A mission, headed by the Bolshevik representative, K. Bravin, arrived in Kabul and was received by Amanullah on September 4, 1919.[33] Negotiations in Kabul resulted in the drafting of an arrangement by which Russia ceded territory to Afghanistan in the Panjdeh area and supplied money, arms, ammunition, and technical assistance in return for Afghan cooperation with Russia in anti-British agitation in India and on the frontier.[34] On October 1 British sources reported the arrival in Kabul of a Russian caravan of some two hundred camels which was presumed to have brought ammunition.[35] The Bravin negotiations were, however, overshadowed by Afghan activities in Russian Central Asia. An ever-increasing number of Afghan missions entered Russian territory, ostensibly for the purpose of pro-Bolshevik and Pan-Islamic propaganda, but the Russians suspected the motives of the Amir. Various potentially hostile forces were at work in the area. Kazim Bey had moved from Afghanistan into Khiva and Bukhara in January, 1919, and then proceeded to Ashkhabad where he soon became one of the leading personalities. He collaborated on the *Voice of the Poor,* a Bolshevik, Turkish newspaper, and he had himself made the virtual ruler of Ashkhabad.[36] In October, 1919, he was reported to have helped to consolidate Turkoman feeling and supervised the "Young Bokhara" party in Kagan, assisting in the training of political agitators. Kazim Bey kept in constant touch with Afghanistan and reported on one occasion to the Governor of Herat that vast Bolshevik and Pan-Islamic forces would soon enter Persia and expel the British from that country. About his Bolshevik friends he said: "I give you my strongest personal assurance that the Bolsheviks are the real friends of the Mohammedans. I can tell you privately but with authority, that the Bolsheviks are preparing several fleets, aeroplanes and much heavy artillery for presentation to the Heroic Amir Amanullah." [37]

Maulvi Barakatullah had stayed in Afghanistan until March, 1919, and then moved into Russia and appeared in Moscow in the following May. From there he returned to Russian Central Asia and collaborated in anti-British agitation. He wrote a pamphlet titled "Bolshevism and Islam" which explained Marxist Socialism as a return to the concept of the *bayt al-mal,* the common treasury for the whole community.[38] According to an intercepted message from Tashkent, the Afghan Ambassador in Tashkent had arrived in Kabul in the company of Mahendra Pratap and a German and Turkish legation. The Tashkent Bolsheviks urged the Ambassador to recognize Mahendra Pratap as president of the "Republic of India."[39]

By October 1919, the Afghans had begun a policy of peaceful penetration of the Panjdeh province. Major General Malleson, head of the British mission to Meshed and Ashkhabad, reported that Afghan influence was consolidating in Merv and to the south, and that the Afghan Consul in Merv was recognized as a more important person than the local Bolshevik Commissary.[40] A Sarakhs agent reported to the British on October 20, that there was great alarm in Merv over Afghan advances and an agent from Tejend said that four hundred or five hundred Bolshevik troops had been hurriedly called up in Merv for defense against the Afghans. He further said that the Afghan Consul in Merv was attempting to allay the excitement by explaining that the Afghans had no aggressive designs, and were merely establishing consulates in various important towns of Turkestan and, because of the disturbed state of the country, required large escorts for their consular officers.[41]

The Pan-Islamic policy of the Afghans appeared clearly in a letter by the Afghan Consul at Merv to a friend in Herat, in which he said:

> I am working hard to bring local Shiahs and Sunnis together, and I am paying particular attention to the Persians, many of whom I have won over by saving them from Bolshevik oppression. I also give alms to destitute Persian families. I utilize every opportunity of impressing on the Persians that the safety and national independence of their country lies entirely in closest association with Afghans and Bolsheviks who have sworn to rid the Islamic world of the hated British oppressors. As an instance of the manner in which I am cooperating with the Bolsheviks, I have enlisted many wandering Afghans in the Bolshevik ranks. This measure reassures the local Bolsheviks and gives Persians here a great idea of Bolshevik-Afghan solidarity.[42]

146   THE SETTLEMENT

According to a French source, a conference was held in Bukhara by representatives of Bukhara, Khiva, Afghanistan, and Persian nationalists in which it was decided to form a Muslim confederation. A suggestion was also made to form a corps in the Caucasus under the command of Khalil Bey, auxiliary to the force under Mustafa Kemal. The latter wanted, however, to await the results of the peace conference first.[43]

Other Afghan emissaries to Russian Central Asia included the Herat Shrine custodians, who left Herat in early September with great ceremony to travel via Panjdeh to Karshi, Bukhara, and Samarkand in order to preach jihad against the British and enlist the sympathy and help of Central Asian Muslims for Afghanistan.[44]

When communications were reestablished, Moscow sent a mission headed by the Bolshevik, Z. Suritz, to discuss the situation with Amanullah and to make arrangements for providing aid to Afghanistan.[45] Suritz arrived in Herat on November 11, 1919, with a party of eighteen officials, two Afghan colonels, and the Herat Shrine custodians. The mission was received with great honor. A salute of sixty guns was fired and a *jirga* of all local mullahs and khans and the entire garrison met the mission and accompanied it in procession to a banquet at Char Bagh.[46] The mission left Herat on November 18, and proceeded via Maymana and Mazar-i-Sharif to Kabul.

Suritz reached Kabul in January, 1920, and immediately set about to continue the negotiations started by Bravin. The main features of the proposed treaty were: (1) each country should supply the other with both raw materials and manufactured goods; (2) on the part of Russia all trade with Afghanistan was to be conducted by the government Department of Foreign Trade, but the department was willing to deal with individual Afghan merchants as well as with the Afghan government; and (3) Russia would impose no import duty on goods from Afghanistan. The Soviets insisted that this commercial treaty be concluded as a preliminary to a more general agreement.[47]

Amanullah was reported to be willing to resume hostilities against Britain after delivery at Kabul of 80,000 to 100,000 rifles, with 600 rounds per rifle, 1,500 machine guns, and 50 million rubles in gold. The Amir was further reported willing to conclude a treaty of friendship or mutual support with Russia on the following terms:

(1) the Kerki and Terek districts were to be ceded to Afghanistan; (2) Afghan delegates were to be appointed to the Russo-Bukharan Commission; (3) a subsidy of 10 million rubles in gold was to be paid to Afghanistan; (4) the Bolsheviks were to supply an installation for the production of smokeless powder; and (5) the Bolsheviks were to provide: (*a*) telegraph lines from Kabul directly to Herat, and via Kandahar to Herat, (*b*) 10,000 rifles, (*c*) civil and military interpreters, (*d*) a number of batteries of artillery, (*e*) wireless telegraphy stations at Kabul, Herat, and Kandahar, (*f*) assistance in arming the Indian frontier tribes, and (*g*) permission for Afghanistan's use of two steamers on the Oxus.

A proposal by Suritz to discuss the Afghan demands at Tashkent by a joint commission was declined by the Afghans. Suritz then declared his willingness to agree to the Afghan demands with the exception of the one provision demanding the cession of territory to Afghanistan. He also reserved his decision as to the amount of aid Russia would give to Afghanistan. Suritz seemed eager to obtain a treaty of friendship which would have the following general provisions: (1) neither party should conclude any agreement that might be injurious to the other; (2) the Afghans would keep the Bolsheviks informed of any negotiations with the British which might affect Russia; (3) the Bolshevik representative should be formally recognized; and (4) factories should be established by the Bolsheviks at Kandahar, Ghazni, and Jalalabad.[48]

It appears that Suritz did not have a free hand in these talks, and that he had to refer to Moscow for approval. Moscow evidently was reluctant to conclude an alliance with the Afghans which might force Russia into a war with the British, since they hoped for Western recognition and resumption of commercial relations with Britain.[49] What Russia apparently wanted was to draw Afghanistan away from Britain and to gain an ally who would support her in the consolidation of her power in the East.[50] The government of India also thought that it would be better to come to an understanding with Russia to avoid having Afghanistan play off one country against the other.[51] Lord Chelmsford even submitted to London the draft of an Anglo-Russian treaty permitting both to establish consular relations, but pledging both states to refrain from supporting Afghanistan against each other.[52]

148   THE SETTLEMENT

Suritz was not successful in obtaining a treaty; it appears that he had exceeded his instructions, and the negotiations were temporarily suspended on orders from Moscow. The period of temporary weakness of the Russians in Turkestan ended when Bolshevik troops finally defeated the anti-Bolshevik forces in Ferghana and Semirechia and deposed the Khan of Khiva. The Afghans were gradually forced out of their de facto recovery of Panjdeh and Merv.[53]

THE MUSSOORIE CONFERENCE

Afghan activities on the Indian frontier had not ended with the signing of the peace treaty at Rawalpindi. The peace was reported to the tribes as merely a cease-fire for six months, after which the Afghans, strengthened by assistance from other powers, were to renew their attacks. The tribes were told that the British would evacuate all trans-Indus areas in six months.[54] Militia deserters from India attended the Amir's durbar at Kabul and were feted by the populace, and Afghan officers remained in Waziristan to work with the tribes.[55]

The "Provisional Government of India" in Afghanistan, headed by Mahendra Pratap as president, Barakatullah as prime minister, and Obeidullah as administrative minister, continued to direct its propaganda into India and to supply Indian revolutionaries with bombs and arms.[56]

When the Mussoorie Conference began, Afghanistan's position vis-à-vis Britain was stronger than ever. Policy clashes between Afghanistan and Soviet Russia had not reached a point where cooperation between them was impossible. On the eve of the conference, Lord Chelmsford reported to the India Office, discussing the points that were likely to be raised. The government of India was willing to permit the establishment of Afghan consulates at Bombay, Karachi, and Calcutta, but not in Peshawar. A simple postal exchange arrangement would have to be devised. India would grant Afghanistan the same rebates on customs duty as Kashmir, Persia, and China received. The Viceroy wanted to explain to the Afghans that there had been no response from the British King to the Afghan ruler's letter because no friendship agreement existed between the two countries. The question of subsidy payments would not be mentioned, but if it came up India would refer the matter to London for advice. India hoped to be permitted to recognize the Amir's title of "Majesty."[57] London approved the above points with the exception of recognizing the title of Majesty, on which the Secretary of State did not want to commit himself in advance, owing to strong opposition in England.[58]

Major F. Humphrys and Ghulam Muhammad Khan held informal talks prior to the first meeting of the conference in which the latter gave an indication of Afghan demands, declaring "that Englishmen bore the reputation in Kabul, and probably all over the world, of being land grabbers with an insatiable appetite for new conquests. They had laid their hands on half the world and were ever pressing forward." He recounted how the British took Ali Masjid, Landi Khana, and other areas, but made the mistake of taking tribes they could not control. Ghulam Muhammad Khan stated that "only a Muhammadan king could keep these tribes in order and the Amir would willingly undertake the task at half the expense and succeed where the British had failed." The Afghan official further indicated that if the Afghan conditions were not accepted the Afghans would be determined to fight to the bitter end. He also indicated that the Amir wanted a Peshawar–Kabul railroad, but it would have to be under Afghan control.[59]

The first meeting took place on April 17, 1920, and the heads of the two delegations, Dobbs, the foreign secretary to the government of India, and Mahmud Tarzi Khan, the Afghan foreign minister, made their opening statements.[60] The British raised the question of Afghan propaganda against Britain and the incitement of the tribes on the frontier. They also commented on the apparent readiness of Afghanistan to assist Bolshevik policy by acting as a corridor for the passage of anti-British emissaries and propaganda.

The Afghans on their part wanted to know what the British attitude toward Turkey and the question of the Caliphate was. Tarzi claimed that the Muslims of Ferghana, Bukhara, Turkoman country, and even Persia "have appealed to Afghanistan and are asking our king for help and have submitted documents of allegiance." The Afghans further wanted to know British intentions regarding the Afghan tribes on the British side of the frontier, and, finally, the real British attitude toward Afghan independence.[61]

Tarzi incidentally but definitely stated that it was the desire of Afghanistan henceforth to abandon her policy of isolation and to have free intercourse with other nations.

During the second meeting, on April 19, Dobbs reassured the Afghans that Britain recognized Afghan independence, but that an Afghan representative could not be established in London before the conclusion of a friendship treaty. Dobbs commented on the difficulty of conducting Anglo-Afghan relations by way of London, since most questions are related to Indo-Afghan affairs, and referral to London would cause great delay. Dobbs gave Canada and the United States as an example of having such direct relations, disregarding the fact that their power relationship and cultural factors were unlike those of India and Afghanistan. But Tarzi was not to be moved in this matter which he considered one of national sentiment and insisted that Afghanistan wanted to be treated just like any other independent state. He considered representation in England especially necessary at this point since Afghanistan wanted to send students to England and intended to make purchases in England directly and not with the help of India. Tarzi further held that Afghanistan had to be able to bring her point of view directly to the attention of the British government in case a difference of opinion developed with India. The Afghans were prepared to accept a British representative in Kabul. Dobbs replied that he could not give any assurances on this matter.[62]

The Afghans showed themselves greatly concerned with the problem of national independence. As long as their foreign relations with Britain had to be conducted through India, the Afghans felt they had little protection from an Indian forward policy; they also had doubts about the sincerity of the British assurances. The Afghans were disturbed about the failure of the British King to answer the Amir's letter. They suspected sinister motives behind the nonpublication of Grant's letter conceding Afghanistan freedom in foreign relations. On the arrival of the Afghan Envoy in India, the British held that his functions would be the same as before. The nonrecognition of the title of "Majesty" for the Amir seemed a further example of British unwillingness to act on their promises of Afghan independence. The Afghans expected that the change of the status of Afghanistan would be reflected by an exchange of ministers with London and the establishment of Afghan consuls general in Simla and Delhi, as well as consuls and vice consuls in other areas in India.[63]

To this Dobbs could only declare that British policy had always been to favor a strong and independent Afghanistan. He excused Afghan accusations of Britain's "nibbling away at Afghanistan" by the need of Britain to "create safe doors for itself to Afghanistan to defend Kabul and Kandahar from Russian aggression." British policy was, according to Dobbs, almost identical with her policy toward Belgium. Dobbs excused the failure of London to reply to the Amir's letter on grounds of the existing period of doubt as to who was the de facto ruler, and he claimed that Grant's letter was not published because of the hostility of British opinion.[64]

During the fourth meeting, on April 22, the matter of consular representation was further discussed. The Afghans held that dismissal of hostile foreigners from Afghanistan could not be demanded since it was contrary to the Islamic injunction of hospitality and the practice in international law of granting asylum; furthermore such demands were irreconcilable with Afghan independence. But Tarzi conceded "if our material interests are involved and substantial friendship is shown to us, we might, perhaps, be willing to waive some of these moral scruples."

At this point in the negotiations, both parties almost simultaneously suspended the discussions because of aggression on the part of the other. In a verbal message to Tarzi, Sir Abdul Kayyum informed him of the suspension of negotiations and said it was the result of Afghan encroachments at Lambabat, Tandisar, Chaman, and other points on the frontier.[65] A letter from the Afghan delegation stated that it must suspend discussions pending satisfactory settlement of the Waziristan question.[66]

S. E. Pears, political adviser to Dobbs, monitored Afghan correspondence and reported that Amanullah had no information about Afghan aggression and had not given Abdul Kuddus any orders. With regard to Nadir Khan, the Amir was quoted as saying, "You know what I think about raids; so long as the British are perplexed the retort is at your discretion. Send word to Nadir Khan whenever you think necessary and remind him to blow softly."[67]

In a memorandum to the government of India, Dobbs commented on the break in the conference. He thought that the Afghans were merely bluffing about their Waziristan position and he believed it would not constitute a *sine qua non* to continued negotiations. Dobbs hoped to keep the question of the tribes in the background on the chance that the longer the Afghans stayed in India the more likely would be the possibility of a break between Afghanistan and Russia. He also wanted to stall for time in order to obtain London's approval for the permanent British occupation of the Mahsud country to confront the Afghans with a *fait accompli*.[68]

During the break in the negotiations Ghulam Muhammad attempted to end the deadlock when he spoke to Sir Abdul Kayyum, saying:

> We do not understand all the niceties of diplomacy and do not see the object of these long discussions. We wish to get to the point. The truth is this. We can still make a good bargain with the Bolsheviks; but we prefer to deal with Great Britain, because she is firmly established and an ancient state, and is also wealthier than the Bolsheviks. Moreover, she is our old friend and we would prefer to turn towards her first. We can easily settle the question of our relations with the Bolsheviks and of our giving an asylum to the Indian seditionists, if we come to terms; but we want to know what the British will offer us. If they will not offer us enough, we must turn to the Bolsheviks. There is still time to do so. But also we require Waziristan. The British Government must be tired of trying to restrain these tribes and we could keep them in much better order. We cannot possibly desert them since they rose against the British and helped us, and they are Musalmans.[69]

Dobbs believed that Tarzi was serious in his threat to return to Kabul if Britain did not stop her Waziristan operations, because this fact was uncovered in an intercepted, ciphered message to Kabul. He also did not think that the Afghan invasion of Chitral and other border areas was officially sanctioned in Kabul; it seemed to be merely an Afghan response to British moves into Waziristan. Dobbs favored a return to the conference to tell the Afghans that there could be no talks until the Afghan troops withdrew and to give notice that if they refused to negotiate because of British actions in Waziristan they would have to return and the conference would be over.[70]

The Afghans did not neglect the field of propaganda in India

One incident was reported during prayers at the Landour Mosque, where the Imam Abdul Kadir read *khutbah* in the presence of the Afghan delegation in the name of the "Amir al-Mu'minin Amir Aman Allah Khan Ghazi." One person present said that the nonbelievers attempted to extinguish the Light of Islam, and urged all to keep Afghanistan victorious and flourishing.[71] During a meeting in the *Jum'a* Masjid in Mussoorie in which Tarzi and the Afghan delegation participated, the Caliphate question was discussed. Tarzi said that the objective of his mission was to obtain a just peace for Turkey. He stressed the lesson of unity and, referring to a speech of Amanullah, he quoted that the Amir was ready to die for the integrity of the Caliphate and was very happy to receive Indian Muslims who felt compelled to leave their country.[72]

On April 30, 1920, India requested the home government to authorize recognition of the title of "Majesty" and payment to Afghanistan of the same subsidy that was previously granted to Habibullah. The Viceroy wanted this concession because he felt that the hand of his government was forced after the blunt Afghan statement, and he had to declare what he wanted to offer. India feared that if the Afghans returned home tribal tension would result and involve India in military operations.[73] His Majesty's government regretted, however, that it could not accept the Indian point of view in this matter, and did not authorize the above measures.[74] Two weeks of unofficial talks followed in which the Afghans denied charges of aggression and insisted on obtaining a settlement on the question of the tribes, either by cession to Afghanistan or by guarantee of an independent tribal area as a buffer state between India and Afghanistan.[75] Finally, during an unofficial tea on May 9, at which only Mahmud Tarzi, Ghulam Muhammad, and their counterparts, Dobbs and Abdul Kayyum, were present, the Afghans revealed the full scope of their objectives. Tarzi admitted that the Afghans had sent sixty military instructors and six guns to the Amir of Bukhara and were considering the question of assisting the anti-Bolsheviks in Ferghana. If given Waziristan, the Afghans declared themselves willing to conclude an alliance with Britain against the Bolsheviks to extricate the Turkomans, Bukhara, and Khiva from Russian influence. The Afghans also wanted British assistance in the development of their country and professed their willingness to give

Britain a monopoly in such developments. The Afghans further hoped for financial assistance from Britain.[76]

Tarzi admitted that the tribes were kept in a state of agitation, ready for war if Britain should renew it. Dobbs reported the Afghans "crestfallen" when they were told that they could not expect any concessions on the frontier, and they immediately withdrew their own concessions. Dobbs felt however that some way would have to be found to give the Afghans a face-saving device in this matter.[77]

In the meantime the peace terms with Turkey were announced, and Tarzi complained that it looked like a new holy war was afoot against Islam—especially since Germany was not similarly divided.[78] It was now Britain's turn to be intransigent and to pursue a policy of the *fait accompli*. Instead of giving Tarzi a way out and rewarding him for achieving the withdrawal of Afghan troops from the areas into which they had intruded, the British not only continued their operations in Waziristan but also planned the permanent occupation of Mahsud country.[79]

Discussions were officially resumed on June 7, 1920, and in this and subsequent meetings Dobbs brought up British complaints against the Afghans and asserted that no monopolies or concessions were wanted, and all that Britain desired was an end to hostilities. Next the Turkish peace terms were discussed. Dobbs finally recommended to his government that some concessions be made to the Afghans, who could not go away empty-handed. In response to the comment from the home government that the conference was taking place without any definite agenda,[80] Dobbs declared the "whole object of my management of these discussions [is] to present Afghans on matters of importance such as [the] Waziristan policy and Turkish treaty with a series of *faits accomplis* which while open to explanation cannot be modified and against it would be useless for them to protest." He assured His Majesty's government that "I am expounding British policy without any pretense of idealistic aims and without false sentiments."[81]

On June 23, at the eighth meeting of the conference, the tribal question was brought up again, and the British delegate remarked that Wilson's right to self-determination applied only to the defeated. Dobbs said that if Britain admitted self-determination it would mean the end of the Empire. But he reasoned also, trying to win both sides of the argument, that although India had more Pashtu-speaking people than Afghanistan she did not claim any portion of Afghanistan. Abdul Hadi replied that for a hundred years the Afghans had not forgotten that Peshawar belonged to Afghanistan.[82]

The London government in the meantime authorized India to grant a subsidy in exchange for the Afghan promise that they would stop their intrigues with the tribes, deny a base in Afghanistan to aliens hostile to India, and refrain from encouraging Indian agitators. The home government warned that the Afghans might merely use a British bid as a lever to obtain more from the Russians. London, furthermore, was still reluctant to grant a subsidy without maintaining control of Afghan foreign relations and suggested that a treaty and loans be offered similar to those contained in the Anglo-Iranian Agreement of 1919.[83] The government of India saw, however, no chance that Afghanistan would permit control of its foreign affairs or accept a loan that might lead to foreign dependence.[84]

During the Mussoorie Conference (April 17–July 18, 1920) the political situation had again changed. Vusuq al-Daula fell in Persia and the new government dispatched a Persian envoy to Moscow. The Bolsheviks took over in Azerbaydjan, and Mustafa Kemal strengthened his power in Anatolia. In Mesopotamia the Arab uprising occurred, and in India the Caliphate question and the Amritsar atrocities had kept the people agitated. To these problems was added the *hijrat* movement which induced many *muhajirun* to move from infidel-controlled India to the Muslim country of Afghanistan.[85]

Suritz, still in Kabul, finally received permission from Moscow to conclude a treaty with the Afghans. Bukhara seemed on the verge of defeat by the "Young Bokharan" movement which leaned on Soviet support, and Jemal Pasha, accompanied by a group of Turkish and Bolshevik officials, was on his way to Afghanistan.[86]

These events led Dobbs to the belief that the Russians would both want and support an Afghan war. Therefore, he thought the time ripe for stabilizing the situation by concluding a treaty of friendship with Afghanistan. He submitted a draft treaty by which Britain recognized Afghan independence and arranged for consular representation. Afghanistan was to pledge herself to refrain from interfering with the transborder tribes and to prohibit anti-British activities in her territory. Britian would grant Afghanistan a subsidy of 18 lakhs of rupees and an unspecified amount of material support for the development of the country. Britain would also help in the construction of railways and telegraph lines. Other assistance would be given, including the free import of arms and ammunitions through India as well as tax and import reductions for trade and transit of goods. Afghanistan would be permitted to export opium through India to those places where the sale of opium was permitted. Finally there were provisions for a postal arrangement between the two countries.[87]

Lord Chelmsford was skeptical about the value of this draft, and the Indian government ruled not to offer Afghanistan any treaty at this time.[88]

On the final meeting of the conferees, on July 24, 1920, Dobbs presented the Afghan delegation an *aide-mémoire* containing provisions similar to his draft treaty, but postponed the conclusion of a treaty to a later date.[89] The *aide-mémoire* also provided for gifts to Afghanistan of telegraphic material, trucks with spare parts, some military equipment, and an American touring car to be delivered after a friendship treaty was signed by the Afghans. Left for consideration during subsequent meetings was the question of Afghan representation in London, and permission for Afghanistan to export ruble notes to such places where their sale was permitted.[90]

The Afghan delegation returned to Kabul with only the promise of an arrangement, which seemed not at all certain of attainment—not much, indeed, to show for three months of grueling negotiations. Commenting on the *aide-mémoire,* the Viceroy wrote to the Amir on August 9:

> I trust that in this memorandum you will find evidence of the sincere goodwill of the British Government towards Afghanistan, and I wish to assure you that if, after having fully considered this statement, you desire to conclude a Treaty of Friendship, and if the attitude of your Government and officials is clearly consistent with that desire, there will be no obstacle on the part of my Government to negotiating a treaty.[91]

THE SETTLEMENT 157

Back in Kabul the Afghans continued the negotiations with Suritz during August and September, 1920. Since they did not obtain a treaty from Britain, the Afghans readily signed a draft of a Russo-Afghan treaty which was then sent to Moscow for approval. But Suritz had obtained this treaty only by making greater concessions to the Afghans than he was instructed to make and the Soviet government was unwilling to give its approval. Suritz's concessions were prompted by friction between the two countries resulting from Jamshidi raids and the overthrow of the Amir of Bukhara in September, 1920. The Afghans seemed to feel that without having a treaty with Britain they could not break with the Russians. A good opportunity for Britain to obtain a treaty seemed lost when the Afghans became reconciled to the Bukhara situation.[92]

KABUL MISSION—THE SETTLEMENT

The government of India expected that Amanullah would appeal for British aid against the Russians in Bukhara, and Lord Chelmsford telegraphed London on September 24, requesting permission to give Afghanistan immediate military aid, but ruling out the conclusion of a defensive alliance. But the Secretary of State warned of the danger in such a move if this military material fell into the hands of the Bolsheviks and insisted that such aid, if given at all, be given only after conclusion of a treaty of friendship. The home government felt that the best form of assistance would be a substantial grant of money.[93]

Contrary to Indian expectations, the Amir did not ask for British assistance, but he answered the Viceroy's message regarding the *aide-mémoire,* saying that "notwithstanding that some of the items contained in the written statement and the memorandum have been found in our Supreme Council not to be free from possibility of complaint and objection, I can assure Your Excellency that this objection and complaint does not conflict with the basis of the question on which we wish to found the conclusion of a treaty of friendship, but refers to certain things which are considered to be trivial." The Amir then invited a British mission to Kabul.

Dobbs thought that this Afghan willingness to come to terms with the British was caused by events that strengthened the position

158   THE SETTLEMENT

of Britain. The *muhajirun* movement had turned out to be a disappointment to many, and the noncooperation movement in India appeared greatly weakened. The Mahsud were on the verge of accepting the permanent British occupation of their territory. The Treaty of Sèvres had been signed and French forces had occupied Damascus and Aleppo. Furthermore, in Afghanistan there was unrest among the troops, and the Khostwal and Mangal tribes were restive and causing some incidents. Dobbs saw the policy of "pinpricks," the tribal raids and kidnapings, continue along the frontier, but he nevertheless saw the time auspicious for the conclusion of a treaty with the Afghans.[94]

Therefore the government of India recommended to the home government that a mission be dispatched to Afghanistan for conclusion of a friendship treaty, provided that the mission be authorized to address the Amir officially as "His Majesty" and that the Afghans release two kidnaped British officers. London, however, was stubbornly persistent that it would not recognize this title except as a reward for a treaty. When it had become known in India that Afghanistan and Russia had reached an agreement, the government of India reported to London on October 19, deprecating the importance of the agreement and stating that "we do not consider that the acceptance by Afghanistan of help from the Bolsheviks, which we believe now inevitable, should preclude us from carrying out to the end, if possible, the programme laid down by us at Mussoorie."[95] But the government of India found it necessary to add a new condition for granting Afghanistan a treaty of friendship, namely, that the Afghans give "full and accurate" information of the terms of the Russo-Afghan treaty to ascertain whether it did not contain any provisions unfriendly to Britain. Hostile provisions would have to be abrogated before an Anglo-Afghan treaty could be signed.

The Secretary of State wrote on October 20, 1920, that the Russo-Afghan treaty makes it impossible for Britain to authorize the payment of a subsidy and the granting of military assistance to Afghanistan. London also thought that the Amir should be approached and told that Britain would give him an opportunity to repudiate the Russo-Afghan treaty; but until this matter was cleared up and Britain informed of the full details of the treaty London thought that "no useful purpose would result from sending an envoy to Kabul."[96] The Viceroy wrote to the Amir according to these instructions, objecting especially to Bolshevik consulates at Ghazni and Kandahar, and informing the Amir of the British intention of conducting operations against the Wana Wazirs.

The Amir denied that the Russian consulates were being set up in return for a subsidy, saying, "I confidentially assure you that, just as [the] matter of Consulates at Kandahar and Ghazni has not yet been formally and finally arranged, so they will never be established for the purpose of causing harm to and creating mischief in your dominions." The Amir, however, did not reveal any details of the treaty with Russia. On the subject of Waziristan, the Amir said that the sending of a mission would also solve this problem without harm or injury to anyone.[97]

The government of India had become anxious to see her relations with Afghanistan settled on a satisfactory basis and it felt convinced that the Amir sincerely wanted an early agreement. Therefore it urged London to authorize the sending of a mission to Kabul. The question was discussed in the English cabinet and finally, not without serious misgivings, permission was granted to India to send a mission to Kabul. London held that "no treaty of friendship can be concluded with Afghanistan if it ultimately appears that the Afghans have committed themselves definitely to a treaty with the Bolsheviks including obviously anti-British provisions such as the establishment of Consulates in Eastern Afghanistan," but the home government was reluctant to override the "deliberate judgement" of the government of India in a matter "lying so peculiarly within its province."[98]

The Viceroy then informed the Amir that he accepted his invitation, and the British mission crossed the Afghan frontier on January 5, 1921, and arrived two days later in Kabul. The discussions between the Delhi and London governments about the advisability of sending a mission had delayed its arrival in Kabul for about two months, and, as so often during the early postwar period, the political situation had again changed. The Russo-Afghan treaty was near ratification, and Russia, after overrunning Azerbayjan and establishing Soviet rule in Armenia, came in direct contact with the Anatolian forces of Mustafa Kemal. Germany, reluctant to pay her reparations, seemed preparing for a new war. Jemal Pasha had established himself in Kabul and began the training of Afghan forces; while Talaat Bey and Enver Pasha encouraged the Afghans by sending word that Germany, after solving her internal divisions, would renew the war.[99]

Overshadowed and continually influenced by changes in the international situation, the British mission, headed by Dobbs, conducted eleven months of grueling negotiations which finally led to a permanent settlement in Anglo-Afghan relations. Dobbs was instructed to negotiate a treaty according to the lines set in the Mussoorie *aide-mémoire*. Afghanistan would have to follow a good-neighbor policy and, furthermore, not permit Russian consulates along the Indian frontier, but Britain would not end her policy of tribal pacifications and annexation in the Waziristan area—a fateful decision which never permitted really cordial relations between Afghanistan and her southeastern neighbor.

Dobbs describes the course of negotiations as falling into four distinct phases: First, from January 20, 1921, to April 9; second, from April 9 to mid-July; third, from mid-July to September 18; and fourth, from September 18 to December 8, 1921.

During the first phase the Afghans began by demanding territorial concessions from the British. They based their demands on the principle of self-determination and asked that those tribes who so desired be permitted to join Afghanistan. In the Chitral area, the Afghans wanted the cession of the Arneway village. They further demanded payment of 4 crores and 36 lakhs of rupees as a reward for Afghan neutrality during the war. The Afghans did not want any development assistance which required British supervision, and they would not promise the exclusion of Russian consulates from the Afghan border. Internationally, the Afghans demanded a revision of the Turkish peace treaty.

Dobbs expressed his willingness to grant Afghanistan an initial payment of 36 lakhs and a yearly subsidy of 20.5 lakhs of rupees. Dobbs also agreed to the establishment of an Afghan legation in London. Furthermore, Britain was willing to give the concessions listed in the Mussoorie *aide-mémoire,* except for the unwanted development projects. But Dobbs insisted on the exclusion of Russian consular offices from southeastern Afghanistan. He also offered to inform the Afghan government in advance of any military action taken by Britain against the frontier tribes.[100]

The tribal question threatened several times to lead to a rupture in the negotiations and, according to Dobbs, a breakdown was averted only when Britain signed the trade agreement with Russia on March 17, 1921. Russian internal difficulties and famine, leading to the New Economic Policy and abortive uprisings, and disagreements with Turkey over the division of Armenia, may have induced the Russians to sign treaties with both Britain and Afghanistan. Dobbs thought the Afghans feared that an Anglo-Russian agreement might be reached over their heads; therefore they appeared reluctant to break with the British at this time.

The second phase in the negotiations started with the conclusion of a friendship treaty between Russia and Turkey. The Amir told the British delegates that their insistence on exclusion of Russian consulates from the border areas forced Afghanistan to decide for friendship with one or the other. If Afghanistan failed to uphold the Russo-Afghan treaty, Britain would have to be ready to defend her with arms and money from a Russian attack. The Amir intimated that Russia's unwillingness to give independence to her Central Asian states inclined him toward Britain, and all he wanted was an amnesty from Britain for the tribes who supported him against the British in the war.

His Majesty's government suggested that the Amir be induced to break completely with Russia by giving him liberal grants in arms and money. This suggestion was readily accepted in India. On June 4, 1921, after the Afghans had unsuccessfully attempted to obtain an offensive–defensive alliance from Britain, they made the following proposal: Afghanistan would break with Russia, using the Soviet inroads in Bukhara and Khiva as a pretext. Britain, in turn, would pay Afghanistan a subsidy of 40 lakhs of rupees and give an immediate present of 20,000 rifles, 200 machine guns, and two 18-pounder batteries with an adequate supply of ammunition. Furthermore, Britain was to provide six airplanes and material for a telegraph line extending from Kabul to Kandahar and Herat. In case Russia responded with unprovoked aggression, Britain should supply additional military assistance. The Amir further wanted a face-saving device by which Britain would recognize the Amir's efforts as helpful in getting a favorable and lenient arrangement for the Waziristan tribes.

Dobbs was permitted to grant all these concessions, but not before June 15, 1921, was he authorized to give assurances regarding the tribes. In the meantime Suritz pressed the Afghans to sign the Russo-Afghan treaty that had been ratified by the Soviets on May 26 and brought back from Moscow. Dobbs believed that the two-month delay had cooled the Afghans' enthusiasm for the British treaty, causing them to raise their demands, reasonably enough, to include the reservation that they not be forced to break with Russia until they had had time to transport British arms up to the border.

On June 21, the Afghans asked for an increase in ammunition and some tribal concessions, but did not commit themselves not to make any agreement with a third power which might affect the mutual interests of Britain and Afghanistan. When Britain refused to grant these concessions, the Afghans turned again to Suritz who now promised that Russia would not press for consulates on the Afghan frontier.

The arrival in Kabul of the new Russian Ambassador, F. Raskolniknoff, on July 6 and new Turkish victories against the Greeks appeared to lead to a stiffening in the Afghan attitude and to their refusal, on July 14, of the British stipulation regarding treaties between Afghanistan and other powers. The Afghans viewed this stipulation, which prohibited the making of agreements with third powers if they affected the mutual interests of Britain and Afghanistan, as control of their foreign relations under a new disguise.

In the beginning of the third phase, the Afghans were quite doubtful as to the honesty and intentions of Britain. An Afghan mission, headed by Sirdar Muhammad Wali Khan, had finally succeeded in getting to Europe and attempted to establish consular relations after talks with government officials in a number of countries.[101] The Afghans were to inform the world that their country had become an independent member of the community of nations and they were to establish diplomatic relations with various countries and to contract for experts in various specialties to come to Afghanistan and work on development projects. When Britain heard that Italy was about to sign a treaty for commercial and consular relations with Afghanistan, His Majesty's Foreign Office protested, informing the Italian government that Britain was about to conclude an agreement with Afghanistan which would "admit the superior and predominant political influence of Britain" in that country.[102] The British government further declared that it "still considered Afghanistan to lie within the sphere of British political influence."

When news of this reached Kabul on July 17, it aroused bitter resentment in the capital. The Afghans expressed their feelings by inviting the representatives of Russia, Anatolia, and Revolutionary Bukhara to a banquet at the Foreign Ministry and treated them to a feast of anti-British pronouncements.

The Afghans now refused to accept the British treaty and sought to return to a more general agreement that would exclude from eastern Afghanistan consulates of "any power opposed to the British" and provide an amnesty for the tribes together with a promise of lenient terms for the Wazirs. The Afghans also did not want any provision that would bind them to refrain from having relations with the frontier Afghans. The Afghan government wanted the right to import arms by way of India and it wanted to be paid a subsidy of 20.5 lakhs of rupees and a gift of 31 lakhs. The Afghan provisions regarding tribal relations and the import of arms made the treaty unacceptable to Britain.

On July 31, the mailbag of the British mission was seized by unknown persons while it was en route from Kabul to the border and Dobbs suspended the negotiations pending its return.

In the meantime, His Majesty's government suggested that the Indian government settle for a general treaty with Afghanistan such as would exist between two civilized powers, containing provisions merely for the exchange of envoys and consuls and for the continuance of neighborly relations without any provisions for a subsidy or alliance.

On August 13 the *Amān-i-Afghān* announced the ratification of a treaty with Russia. A week later the mailbag was restored to the British. Dobbs thereupon wrote to Mahmud Tarzi, asking him to reveal the content of the Russo-Afghan treaty.

Lord Curzon, who had in 1919 become Secretary of State of Foreign Affairs, now again fanned the passions of the Afghans. The

Afghan mission to Europe and the United States had finally arrived in London and had an interview with the Foreign Secretary. When Sirdar Muhammad Wali mentioned the discussions in Kabul, Lord Curzon curtly broke off the conversation, saying that the negotiations in Kabul were the affair of Afghanistan and India and not his concern. The Afghan mission wanted to be introduced to the King by Lord Curzon, but the latter refused and referred them to the India Office for this purpose.

The Afghan Foreign Minister reacted angrily. He sent Dobbs a letter, dated August 28, which was "couched in language of studied insult," omitting all titles and merely addressed to "Janab-i-Dobb," and complaining about the treatment of the Afghan mission in London.[103] In a second letter, Tarzi refused to give Dobbs any information about the Russo-Afghan treaty, telling him he could read the text in the newspaper. Finally on September 3, the Afghan government officially informed the British delegates of the text of the treaty.[104] But in this copy the clause which promised Afghanistan a subsidy and military and technical assistance was omitted. His task being completed, Suritz left Afghanistan in August and a month later Jemal Pasha left Kabul to return to Turkey.

The fourth and final phase in the negotiations was marked by a serious impasse, and twice the government of India sent transportation from Peshawar to the Afghan border to bring the British mission back to India, but a solution was finally reached.[105]

Dobbs had become reluctant to return without a treaty and he asked the Indian government whether or not he might try for the kind of neighborly treaty which the Secretary of State had previously suggested. His request was granted, provided he could obtain such a treaty without any loss of dignity to the British government. Dobbs' departure had been set for September 18, and on the day before he sent two of his officers, Pipon and Acheson, to visit Mr. Tarzi at Paghman and to inform him that the government of India was prepared to conclude a neighborly treaty with Afghanistan. An official meeting was held on the next day at which Dobbs produced a new treaty.

When no progress was made, the Amir stepped into the picture, inviting Dobbs to Paghman on September 27, and personally took part in the negotiations. The Amir now declared himself ready to break with the Russians, as suggested before, if Britain reverted to her "exclusive treaty" and gave additional aid, but permitted the Amir more time for repudiation of the Russo-Afghan treaty. The Amir also wanted the Afghan Ambassador in London to be permitted to deal directly with the British Foreign Office rather than with the India Office. The following six weeks were spent in discussions between the Delhi and London governments with the result that the home government ruled that Afghan acceptance of a Russian treaty precluded the conclusion of a treaty of friendship with Afghanistan.

When Dobbs informed the Amir of this decision, the Amir told him that he must leave. A farewell interview was set for November 12 at which no business was to be discussed. During this visit, faint hopes for a treaty were again aroused when the Afghans demanded customs concessions and permission for the free import of arms as long as Afghanistan remained friendly. In return for this they would promise to keep Russian influence away from the border. On November 15, the Amir appeared ready to accept a treaty of neighborly relations, provided that the British Ambassador, who would be residing in Kabul, was empowered to continue the negotiations for a treaty of friendship.

The treaty was finally signed on November 22, 1921, and Dobbs announced that the government of India was ready to give Afghanistan the gifts suggested in the *aide-mémoire*. When Dobbs suggested that Afghan troops evacuate from the Arneway area, which they had occupied during the Third Afghan War before he would arrange for a realignment of the border at Torkham, the cordial atmosphere was again seriously upset.

On December 1, 1921, the Amir announced the conclusion of the treaty in the presence of the British delegation. He emphasized the fact that this was not a friendship treaty, but merely one for neighborly relations. The conclusion of a treaty of friendship the Amir made contingent on the generosity which Britain would show toward Turkey and the frontier tribes, and the treatment it would give to the inhabitants of India.

In his report to the government of India, Dobbs asserted that "in all but name the treaty is one of friendship, giving us what we had wished for more cheaply than had been contemplated." By not paying a subsidy, the government of India had lost some of its influence, but Dobbs saw that the real hold of Britain over Afghanistan lay in the fact that the latter depended on Britain for its supplies and communication with the outside world.

As for the future, Dobbs believed that as long as Britain persisted in her policy of dominating the Khyber and Waziristan, she would be strong enough to discourage any Afghan moves on the frontier. But Dobbs also saw the Amir's "ruling passion" as tending toward expansion, which could be directed only in three directions: India, Central Asia, and Persia. India appeared most attractive, followed by Central Asia; and Dobbs warned that "unless . . . the gaze of the Amir can be safely diverted towards Central Asia, it will almost inevitably be fixed upon India." Dobbs said the Amir had hinted that on the collapse of Bolshevik rule in Russia he would attempt with British assistance to extend his hegemony over the area of Central Asia.

The Viceroy commented to London that the Amir's intentions were disturbing, and no less disturbing was the policy recommended by Dobbs of assisting the Amir in his expansionist policy in Central Asia.[106]

Conclusion

The Anglo-Afghan Treaty of 1921 freed Afghanistan from British suzerainty and marked the beginning of a new era in the history of Afghanistan. While Afghan rulers were successful in preserving their independence, they were unsuccessful in their big-power aspirations. The Third Afghan War was an attempt at reestablishing Afghanistan's former borders with India, of redressing what the Afghans felt was a great injustice to them. The North-West Frontier, which some called the "Alsace of Afghanistan," was Afghan land, and this was never forgotten on both sides of the Afghan border.

The time seemed auspicious, India was in revolt, and the British were weak as seldom before. Amanullah tried his fortunes, but he could not win his objectives in India. For a short time he looked north where Muslim rebels were attacking the Bolshevik forces, where Enver Pasha was riding the tide of popular revolt, and the Afghan King toyed with the idea of seeking compensation in the north for what he could not win in the south. But the forces of the Amir of Bukhara and Enver Pasha and the Basmachis were in turn defeated, and Amanullah's dream of leading a Central Asian Confederation did not come true.

Amanullah may at that time have remembered the words of his grandfather, Abd al-Rahman, who wished that "as long as Russia and Britain exist, my countrymen, the tribes of Afghanistan, should live quietly in ease and peace; and that these two states should find us true and faithful; and that we should rest at peace with them: for my tribesmen are unable to struggle with Empires."

Amanullah gave up all attempts of territorial aggrandizement and turned his attention to internal reforms and the development of his country.

Afghanistan ended its policy of isolation, for independence required political relations with the world. The existence of foreign representatives at Kabul was in itself a guarantee that no single foreign power would gain a preponderant influence in Afghanistan.

Afghan rulers continued to assert their national independence; they remained the masters of their country. The nationals of many countries came to Afghanistan, but they came as temporary guests, working in many professions and trades which needed to be developed and they left after they had finished their tasks. No permanent European colony existed in Kabul. Foreign influences tended to be balanced in Afghanistan and no country obtained a vital monopoly in any particular field.

After World War II when both the United States and the Soviet Union were attempting to draw the "uncommitted" into their orbits, Afghanistan gravitated to the bloc of neutral powers, practicing *bi-tarafi*—now positive neutrality: an old policy indeed.

Appendixes

Appendix 1

TREATIES

1. *Letter from Lepel Griffin to Sirdar Abdur Rahman Khan, June 14, 1880.*

My friend, I have received your letter of the 16th May by the hand of Sirdar Ibrahim Khan, Sirdar Bahadoor, who arrived at Kabul on the 23rd May, and have fully understood its friendly sentiments, and the desire which it expresses for a cordial understanding between the British Government and yourself. This letter, together with the memorandum of the members of the Mission, which was shown to you before despatch, and which mentioned certain matters regarding which you desired further information, has been laid before His Excellency the Viceroy and Governor-General of India; and I am now commanded to convey to you the replies of the Government of India to the questions which you have asked.

Firstly.—With regard to the position of the ruler of Kabul to Foreign Powers, since the British Government admit no right of interference by Foreign Powers in Afghanistan, and since both Russia and Persia are pledged to abstain from all political interference with Afghanistan affairs, it is plain that the Kabul ruler can have no political relations with any Foreign Power except the English; and if any such Power should attempt to interfere in Afghanistan, and if such interference should lead to unprovoked aggression on the Kabul ruler, then the British Government will be prepared to aid him if necessary, to repel it, provided that he follows the advice of the British Government in regard to his external relations.

Secondly.—With regard to limits of territory, I am directed to say that the whole province of Kandahar has been placed under a separate ruler, except Pishin and Sibi, which are retained in British possession. Consequently the Government is not able to enter into any negotiations with you on these points, nor in respect to arrangements with regard to the North-Western Frontier, which were concluded with the ex-Amir Muhammad Yakub Khan. With these reservations the British Government are willing that you should establish over Afghanistan—including

Herat, the possession of which cannot be guaranteed to you, though Government are not disposed to hinder measures which you may take to obtain possession of it—as complete and extensive authority as has been hitherto exercised by any Amir of your family. The British Government desires to exercise no interference in your internal government of these territories, nor will you be required to admit an English Resident anywhere; although, for convenience of ordinary friendly intercourse between two contiguous States, it may be advisable to station, by agreement, a Muhammadan Agent of the British Government at Kabul.

If you should, after clearly understanding the wishes and intentions of the British Government, as stated in former letters and now further explained, desire these matters to be stated in a formal writing, it is necessary that you should first intimate plainly your acceptance or refusal of the invitation of the British Government, and should state your proposals for carrying into effect friendly arrangements.

Sirdar Wazirzada Muhammad Afzal Khan has been ordered to leave Khanabad within five days after receipt of this letter, as it is necessary to understand from him, by word of mouth, the position of affairs, and your wishes and sentiments. Should your reply be sent by his hand, it will prevent delay and accelerate the conclusion of final arrangements, and consequently the Government trusts that you will be able to make use of his agency.

2. *Letter from Sirdar Abdur Rahman Khan to Lepel Griffin, June 22, 1880.*

The kind letter, sent by the hand of Taj Muhammad Khan, telling me of your welfare and friendship, arrived on the 11th Rajab (20th June), and caused me great pleasure. What was the wish and object of myself and my people you yourself have kindly granted.

Regarding the boundaries of Afghanistan which were settled by treaty with my most noble and respected grandfather, Amir Dost Muhammad, these you have granted to me. And the Envoy which you have appointed in Afghanistan you have dispensed with, but what you have left to (be settled according to) my wish is, that I may keep a Mussulman Ambassador, if I please. This was my desire and that of my people, and this you have kindly granted.

About my friendly relations and communication with Foreign Powers, you have written that I should not have any without advice and consultation with you (the British). You should consider well that if I have the friendship of a great Government like yours, how can I communicate with another Power without advice from and consultation with you? I agree to this also.

You have also kindly written that should any unwarranted (improper) attack be made by any other Power on Afghanistan, you will under all circumstances afford me assistance; and you will not permit any other person to take possession of the territory of Afghanistan. This also is my desire, which you have kindly granted.

As to what you have written about Herat. Herat is at present in the possession of my cousin. So long as he does not oppose me, and remains friendly with me, it is better that I should leave my cousin in Herat, rather that any other man. Should he oppose me, and not listen to my words (advice) or those of my people, I will afterwards let you know. Everything shall be done as we both deem it expedient and advisable.

All the kindness you have shown is for my welfare and that of my people, how should I not accept it? You have shown very great kindness to me and my people.

I have written and sent letters containing full particulars to all the tribes of Afghanistan, and I have given copies of these papers to Sirdar Muhammad Afzal Khan, for transmission to you; and I have also communicated verbally to Afzal Khan certain matters.

Three days after this I will give him leave to start. Consider me also, the slave of the threshold of God, as having already arrived at Parwan.

Send me back a verbal reply by Muhammad Afzal Khan, so that he may reach me on the road wherever I may be. Dated 18th Rajab.

(P.S.—In Abdur Rahman's own hand.)

I have signed this and sealed this envelope with wax.

In this letter, and the former letters, all is written by the same hand, and there is no alteration (erasure) anywhere.

3. *Letter from Lepel Griffin to His Highness, Sirdar Abdur Rahman Khan, Amir of Kabul, July, 1880.**

After compliments.—His Excellency the Viceroy and Governor-General in Council has learnt with pleasure that Your Highness has proceeded toward Kabul, in accordance with the invitation of the British Government. Therefore, in consideration of the friendly sentiments by which Your Highness is animated, and of the advantage to be derived by the Sirdars and people from the establishment of a settled government under Your Highness's authority, the British Government recognises Your Highness as Amir of Kabul.

I am further empowered, on the part of the Viceroy and Governor-General of India, to inform Your Highness that the British Government has no desire to interfere in the internal government of the territories in the possession of Your Highness, and has no wish that an English Resident should be stationed anywhere within those territories. For the

---

* This letter (No. 3), which is generally referred to as the letter from the Foreign Secretary, dated the 20th July, 1880, is known to have been sealed by Mr. Griffin and delivered by him on the 31st July, 1880.

convenience of ordinary friendly intercourse, such as is maintained between two adjoining States, it may be advisable that a Muhammadan Agent of the British Government should reside, by agreement, at Kabul.

Your Highness has requested that the views and intentions of the British Government with regard to the position of the ruler at Kabul in relation to Foreign Powers, should be placed on record for Your Highness's information. The Viceroy and Governor-General in Council authorises me to declare to you that since the British Government admits no right of interference by Foreign Powers within Afghanistan, and since both Russia and Persia are pledged to abstain from all interference with the affairs of Afghanistan, it is plain that Your Highness can have no political relations with any Foreign Power except with the British Government. If any Foreign Power should attempt to interfere in Afghanistan, and if such interference should lead to unprovoked aggression on the dominions of Your Highness, in that event the British Government would be prepared to aid you, to such extent and in such manner as may appear to the British Government necessary, in repelling it: provided that Your Highness follows unreservedly the advice of the British Government in regard to your external relations.

4. *Letter from the Viceroy of India (the Marquess of Ripon) to the Amir of Afghanistan, Simla, June 16, 1883.*

After compliments.—Your Highness will remember that, at Sir Lepel Griffin's interview with you at Zimma on the 31st July 1880, he said that the Government of India could only start your administration by giving you a grant to pay your army and officials and your immediate expenses; and that, having recognised you as Amir, it was anxious to see you strong; but after you had taken possession of Kabul, you must rely on your own resources.

I have always interested myself so much in Your Highness's success, and have felt so great a desire for the establishment of a strong and friendly power under Your Highness's auspices in Afghanistan, that I have on various occasions gone beyond the determination then communicated to you and have from time to time aided Your Highness with sums of money and arms, besides devoting some lakhs a year to the support of Afghan refugees and detenus, whose presence in Afghanistan is, I understand, regarded by Your Highness as dangerous to your power. Still my view of the relations to each other of the two countries has throughout been that, in matters of internal policy and finance, India should not seek to interfere with Afghanistan, but should confine herself to the part of a friendly neighbor and ally. On these conditions it would be in accordance with the practice of nations that Afghanistan should regulate her own finance and bear her own burdens as she has always done heretofore.

As regards matters of external policy, Your Highness was informed in the communication from the Foreign Secretary to the Government of India, dated the 20th July 1880, and again in my letter of the 22nd February 1883, that if any Foreign Power should attempt to interfere in Afghanistan, and if such interference should lead to unprovoked aggression on the dominions of Your Highness, in that event the British Government would be prepared to aid you to such extent and in such manner as might appear to the British Government necessary in repelling it; provided that Your Highness follows unreservedly the advice of the British Government in regard to your external relations.

On consideration, however, of your accounts of the condition of your north-west frontier, I have been satisfied that Your Highness has to contend with exceptional difficulties in that quarter. I have understood that, owing to various untoward circumstances, Your Highness has not yet been able to reduce the important frontier province of Herat to the orderly and secure condition so essential for the protection of Afghanistan as a whole; and, therefore, that, for the settlement of the affairs of that frontier, some friendly assistance may be needful to you. I further observe, with satisfaction, Your Highness's assurances of good faith and loyalty to the British Government; and Your Highness's language convinces me that you realise how much it is to the interest of Afghanistan to maintain friendly relations with the Government of India.

Impressed by these considerations, I have determined to offer to Your Highness personally, as an aid towards meeting the present difficulties in the management of your State, a subsidy of 12 lakhs of rupees a year, payable monthly, to be devoted to the payment of your troops, and to the other measures required for the defence of your north-western frontier. I feel that I may safely trust to Your Highness's good faith and practised skill to devote this addition to your resources to objects of such vital importance as those which I have above mentioned.

5. *Agreement Signed at Kabul by H. M. Durand and Amir Abdur Rahman Khan, November 12, 1893.*

Whereas the British Government has represented to His Highness the Amir that the Russian Government presses for the literal fulfilment of the Agreement of 1873 between Russia and England by which it was decided that the river Oxus should form the northern boundary of Afghanistan from Lake Victoria (Wood's Lake) or Sarikul on the east to the junction of the Kokcha with the Oxus, and whereas the British Government considers itself bound to abide by the terms of this Agreement, if the Russian Government equally abides by them, His Highness Amir Abdur Rahman Khan, G.C.S.I.; Amir of Afghanistan and its Dependencies, wishing to show his friendship to the British Government and his readiness to accept their advice in matters affecting his relations with Foreign powers, hereby agrees that he will evacuate all the districts held by him to the north of this portion of the Oxus on the clear understanding that all the districts lying to the south of this portion of the Oxus, and not now in his possession, be handed over to him in exchange. And Sir Henry Mortimer Durand, K.C.I.E., C.S.I., Foreign Secretary to the Government of India, hereby declares on the part of the British Government that the transfer to his Highness the Amir of the said districts lying to the south of the Oxus is an essential part of this transaction, and undertakes that arrangements will made with the Russian Government to carry out the transfer of the said lands to the north and south of the oxus.

6. *Agreement Signed at Kabul by H. M. Durand and Amir Abdur Rahman Khan, November 12, 1893.*

Whereas certain questions have arisen regarding the frontier of Afghanistan on the side of India, and whereas both His Highness the Amir and the Government of India are desirous of settling these questions by a friendly understanding, and of fixing the limits of their respective spheres of influence, so that for the future there may be no difference of opinion on the subject between the allied Governments, it is hereby agreed as follows:—

1) The eastern and southern frontier of His Highness's dominions, from Wakhan to the Persian border, shall follow the line shown in the map attached to this agreement.

2) The Government of India will at no time exercise interference in the territories lying beyond this line on the side of Afghanistan, and His Highness the Amir will at no time exercise interference in the territories lying beyond this line on the side of India.

3) The British Government thus agrees to His Highness the Amir retaining Asmar and the valley above it, as far as Chanak. His Highness agrees, on the other hand, that he will at no time exercise interference in Swat, Bajaur, or Chitral, including the Arnawai or Bashgal valley. The British Government also agrees to leave to His Highness the Birmal tract as shown in the detailed map already given to His Highness, who relinquishes his claim to the rest of the Waziri country and Dawar. His Highness also relinquishes his claim to Chageh.

4) The frontier line will hereafter be laid down in detail and demarcated whereever this may be practicable and desirable, by Joint British and Afghan Commissioners, whose object will be to arrive by mutual understanding at a boundary which shall adhere with the greatest possible exactness to the line shown in the map attached to this agreement, having due regard to the existing local rights of villages adjoining the frontier.

5) With reference to the question of Chaman, the Amir withdraws his objection to the new British Cantonment and concedes to the British

Government the rights purchased by him in the Sirkai Tilerai water. At this part of the frontier the line will be drawn as follows:—

From the crest of the Khwaja Amran range near the Peha Kotal, which remains in British territory, the line will run in such a direction as to leave Murgha Chaman and the Sharobo spring to Afghanistan, and to pass half-way between the New Chaman Fort and the Afghan outpost known locally as Lashkar Dand. The line will then pass half-way between the railway station and the hill known as the Mian Baldak, and turning southwards, will rejoin the Khwaja Amran range, leaving the Gwasha Post in British territory, and the road to Shorawak to the west and south of Gwasha in Afghanistan. The British Government will not exercise any interference within half-a-mile of the road.

6) The above articles of agreement are regarded by the Government of India and His Highness the Amir of Afghanistan as a full and satisfactory settlement of all the principal differences of opinion which have arisen between them in regard to the frontier; and both the Government of India and His Highness the Amir undertake that any differences of detail, such as those which will have to be considered hereafter by the officers appointed to demarcate the boundary line, shall be settled in a friendly spirit, so as to remove for the future as far as possible all causes of doubt and misunderstanding between the two Governments.

7) Being fully satisfied of His Highness's goodwill to the British Government, and wishing to see Afghanistan independent and strong, the Government of India will raise no objection to the purchase and import by His Highness of munitions of war, and they will themselves grant him some help in this respect. Further, in order to mark their sense of the friendly spirit in which His Highness the Amir has entered into these negotiations, the Government of India undertake to increase by the sum of six lakhs of rupees a year the subsidy of twelve lakhs now granted to His Highness.

7. *Letter from Sir Mortimer Durand, K.C.I.E., C.S.I., to His Highness, the Amir of Afghanistan and Its Dependencies, Kabul, November 11, 1893.*

After compliments.—When Your Highness came to the throne of Afghanistan Sir Lepel Griffin was instructed to give you the assurance that, if any Foreign Power should attempt to interfere in Afghistan, and if such interference should lead to unprovoked aggression on the dominions of Your Highness, in that event the British Government would be prepared to aid you to such and extent and in such manner as might appear to the British Government necessary in repelling it, provided that Your Highness followed unreservedly the advice of the British Government in regard to your external relations.

I have the honour to inform Your Highness that this assurance remains in force, and that it is applicable with regard to any territory which may come into your possession in consequence of the agreement which you have made with me to-day in the matter of the Oxus frontier.

It is the desire of the British Government that such portion of the northern frontier of Afghanistan as has not yet been marked out should now be clearly defined; when this has been done, the whole of Your Highness's frontier towards the side of Russia will be equally free from doubt and equally secure.

8. *Translation of Treaty Signed at Kabul by Amir Habibulla and Louis W. Dane, Foreign Secretary, March 21, 1905.*

He is God. Extolled be His Perfection.

His Majesy Siraj-ul-millat-wa-ud-din Amir Habibulla Khan, Independent King of the State of Afghanistan and its Dependencies, on the one part, and the Honourable Mr. Louis William Dane, C.S.I., Foreign Secretary of the Mighty Government of India and Representative of the Exalted British Government, on the other part.

His said Majesty does hereby agree to this, that in the principles and in the matters of subsidiary importance of the Treaty regarding internal and external affairs, and of the engagements which His Highness, my late father, that is Zia-ul-millat-wa-ud-din, who has found mercy, may God enlighten his tomb! concluded and acted upon with the Exalted British Government, I also have acted, am acting, and will act upon the same agreement and compact, and I will not contravene them in any dealing or in any promise.

The said Honourable Mr. Louis William Dane does hereby agree to this, that as to the very agreement and engagement which the Exalted British Government, concluded and acted upon with the noble father of His Majesty Siraj-ul-millat-wa-ud-din, that is, His Highness Zia-ul-millat-wa-ud-din, who has found mercy, regarding internal and external affairs and matters of principle or of subsidiary importance, I confirm them and write that they (the British Government) will not act contrary to those agreements and engagements in any way or at any time.

Made on Tuesday, the fourteenth day of Muharram-ul-haram of the year thirteen hundred and twenty-three, Hijri, corresponding to the twenty-first day of March of the year nineteen hundred and five A.D.

9. *Extracts from Seiler's Shorthand Diary, May 23, 1916.*

Kabul, Jan. 24, 1916. Foreign Office, Berlin. Previous reports summarised. Up till now Amir harping on declared neutrality and traditional friendship with England; undecided; leaning (doubtful) on English party alone. By November our work so far successful that, in spite of complete isolation, tide took a perceptible turn in our favor. On our side came in PM, brother and successor, and his father-in-law. When toward the end of December we tried to force on a decision, we were asked by Nasr Allah whether we had full powers to conclude a treaty. Said no; declared myself ready to draft if he wished. He received promise of German help in money and material so far as actually possible, as also of claims to a subvention proportionate to achievements at the conclusion of peace, provided Afghanistan made preparations for war forthwith. The foregoing has been made by the Amir, after and in spite of every conceivable objection each more impossible than the last, (into) the following Treaty draft.

The following Friendship Treaty is concluded between the *All-highest God-given Afghan Government* and the *Highest German Government*.
This Treaty and Friendship shall exist for the present and future between the *All-highest God-given Afghan Government* and the *Highest German Government* and their revered masters.

1) The Afghan Government postulates her complete independence and political freedom.

2) The German Government takes it upon herself to help the Afghan Government so far as she can do so. Recognises the independence of Afghanistan, and will cause the Austrian and Bulgarian Governments to recognise it on their part.

3) The Afghan Government begins forthwith with the perfecting of her military resources and administration, as also with political relations with the peoples of Persia, India and Rusian Turkestan.

4) The German Government is pledged to furnish the Afghan Government as assistance as quickly as possible, gratis and without return, 100,000 rifles of the newest pattern, and 300 guns, small and big, with complete new pattern equipment of the appropriate munitions, and other necessary war material, and a crore fund, i.e., 10 mil. sterling. She takes it upon herself, moreover, to open the way through Persia in order that the German Empire may give the Afghan Kingdom officers, engineers, and other officials, of whom Afghanistan stands in need, and that these may remain officials of the Afghan Kingdom and be honored as such.

5) The Afghan Kingdom lays down categorically that these measures are for this purpose, that when they are taken she may strengthen herself and will draw benefit from them in time of necessity.

6) The German Government is pledged in the event of Afghanistan having entered into the war or making expeditious preparations of a military or external political character, to enter the lists for the possession of lost and conquered territories and always to defend the Afghan Kingdom with all measures against foreign conquest in the rear of the Afghan Kingdom.

7) The Afghan Government recognises the Embassy Secretary of the German Empire, Herr von Hentig, and sends forthwith her own envoy with limited powers to the Persian capital in order to negotiate there in secrecy with the German, Turkish, and Austrian envoys. As soon as the time is come and he can show openly that he is the deputy of the Afghan Government, he will openly declare himself Minister of Afghanistan; and at the time of the general conclusion of peace a plenipotentiary, qualified for the Conference, will be appointed with plenary powers as Afghanistan's Plenipotentiary on behalf of the rights of the Afghan Government.

8) Relating to the Embassy are:

a) The escort of the Embassy shall not be more than 20 to 30 strong.

b) It will be permitted to buy up to 20 jaribs of land for the Ambassador's residence and to build the Embassy on it.

c) If a subject of Afghanistan or some other Power seeks refuge in the Embassy after the commission of a crime, it is essential that the Embassy should give him no protection.

d) If a subject of the Kingdoms possessing an Embassy in Afghanistan has a lawsuit, the decision shall be pleaded according to Afghan laws, and his Ambassador shall have no concern with it. For various commercial suits and others which have not yet arisen in any form in Afghanistan, the Afghan Government will make new laws.

9) After the general peace a Commercial Treaty will be concluded between the Afghan and German Governments with mutually binding conditions.

10) Both parties shall regard themselves bound when the Afghan envoy in the Persian capital receives news from the German Government that this Treaty has been ratified by the German Government.

True copy of His Majesty's endorsement.

I, on behalf of the Highest Afghan Government, in accordance with the conditions of the above Treaty with the German Government, desire that an alliance shall be concluded.

Signed. Lamp of the Nation and Religion, Kabul, the 18th Rabi-ul-Awal, 1916.

True copy of the endorsement by Captains Niedermayer and von Hentig.

The Afghan Government desires the friendship of the German Government and to conclude a treaty in accordance with this draft. I send this copy of the Afghan Treaty to the German Government. Now that I have seen Afghanistan I recommend one to the German Government, and I hope that she will accept this Friendship Treaty.

24th January 1916. Niedermayer. von Hentig.

APPENDIXES 181

The remarks by Niedermayer and myself that stand below the draft were added at the request of the Amir and Nasr Allah, to whom I made it quite clear that none of the conditions protocolled by me were withdrawn, and that a recommendation of acceptance was simply to serve the purpose they themselves had mentioned, viz., the facilitating for them of the work over the draft with the notables. I beg, however, that the draft may be taken as successful in so far as it affords the basis for immediately getting to work, and on the arrival of Germans in the sense of Niedermayer's proposal means war. Summonses issued. Connections established with Indian leaders. Niedermayer admitted to General Staff work. Emissary sent across Persia to Central Powers. Shall hand to Amir on next opportunity the large cross hitherto held back. Beg appropriate distinctions for his brother and crown prince, two princes, and the three governor-generals. Portraits of the Kaiser, illustrated war literature greatly wanted. General health good. Hentig.

(Possibly to General Staff, Berlin)

Regular Afghan Army to be reckoned at 80,000 strong, 42,000 of them mobilised; 16,000 modern rifles; capable of expansion to 400,000–500,000 on money and arms being furnished. General feeling and prospects of military success appear everywhere favorable. The English have concentrated strong troops, chiefly European and also Canadians, on Afghan frontier. Sharp look-out also on Indian frontier for some weeks past. Extension of field works at Ford Jamrud. Great nervousness on the part of the English. Wireless station urgently required. Large number of rifles, guns and munitions. Money, if possible, not less than a million pounds. Aeroplanes or at least one (of) or two fliers wanted. On the appearance of 10,000 men, whether German or Turkish, well equipped, on Afghan soil, war might begin even without Amir's large demands being fulfilled. It would give us desired support in present situation. Most favorable time for war to begin, end of April. Our work in the meantime: secret mobilisation; construction of field works on the frontier; release of prisoners in Turkestan; attack on English arms and bullion transports; destruction of factories in India and Turkestan, and agitation work in India. External work to be done: covering Afghanistan's rear urgently necessary; expulsion of Russians from Khorasan; securing the Persian frontier; keeping open at least the central Persian roads over Kerman and Tabriz; two gendarmerie regiments to Khorasan; one to Kerman. War situation in Persia of decisive significance. Afghan frontier station informed. Middle January 1916. Niedermayer.

P.S. Kabul, 25th January. According to the Amir's statement war begins at once as soon as 20,000 to 100,000 German or Turkish soldiers arrive in Afghanistan. On these would devolve above all the covering the rear against Russia. Recommend collection of troops in Kerman and making general advance along the line of the Helmand and Kandahar. Flank column via Birjand or Herat. Breaking down of strong English opposition in east Persia to be calculated for. There 12,000 to 15,000 Indian troops. Further troops lately sent from India to Egypt. Conditions for offensive at present very favorable. All possible preparations will be made on our side. Urgently request despatch of desired support. Niedermayer.

10. *Treaty of Peace between the Illustrious British Government and the Independent Afghan Government, Concluded at Rawalpindi on August 8, 1919 (11th Ziqada 1337 Hijra), Signed by A. H. Grant, Foreign Secretary, and Ali Ahmad Khan, Commissary for Home Affairs.*

The following Articles for the restoration of peace have been agreed upon by the British Government and the Afghan Government:

Article I

From the date of the signing of this Treaty there shall be peace between the British Government, on the one part, and the Government of Afghanistan on the other.

Article II

In view of the circumstances which have brought about the present war between the British Government and the Government of Afghanistan, the British Government, to mark their displeasure, withdraw the privilege enjoyed by former Amirs of importing arms, ammunition or warlike munitions through India to Afghanistan.

Article III

The arrears of the late Amir's subsidy are furthermore confiscated, and no subsidy is granted to the present Amir.

Article IV

At the same time, the British Government are desirous of the reestablishment of the old friendship that has so long existed between Afghanistan and Great Britain, provided they have guarantees that the Afghan Government are, on their part, sincerely anxious to regain the friendship of the British Government. The British Government are prepared, therefore, provided the Afghan Government prove this by their acts and conduct, to receive another Afghan mission after six months for the discussion and settlement of matters of common interest to the two Governments and the re-establishment of the old friendship on a satisfactory basis.

Article V

The Afghan Government accept the Indo-Afghan frontier accepted by the late Amir. They further agree to the early demarcation by a British Commission of the undemarcated portion of the line west of the Khyber, where the recent Afghan aggression took place, and to accept such boundary as the British Commission may lay down. The British troops on this side will remain in their present positions until such demarcation has been effected.

Annexure, Rawalpindi, August 8, 1919, from the Chief British Representative, Indo-Afghan Peace Conference, to the Chief Afghan Representative.*

After compliments.—You asked me for some further assurance that the Peace Treaty which the British Government now offer, contains nothing that interfered with the complete liberty of Afghanistan in internal or external matters.

My friend, if you will read the Treaty carefully you will see that there is no such interference with the liberty of Afghanistan. You have told me that the Afghan Government are unwilling to renew the arrangement whereby the late Amir agreed to follow unreservedly the advice of the British Government in regard to his external relations. I have not, therefore, pressed this matter: and no mention of it is made in the Treaty. Therefore, the said Treaty and this letter leave Afghanistan officially free and independent in its internal and external affairs.

Moreover, this war has cancelled all previous Treaties.

11. *Treaty between Great Britain and Afghanistan Establishing Friendly and Commercial Relations, Signed at Kabul, November 22, 1921 (30th Aqrab 1300 Hijra Shamsi), by Henry R. C. Dobbs, Envoy Extraordinary and Chief of the British Mission to Kabul, and Mahmud Tarzi, Chief of the Delegation of the Afghan Government for the Conclusion of the Treaty. Ratifications Exchanged at Kabul, February 6, 1922.*

The British Government and the Government of Afghanistan, with a view to the establishment of neighbourly relations between them, have agreed to the Articles written hereunder whereto the undersigned duly authorised to that effect have set their seals:

---

* For appended Schedules I and II and Appendixes 1, 2, 3, 4 see C. U. Aitchison, *Treaties, Engagements and Sanads* (Calcutta, 1933), Vol. XIII.

Article I

The British Government and the Government of Afghanistan mutually certify and respect each with regard to the other all rights of internal and external independence.

Article II

The two High Contracting Parties mutually accept the Indo-Afghan frontier as accepted by the Afghan Government under Article V of the Treaty concluded at Rawalpindi on the 8th August, 1919, corresponding to the 11th Ziqada, 1337 Hijra, and also the boundary west of the Khyber laid down by the British Commission in the months of August and September 1919, pursuant to the said Article, and shown on the map * attached to this Treaty by a black chain line; subject only to the re-alignment set forth in Schedule I annexed, which has been agreed upon in order to include within the boundaries of Afghanistan the place known as Tor Kham, and the whole bed of the Kabul River between Shilman Khwala Banda and Palosai and which is shown on the said map by a red chain line. The British Government agrees that the Afghan Authorities shall be permitted to draw water in reasonable quantities through a pipe which shall be provided by the British Government from Landi Khana for the use of Afghan subjects at Tor Kham, and the Government of Afghanistan agrees that British officers and tribesmen living on the British side of the boundary shall be permitted without let or hindrance to use the aforesaid portion of the Kabul River for purposes of navigation and that all existing rights of irrigation from the aforesaid portion of the river shall be continued to British subjects.

Article III

The British Government agrees that a Minister from His Majesty the Amir of Afghanistan shall be received at the Royal Court of London like the Envoys of all other Powers, and to permit the establishment of an Afghan Legation in London, and the Government of Afghanistan likewise agrees to receive in Kabul a Minister from His Britannic Majesty the Emperor of India and to permit the establishment of a British Legation at Kabul.

Each Party shall have the right of appointing a Military Attaché to its Legation.

Article IV

The Government of Afghanistan agrees to the establishment of British Consulates at Kandahar and Jalalabad, and the British Government agrees to the establishment of an Afghan Consul-General at the head-

---
* Not reproduced.

quarters of the Government of India and three Afghan Consulates at Calcutta, Karachi and Bombay. In the event of the Afghan Government desiring at any time to appoint Consular officers in any British territories other than India a separate agreement shall be drawn up to provide for such appointments if they are approved by the British Government.

Article V

The two High Contracting Parties mutually guarantee the personal safety and honourable treatment each of the representatives of the other, whether Minister, Consul-General or Consuls, within their own boundaries, and they agree that the said representatives shall be subject in the discharge of their duties to the provisions set forth in the Second Schedule annexed to this Treaty. The British Government further agrees that the Minister, Consul-General or Consuls of any other Government in the countries in which the places of residence of the said Minister, Consul-General and Consuls of Afghanistan are fixed; and the Government of Afghanistan likewise agrees that the Minister and Consuls of Great Britain shall, within the territorial limits within which they are permitted to reside or to exercise their functions, notwithstanding the provisions of the said Schedule, receive and enjoy any rights or privileges which are or may hereafter be granted to or enjoyed by the Minister or Consuls of any other Government in the countries in which the places of residence of the said Minister and Consuls of Great Britain are fixed.

Article VI

As it is for the benefit of the British Government and the Government of Afghanistan that the Government of Afghanistan shall be strong and prosperous, the British Government agrees that whatever quantity of material is required for the strength and welfare of Afghanistan, such as all kinds of factory machinery, engines and materials and instruments for telegraph, telephones, etc., which Afghanistan may be able to buy from Britain or the British Dominions or from other countries of the world, shall ordinarily be imported without let or hindrance by Afghanistan into its own territories from the ports of the British Isles and British India. Similarly the Government of Afghanistan agrees that every kind of goods, the export of which is not against the internal law of the Government of Afghanistan and which may in the judgment of the Government of Afghanistan be in excess of the internal needs and requirements of Afghanistan and is required by the British Government, can be purchased and exported to India with the permission of the Government of Afghanistan. With regard to arms and munitions, the British Government agrees that as long as it is assured that the intentions of the Government of Afghanistan are friendly and that there is no immediate danger to India from such importation in Afghanistan, permission shall be given without let or hindrance for such importation. If, however, the Arms Traffic Convention is hereafter ratified by the Great Powers of the world and comes into force, the right of importation of arms and munitions by the Afghan Government shall be subject to the proviso that the Afghan Government shall first have signed the Arms Traffic Convention, and that such importation shall only be made in accordance with the provisions of that Convention. Should the Arms Traffic Convention not be ratified or lapse, the Government of Afghanistan, subject to the foregoing assurance, can from time to time import into its own territory the arms and munitions mentioned above through the ports of the British Isles and British India.

Article VII

No Customs duties shall be levied at British Indian ports on goods imported under the provisions of Article VI on behalf of the Government of Afghanistan, for immediate transport to Afghanistan, provided that a certificate signed by such Afghan authority or representative as may from time to time be determined by the two Governments shall be presented at the time of importation to the chief Customs officer at the port of import setting forth that the goods in question are the property of the Government of Afghanistan and are being sent under its orders to Afghanistan, and showing the description, number and value of the goods in respect of which exemption is claimed; provided, secondly, that the goods are required for the public services of Afghanistan and not for the purposes of any State monopoly or State trade; and provided, thirdly, that the goods are, unless of a clearly distinguishable nature, transported through India in sealed packages, which shall not be opened or sub-divided before their export from India.

And also the British Government agrees to the grant in respect of all trade goods imported into India at British ports for re-export to Afghanistan and exported to Afghanistan by routes to be agreed upon between the two Governments of a rebate at the time and place of export of the full amount of Customs duty levied upon such goods, provided that such goods shall be transported through India in sealed packages which shall not be opened or sub-divided before their export from India.

And also the British Government declares that it has no present intention of levying Customs duty on goods or livestock of Afghan origin or manufacture, imported by land or by river into India or exported from Afghanistan to other countries of the world through India and the import of which into India is not prohibited by law. In the event, however, of the British Government deciding in the future to levy Customs duties on goods and livestock imported into India by land or by river from neighbouring States, it will, if necessary, levy such duties on imports from Afghanistan; but in that event it agrees that it will not levy higher duties on imports from Afghanistan than those levied on imports from such neighbouring States. Nothing in this Article shall prevent the levy on imports from Afghanistan of the present Khyber tolls and of octroi in any town of India in which octroi is or may be hereafter levied, provided that there shall be no enhancement over the present rate of the Khyber tolls.

Article VIII

The British Government agrees to the establishment of trade agents by the Afghan Government at Peshawar, Quetta and Parachinar, provided that the personnel and the property of the said agencies shall be subject to the operations of all British laws and Orders and to the jurisdiction of British Courts; and that they shall not be recognised by the British authorities as having any official or special privileged position.

Article IX

The trade goods coming to (imported to) Afghanistan under the provisions of Article VII from Europe, etc., can be opened at the railway terminuses at Jamrud, in the Kurram and at Chaman for packing and arranging to suit the capacity of baggage animals without this being the cause of reimposition of Customs duties; and the carrying out of this will be arranged by the trade representatives mentioned in Article XII.

Article X

The two High Contracting Parties agree to afford facilities of every description for the exchange of postal matter between their two countries, provided that neither shall be authorised to establish post offices within the territory of the other. In order to give effect to this Article, a separate Postal Convention shall be concluded, for the preparation of which such number of special officers as the Afghan Government may appoint shall meet the officers of the British Government and consult with them.

Article XI

The two High Contracting Parties having mutually satisfied themselves each regarding the goodwill of the other and especially regarding their benevolent intentions towards the tribes residing close to their respective boundaries, hereby undertake each to inform the other in future of any military operations of major importance which may appear necessary for the maintenance of order among the frontier tribes residing within their respective spheres, before the commencement of such operations.

Article XII

The two High Contracting Parties agree that representatives of the Government of Afghanistan and of the British Government shall be appointed to discuss the conclusion of a Trade Convention, and the

Convention shall in the first place be regarding the measures (necessary) for carrying out the purposes mentioned in Article IX of this Treaty. Secondly. (They) shall arrange regarding commercial matters not now mentioned in this Treaty which may appear desirable for the benefit of the two Governments. The trade relations between the two Governments shall continue until the Trade Convention mentioned above comes into force.

Article XIII

The two High Contracting Parties agree that the First and Second Schedules attached to this Treaty shall have the same binding force as the Articles contained in this Treaty.

Article XIV

The provisions of this Treaty shall come into force from the date of its signature, and shall remain in force for three years from that date. In case neither of the High Contracting Parties should have notified twelve months before the expiration of the said three years the intention to terminate it, it shall remain binding until the expiration of one year from the day on which either of the High Contracting Parties shall have denounced it. This Treaty shall come into force after the signatures of the Missions of the two parties and the two ratified copies of this shall be exchanged in Kabul within two and a half months after the signature.

12. *Agreement between Russia and Afghanistan, February, 1921.*

With a view to strengthening friendly relations between Russia and Afghanistan and confirming the actual independence of Afghanistan, the Russian Socialist Federated Soviet Republic of the one part and the Sovereign State of Afghanistan of the other part have decided to conclude the present treaty, for which purpose there have been appointed as their plenipotentiaries:—

For the Government of the Russian Socialist Federated Soviet Republic: Georgy Vasilievich Chichérin, Lyov Mihailovich Karahan, and for the Government of the Sovereign State of Afghanistan: Muhammad Wali Khan, Mirza Muhammad Khan, Gulyam Sadlik * Khan.

The above-named plenipotentiaries, after mutual presentation of their credentials, which were found to be in due and proper form, have agreed as follows:—

I

The High Contracting Parties, recognising their mutual independence and binding themselves to respect it, now mutually enter into regular diplomatic relations.

* Ghulam Sadiq. (Tr.)

II

The High Contracting Parties bind themselves not to enter into any military or political agreement with a third State which might prejudice one of the Contracting Parties.

III

The Legations and Consulates of the High Contracting Parties shall mutually and equally enjoy diplomatic privileges in accordance with the uses of International Law.

Note I.—There shall be included in that category—
a) The right to hoist the State flag.
b) Personal inviolability of registered members of Legations and Consulates.
c) Inviolability of diplomatic correspondence and of persons fulfilling the duties of couriers with every kind of mutual assistance in these matters.
d) Communication by telephone, wireless and telegraph, in accordance with the privileges of diplomatic representatives.
e) Exterritoriality of premises occupied by Legations and Consulates, but without the right of giving asylum to persons who are officially recognised by their Local Government as having broken the laws of the country.

Note II.—The Military Attachés of both Contracting Parties shall be attached to their Legations on the basis of equality as regards the above.

IV

The High Contracting Parties mutually agree to the opening of five consulates of the Russian Socialist Federated Soviet Republic on Afghan territory and of seven consulates of Afghanistan on Russian territory, of which five shall be within the boundaries of Russian Central Asia.

Note.—In addition to the above, the opening of further consulates and consular points in Russia and Afghanistan shall be arranged in each particular case by special agreement between the High Contracting Parties.

V

Russian consulates shall be established at Herat, Meimen, Mazar-i-Sharif, Kandahar and Ghazni. Afghan consulates shall be established as follows:—A Consulate-General at Tashkend and consulates at Petrograd, Kazan, Samarkand, Merv and Krasnovodsk.

Note.—The manner and time of the actual opening of the Russian consulates in Afghanistan and of the Afghan consulates in Russia shall be defined by special agreement between the two Contracting Parties.

VI

Russia agrees to the free and untaxed transit through her territory of all kinds of goods purchased by Afghanistan either in Russia herself, through State organizations, or from abroad.

VII

The High Contracting Parties recognise and accept the freedom of Eastern nations on the basis of independence and in accordance with the general wish of each nation.

VIII

In confirmation of Clause VII of the present treaty, the High Contracting Parties accept the actual independence and freedom of Bokhara and Khiva, whatever may be the form of their government, in accordance with the wishes of their peoples.

IX

In fulfilment of and in accordance with the promise of the Russian Socialist Federated Soviet Republic, expressed by Lenin as its head to the Minister Plenipotentiary of the Sovereign State of Afghanistan, Russia agrees to hand over to Afghanistan the frontier districts which belonged to the latter in the last century, observing the principles of justice and self-determination of the population inhabiting the same. The manner in which such self-determination and will of the majority of the regular local population shall be expressed shall be settled by a special treaty between the two States through the intermediary of Plenipotentiaries of both parties.

X

In order to strengthen friendly relations between the High Contracting Parties, the Government of the Russian Socialist Federated Soviet Republic agrees to give to Afghanistan financial and other assistance.

XI

The present treaty is drawn up in the Russian and Persian languages; both texts are accounted authentic.

XII

The present treaty shall come into force upon its ratification by the Governments of the High Contracting Parties. The exchange of ratifications shall take place at Kabul, in witness wherof the Plenipotentiaries of both parties have signed the present treaty and set their seals thereto.
Drawn up in Moscow on the 28th day of February 1921.

Supplemental Clause

In amplification of Clause X of the present treaty, the Government of the Russian Socialist Federated Soviet Republic gives the following assistance to the Sovereign State of Afghanistan:—

1) A yearly free subsidy to the extent of one million gold or silver roubles in coin or bullion.
2) Construction of the Kushk-Herat-Kandahar-Kabul telegraph line.
3) In addition to this, the Government of the Russian Socialist Federated Soviet Republic expresses its readiness to place at the disposal of the Afghan Government technical and other specialists.

The Government of the Russian Socialist Federated Soviet Republic shall afford this assistance to the Government of the Sovereign State of Afghanistan within two months after the coming into force of the present treaty.

The present supplementary clause shall have the same legal validity as the other clauses of the present treaty.

Moscow, this 28th day of February 1921.

N.B.—The second half of XII appears to consist of the witnessing clause, which should surely have a paragraph to itself. Otherwise, it would only appear to refer to the ratification—(Translator).

13. *Translation of Treaty of Alliance between Turkey and Afghanistan, Signed at Moscow, March 1, 1921, by Youssouf Kemal, Dr. Reza Nour, and Muhammad Wali.* Ratifications Exchanged at Kabul, October 20, 1922.*

(The blessed clauses which bind together two brother Governments of the East united in faith and interest.)

In the name of God, the Merciful, the Compassionate!

The Turkish and Afghan Governments, convinced that they are bound together by sincere ties of sympathy, are imbued with one desire and one sacred purpose, and each possess the same high moral and material interests, and that the happiness or misfortune of one State will redound to the happiness or misfortune of the other, and recognising that it is no longer possible that they should remain disconnected and isolated as in the past, and that certain historical duties necessarily devolve upon them at this moment, when is seen with infinite thankfulness that an era of awakening and deliverance of the Eastern world has begun.

These two brother States and nations, therefore, observing that as with the members of one body the troubles and afflictions of one of the

* Signed in the Turkish and Persian languages.

parties must affect and pain the other, have resolved to transfer their age-long moral unity and natural alliance to the political sphere, to bring about a state of material and official alliance, and, in the name of the future welfare of the whole East, to conclude a Treaty of Alliance as a prelude to future welfare.

For this purpose Delegates have been nominated—Youssouf Kemal Bey, Commissioner (Minister) of Economic Affairs; and Dr. Reza Nour Bey, Commissaire of Public Instruction, Members of the Government, on behalf of the Government of the Grand National Assembly of Turkey; and His Highness General Muhammad Wali Khan, Ambassador Extraordinary on behalf of Afghanistan; who, having communicated their full powers, found to be in due and proper order, have accepted the following Articles:—

Article I

The Turkish nation, in possession of an independent existence for such time as God wills, considers it to be a sacred duty to recognise the independence, in the full significance of the term, of the Afghan nation, to which she is bound with ties of the utmost sincerity and conscientiousness.

Article II

The two High Contracting Parties recognise that all Eastern nations possess complete liberty and right of independence, and that each of these nations is free to administer itself by such form of administration as it may particularly desire, and they recognise the independence of the States of Bokhara and Khiva.

Article III

Turkey having for centuries given guidance to and rendered distinguished services to Islam, and holding in her hand the standard of the Caliphate, Afghanistan in this connection recognises the leadership of Turkey.

Article IV

Each of the High Contracting Parties will consider as directed against herself personally, and will oppose with all the means at her disposal, any attack made against the other by any Imperialistic State in pursuance of the policy of invasion and exploitation of the East.

Article V

Each of the Contracting Parties undertakes not to conclude any Treaty or Convention injurious to the interests of the other party or which would be in the interests of a third State with which the other is not on friendly terms, and to give prior notice to the other of the forthcoming conclusion of an Agreement with any nation whatsoever.

Article VI

With a view to the regularisation of commercial and economic relations and Consular affairs, the two Contracting Parties will conclude the necessary Conventions separately, and Ambassadors will from henceforth be sent by each to the capital of the other.

Article VII

Turkey agrees to help Afghanistan militarily and to send instructors and officers. These missions of teachers and officers will serve for a minimum period of five years, and on the expiration of that period, if Afghanistan so desires, a new mission of instructors will be sent.

Aricle VIII

This Treaty will be ratified with the least possible delay, and its clauses will be in force from that time.

Article IX

This Treaty has been drawn up at Moscow in duplicate signed and exchanged by the Delegates of the two parties.

14. *Agreement To Facilitate Commercial Relations between France and Afghanistan, Signed at Paris, April 28, 1922 by R. Poincaré and Mohammed Waly Khan.*

Désireux de faciliter les relations de commerce et d'amitié entre la France et l'Afghanistan, son Excellence M. Raymond Poincaré, Président du Conseil, Ministre des Affaires étrangères de la République française, et son Excellence le Général Mohammed Waly Khan, Ambassadeur extraordinaire de Sa Majesté l'Emir d'Afghanistan, sont convenus des dispositions suivantes:

1. Le Gouvernement français consent à recevoir une mission diplomatique permanente du Gouvernement afghan.

Le Gouvernement afghan consent à recevoir une mission diplomatique permanente du Gouvernement français.

Ces missions jouiront, dans l'un et l'autre pays, d'un traitement égal conforme au droit international public européen.

2. Les missions de l'un et l'autre pays pourront être composées de:—un représentant du rang de Ministre plénipotentiaire; un conseiller; un secrétaire; un attaché commercial; un attaché militaire; trois interprètes et fonctionnaires de chancellerie.

3. Les représentants de l'un et de l'autre pays pourront arborer leur

pavillon national sur l'immeuble de leur résidence. Ils pourront communiquer, en langage clair et en language conventionnel, par télégramme et par radiotélégramme, avec leur Gouvernement et ses autres représentants.

4. En attendant la conclusion d'un traité de commerce et d'etablissement, les ressortissants de chacun des deux pays jouiront, sur le territoire de l'autre, de la pleine liberté de commerce sous la protection de l'un et l'autre Gouvernements.

15. *Afghan-Italian Treaty, Signed at Rome, June 3, 1921, by Muhammad Vali Khan and Count Sforza.**

I. The high contracting Governments are agreeing to establish permanent diplomatic representations and are ready to grant them all equal rights recognized by the European International Public Law.

The Missions may contain the following persons:

II. *a*) Minister Plenipotentiary
  b) Councellor
  c) Secretary
  d) Commercial Attaché
  e) Military Attaché
  f) Director, Office of Chancellor
  g) Praying Master
  h) Clerks and Interpreters
  i) Diplomatic Couriers
  j) Servants.

III. The High Contracting Governments are also recognizing the following mutual rights of each other's diplomatic Missions:
  1) to take up the national flag
  2) to use Telegraph, Telephone and Radio services
  3) to use conventional codes.

16. *Translation of Treaty between the Exalted Governments of Afghanistan and Persia, Signed at Tehran, June 22, 1921, by Mohtashem-es-Sultaneh, Minister for Foreign Affairs, for Persia, and Abdul Aziz, Envoy, for Afghanistan.*

In the name of Allah, the Compassionate, the Merciful! There is no God but Allah, Mohammed is his Prophet! Hold fast by the rope of Allah all together and be not disunited!

Whereas Islamic unity, the ties of race and the bond of good and neighbourly relations between the two States required that friendly

---

* From an unofficial, unpublished copy in the United States National Archives, Washington (call number 701.6590h/orig.).

intercourse should be consolidated by the conclusion of a Treaty; therefore, in order to carry out this holy purpose, His Majesty the Shah of Persia appointed His Excellency Hajji Mohtashem-es-Sultaneh, the Minister for Foreign Affairs, and His Majesty the Ameer of Afghanistan appointed His Excellency Sardar Abdul Aziz Khan, his Minister Plenipotentiary and accredited Envoy, as their authorised agents, who after exchange of their official credentials, concluded the following Articles:—

Article I

From this day henceforth, sincere friendship and good relations will be established between Persia and Afghanistan and the subjects of the two Governments.

Article II

The Ambassadors, Ministers Plenipotentiary, Chargés (d'Affaires) and Officers of the High Contracting Parties at the Court of the other will enjoy all the rights and privileges which are ordained and customary according to international law and usage.

Article III

The subjects of the two Contracting Governments, whether residing or travelling (in the other's country) will be respected and wholly under the protection of the officials of their own Governments.

Article IV

The subjects of the two Contracting Governments, whether residing or travelling in the territory of the other, will be subjected to the laws of such territory. Civil and criminal cases will be heard and decided by the local judicial Courts of Persia and Afghanistan.

Diplomatic and Consular Officers of the High Contracting Parties will have no right of interference in civil and criminal cases in each other's territory, and the internal Courts of the country in which they are staying will be those to which all claims must be referred by the subjects of either Government.

Article V

The Two High Contracting Parties will have the right to appoint Consuls General, Consuls, Vice-Consuls, and Consular Agents in the important towns and trading centres of each other's country; but the said officials will not enter upon the duties of their appointments until after the exequaturs of their commissions have been issued according to the custom of the country in which they are staying.

Article VI

The subjects of either Government staying in the territory of the other will be exempt from military service and all other duties incumbent only on subjects of the country.

Article VII

If a subject of either of the two Contracting Governments commits a crime and absconds to the territory of the other, the officers of his Government will have the right to demand, through diplomatic channels, his extradition, and the local authorities will not fail to give assistance in the matter. Political offenders, however, will be excepted from this arrangement.

Article VIII

In order to strengthen friendly relations and to establish trade connections, the two Contracting Parties will, at the first opportunity, conclude such Agreements and Conventions as may be necessary in regard to trade relations, Customs duties, postal and telegraphic exchanges, which will come into force after signature and ratification.

Article IX

The outbreak of war between one of the Contracting Parties and a third State will not operate to cause a rupture of the friendly relations of the two parties. The other party will be bound, according to the rules of neutrality, to avoid giving facilities to the enemy.

Article X

The Contracting Parties, in order to manifest the friendship and trust existing between the Imperial Government of Persia and the Kingdom of Afghanistan, have decided that all important difficulties and disputes, which they may not be able to settle satisfactorily by negotiation, should be referred to arbitration according to international law and custom. The Contracting Parties engage to carry out the award with all sincerity.

Article XI

This treaty will be drawn up in duplicate in the Persian language.

Article XII

The representatives of the two Contracting Parties undertake that within three months of the signature of this Treaty, or, if possible, at an earlier date, all documents necessary for its ratification will be exchanged at Tehran or Kabul.

16a. *Supplementary Articles, Signed by Muhammed Wali Khan, Minister for Foreign Affairs, for Afghanistan, and Nasrullah Itela-ul-Mulk, Minister Plenipotentiary and Envoy, for Persia.*

Article I

The meaning of the sentence in Article III of this Treaty, viz., "The subject of the two Contracting Governments, whether residing or travelling (in the other's country) will be respected and wholly under the protection of the officials of their own Governments," is that the officials of either Government can, within the scope of the laws of the country in which they reside, refer to the officials of that country, for the arrangement of facilities for their subjects.

Article II

The tribes and nomads who have previously emigrated from Afghanistan to Persia (including Barbaris, &c.) will remain Persian subjects as before. The Barbaris who intend to travel to Afghanistan shall not be allowed to enter Afghan territory unless their passports have been visé by the Afghan officials residing in Persia. The frontier tribes, who have their summer quarter in one country and their winter quarters in the other, will be treated as Persian subjects during their stay in Persia, and as Afghan subjects during their stay in Afghanistan. Persons who have come from Afghanistan and settled in Persia previously to the establishment of an Afghan Legation in Tehran will remain Persian subjects as before. Merchants, who have come to Persia from Afghanistan only for purposes of trade and have not settled permanently in Persia, and who are proved by documentary evidence not to have been treated as Persians by Persian Government Departments, will be recognised as Afghan subjects.

Article III

Similarly, the tribes and nomads who have emigrated from Persia to Afghanistan will remain subjects of the Government of the country in which they reside, and will have no right to enter Persia unless their passports have been visé by the Persian representatives. The same treatment, as detailed in supplementary Article II, will be applicable to the tribes and nomads who have previously emigrated from Afghanistan to Persia. Persons who have previously to the establishment of a Persian Legation in Kabul emigrated from Persia to Afghanistan and settled there, will remain Afghan subjects as before.

Merchants, who have gone to Afghanistan from Persia only for purposes of trade, and have not settled there permanently, and who are proved by documentary evidence not to have been treated as Afghans by Afghan Government Departments, will be recognised as Persian subjects.

16b. *Ratification of Treaty and Supplementary Articles, Signed by His Majesty the Ghazi on September 7, 1923.*

In the name of God, Most Holy!

We, the slave of Allah, the toiler in the path of God, Ameer Amanullah, King of the Exalted State of Afghanistan, ratify this friendly Treaty, consisting of twelve Articles and three supplementary Articles, which has been concluded through the authorised representatives of the two exalted Governments on the different dates specified, between us and His Majesty Sultan Ahmed Shah, Kajar, Shah of all territories comprised in Persia, and undertake to carry it out without any alteration.

Appendix II

DOCUMENTS

1. *Letter from von Bethmann-Hollweg, German Chancellor, to Amir Habibullah Khan.*

Der Ueberbringer dieses Schreibens, der Kaiserliche Legationssekretaer Leutnant von Hentig, ist beauftragt, den Kumar Raja Mahendra Pratap von Mursen nach Eurer Majestaet Hauptstadt zu begleiten. Der Kumar Raja, den Seine Majestaet der Kaiser und Koenig, mein erhabener Herr, in Audienz zu empfangen geruht haben, und der hier Gelegenheit gehabt hat, sich davon zu ueberzeugen, dass Deutschland und seine Verbuendeten, Oesterreich-Ungarn und das Osmanishe Reich, als Sieger hervorgehen werden aus dem Kampf gegen England, Russland und Frankreich, gedenkt Eurer Majestaet eine Schilderung von den Eindruecken zu machen, die er in Deutschland gewonnen hat und Eurer Majestaet Rat zu erbitten, wie Indien, das unter dem Joche einer ihm aufgezwungenen Fremdherrschaft seufzt, entgueltig befreit werden kann, so dass es wieder den ihm gebuehrenden Platz im Rate der Voelker einnimnt. Die Kaiserliche Regierung ist davon ueberzeigt, dass Eure Majestaet, deren heldenhafte Heere die Englaender und Russen schon oft zu Paaren getrieben haben, dem Kumar Raja den richtigen Weg zur Erreichung seines hohen Zieles weisen werden.

Die Kaiserliche Regierung ergreift mit ausserordentlicher Genugtuung diese Gelegenheit, um Eurer Majestaet ihre besondere Wertschaetzung und Hochachtung zu versichern in der Hoffnung, dass zwischen dem erhabenen Koenigreich Afghanistan und dem Deutschen Reich von nun an dauernde Beziehungen hergestellt werden moegen zum Nutzen und Gedeihen beider Laender.

Der Kaiserliche Legationssekretaer von Hentig hat Weisung, Eurer Majestaet jeden Aufschluss ueber die gegenwaertige Kriegslage zu geben und Eurer Majestaet wichtige Eroeffnungen zu machen ueber die von der kaiserlichen Regierung erhoffte kuenftige Gestaltung des Verhaeltnisses zwischen Afghanistan, dem Deutschen Reiche, Oesterreich-Ungarn und der Turkei.

2. *Letter from Zimmermann, German Foreign Office, to Werner Otto von Hentig, April 17, 1915.*

Euer Hochwohlgeboren beauftrage ich hierdurch sich nach Kabul zu begeben, um eine Verbindung mit dem Emir von Afghanistan herzustellen und den Kumar Mahendra Pratap bei ihm einzufuhren. Dieser ueberbringt seiner Majestat dem Emir von Afghanistan ein Allerhoechstes Handschreiben Seiner Majestaet des Kaisers und Koenigs und ein Begruessungsschreiben der Kaiserlichen Regierung.

Euer Hochwohlgeboren ersuche ich ergebenst, den Kumar Pratap bei der Behandlung indischer Angelegenheiten, die ihm ausschliesslich uberlassen bleibt, in jeder Weise zu unterstuetzen.

Die Leitung der Expedition nach Kabul und alle Massnahmen zu ihrer Durchfuehrung, insbesondere alle Anordnungen bezueglich der Reise, der Aufenthalte pp. und die Verwaltung des Expeditions fonds ubertrage ich hiermit Eurer Hochwohlgeboren und ueberlasse ihnen gegebenenfalls die Bestellung eines Vertreters.

3. *Letter from Sirdar Nasrullah Khan to von Bethmann-Hollweg, German Chancellor, May 12, 1916.*

Der Kaiserliche Vertreter Leutnant von Hentig hat Euer Exzellenz Brief an Seine Majestät meinen erhabenen Herrscher gelangen lassen und er hat auch Seine Hoheit den Radscha Mahandra Puratab Mursani Seiner Majestaet meinem erhabenen Herrscher vorgestellt. Seine Majestaet haben sie in Gnaden aufgenommen und zaehlen sie unter die teuren Gaeste der afghanischen Regierung. Und Seine Hoheit der Radscha Mahandra Puratab Mursani widmet sich in Kabul seiner Sache und die afghanische Regierung wird bei den Arbeiten des genannten Radscha Beistand und Mitarbeit leisten.

Ferner war in Euer Exzellenz Brief geschrieben worden, dass die Kaiserliche Regierung mit groesster Lust und Freude diese guenstige Gelegenheit ergreift, ihre ausgezeichnete Hochachtung und ihre aufrichtige Anerkennung Seiner Majestaet zu entbieten, in der Hoffnung, dass zwischen dem maechtigen Kaiserreich Afghanistan von Gottes Gnaden und dem Kaiserreich Deutschland kuenftighin bis in Ewigkeit die freundschaftlichen Beziehungen und die andauernde Freundschaft im gegenseitigen Interesse und die Macht und der Glanz der beiden Reiche von Bestand sein moegen. Der Kaiserliche Vertreter von Hentig ist beauftragt worden, dass er Seiner Mafestaet jedwede noetigen Aufklaerungen ueber die jetzige Kriegslage unterbreite und ueber die Staerkung der kuenftigen Beziehungen zwischen dem afghanischen Reiche und den Staaten Deutschland, Oesterreich-Ungarn und Tuerkei, deren Verwirklichung die Kaiserlich Deutsche Regierung ins Auge fasst, und dass er wichtige Fragen dem allerhoechsten Throne aufklaere.

Euer Exzellenz! Ueber diesen aufrichtigen Wunsch der Kaiserlich Deutschen Regierung ist Seine Majestaet men Herrscher und die afghanische Regierung sehr erfreut und entzueckt. Auch die afghanische Regierung wuenscht mit aeusserster Bereitwilligkeit (?) die andauernde Freundschaft der Kaiserlich Deutschen Regierung im Interesse der beiden Laender und hofft, dass die Freundschaft der beiden Staaten, die beiden Laendern zum Vorteil gereicht, bald die Gestalt des Vertragsabschlusses finden moege.

Euer Exzellenz! Die afghanische Regierung bat Herrn von Hentig, dass der offizielle Freundschaftsvertrag zwischen der afghanischen Regierung und der Kaiserlich Deutschen Regierung zum Abschluss komme, und sie hat Herrn von Hentig auch die Bedingungen unterbreitet. Er sagte: "Ich kann den Vertrag nicht in offizieller Weise zum Abschluss bringen, aber ich werde es der Kaiserlich Deutschen Regierung unterbreiten. Wenn man mir oder einer anderen Person die Vollmacht erteilt, dann wird der offizielle Vertrag zwischen der afghanischen Regierung und der Kaiserlich Deutschen Regierung abgeschlossen werden."

Da jetzt Herr von Hentig gebeten hat, dass fuer ihn die Erlaubnis zur Heimkehr gegeben werde, so schreibe ich an Euer Exzellenz diesen Brief und entbiete die aufrichtigen, freundschaftlichen Gefuehle seitens des Kaiserreiches Afghanistan von Gottes Gnaden an die hohe Kaiserlich Deutsche Regierung, in der Hoffnung, dass in sehr grosser Eile die Freundschaft der beiden Regierungen Afghanistan und der Kaiserlich Deutschen Regierung aus dem Projekt zur Tat werde. Ich hoffe, dass Euer Exzellenz bei vollster Gesundheit und bei vollstem Wohlbefinden sein moegen.

4. *Proposed German-Afghan Treaty of Friendship.*

Es ist der Wille und das Glueck der Herrscher und der Voelker des Deutschen Reiches und Afghanistans, dass sie in alle Zukunft in angestammter Freiheit ihre Gebiete bewohnen und nach ihren eigenen Gesetzen und Sitten leben sollen. Die Weisheit der Herrscher aber hat es erkannt, dass Wohlfahrt und Wachstum der Voelker nur moeglich sind, wenn sie gleichberechtigt in Freundschaft mit anderen freien Voelkern verbunden sind und mit ihnen geistige Gueter und Handelswaren austauschen und so das Wissen und den Reichtum ihrer Untertanen erhoehen. So haben denn die beiden erhabenen Herrscher Seine Majestaet der Deutsche Kaiser, Koenig von Preussen, im Namen des Deutschen Reiches, und Seine Majestaet Straj-ul-Millat-wa-ud-Din, Emir Habib-Ullah-Khan, Koenig von Daulat-i-Khudadad, Afghanistan und den vom Koenigreich Afghanistan abhaengigen Staaten, beschlossen, den folgenden gerechten Vertrag miteinander zu schliessen, zu welchem Gott der Allmaechtige, zum Heile der Herrscher und der Voelker, seinen Segen geben wolle.

Satz I

Ich, der Deutsche Kaiser, erkenne feierlich und fuer alle Zeiten die Wahrheit dessen an, dass Seine Majestaet der Koenig von Daulat-i-Khudadad, Afghanistan und der vom Koenigreich Afghanistan abhaengigen Staaten Siraj-ul-Millat-wa-ud-Din, Habib-Ullah-Khan Sohn des grossen Abd-er-Rahman, aus dem erlauchten Geschlecht der Barakzai, welches von Alters her dem Lande der Afghanen seine Emire geschenkt hat, von Gottes Gnaden den Thron Seiner Vaeter in Kabul einnimmt und in voller Unabhaengigkeit von seinen Nachbarn Seines hohen Amtes waltet.

Es ist daher Mein aufrichtiger Wunsch, einen Vertreter Seiner Majestaet des Emirs, wie solche von allen unabhaengigen Fuersten an Meinem Hofe beglaubigt sind, bei Mir zu empfangen und dauernd in Meiner Naehe zu sehen. Durch seinen Mund werde ich erfahren, welches die Gefuehle und welches die Auffassung seines erhabenen Herrn fuer Mich und Mein Land in allen Angelegenheiten sein werden. Er soll alle Vorrechte, Befreiungen und Ehren geniessen, wie sie den uebrigen Vertretern unabhaengiger Staaten im Deutschen Reiche zugebilligt werden.

Satz II

Ich, Habib-Ullah-Khan, Emir aller Provinzen Afghanistans, trage den Wunsch, einen Vertreter Seiner Majestaet des Deutschen Kaisers an Meinem Hofe zu empfangen und dauernd in Meiner Naehe zu sehen. Meinen starken Schutz fuer seine Person und alle Vorrechte, Befreiungen und Ehrungen, wie sie dem Vertreter eines befreundeten und unabhaengigen Reiches zukommen, werde ich ihm gewaehren. Aus seinen Worten werde Ich die Gefuehle und die Auffassung seines erhabenen Herrn in allen Angelegenheiten erkennen.

Satz III

Ausser diesen diplomatischen Vertretern haben die beiden hohen Vertragschliessenden das Recht, in dem Lande des anderen konsularische Vertreter an einzelnen fuer den Handel und Verkehr besonders wichtigen Posten zu ernennen, deren Zulassung und Anerkennung vor Beginn ihrer Taetigkeit jedesmal durch den diplomatischen Vertreter erbeten werden wird. Diese Konsuln werden den gleichen persoenlichen Schutz geniessen, wie die diplomatischen Vertreter.

Satz IV

Alle unter I–III erwaehnten Vertreter werden eine von ihrem Herrscher selbst unterzeichnete Bestallung erhalten, die bei ihrer Ankunft zum Zwecke ihrer Zulassung an hoechster Stelle vorzulegen sein wird. Nachdem sie anerkannt und zugelassen sind, haben diese Vertreter das Recht, in allen Angelegenheiten ihrer Staatsangehoerigen und Schutzgenossen mit den Behoerden ihres Amtsbezirks unmittelbar zu verkehren und sich fuer sie zu verwenden. Sollte es sich als erwuenscht herausstellen, so werden die hohen Vertragschliessenden noch naehere Vereinbarungen ueber einzelne Befugnisse der Konsuln treffen. Alle Vorrechte, Befreiungen und Befugnisse, die einer der hohen Vertragschliessenden den konsularischen Vertretern eines dritten Staates gewaehrt oder gewaehren wird, wird er auch denen des anderen Vertragschliessenden gewaehren.

Satz V

Beide vertragschliessenden Teile sichern den Staatsangehoerigen und Schutzgenossen des anderen in ihrem Gebiete vollkommenen Schutz der Person und des Eigentums zu. Bei ihrem Eintritt in das Gebiet des anderen, ebenso wie bei ihrem Ausgang soll ihnen nichts in den Weg gelegt werden. Sie sollen freien und ungehinderten Zutritt zu allen Orten der Gebiete des anderen Teiles haben, zu welchen allgemein den eigenen Angehoerigen der Zutritt freisteht.

Satz VI

Den Angehoerigen und Schutzgenossen der beiden Teile soll gegenseitig vollstaendige Freiheit des Handels in und mit den Gebieten der beiden hohen vertragschliessenden Teile gewaehrt sein. Sie sollen gegenseitig dieselben Rechte und Freiheiten im Handel und Verkehr (z.B. bei Benutzung der Bahn, der Post und des Telegraphen) geniessen, welche den eigenen Angehoerigen allgemein zustehen und kuenftig zustehen werden, ohne dass sie hoehere Gebuehren oder Steuern als diese oder als andere Fremde zu zahlen haetten.

Satz VII

Fuer Ein- und Ausfuhr der afghanischen und der deutschen Waren werden keine hoeheren Zoelle in den beiden Laendern erhoben werden als bei den gleichen Waren aus anderen Laendern.

Satz VIII

Die Deutschen in Afghanistan und die Afghanen in Deutschland sollen frei von allen persoenlichen oder sachlichen Diensten fuer das Heer sein.

Satz IX

Der gegenwaertige Vertrag soll von unbegrenzter Dauer sein und soll auch fuer alle Nachfolger der hohen Vertragschliessenden bindend sein. Gefaellt es aber einem der Vertragschliessenden oder einem seiner Nachfolger, dass der Vertrag wieder anfgehoben werden soll, so wird er es ein

Jahr vorher dem anderen Vertragschliessenden durch den Mund seines Vertreters an dessen Hofe kund tun.

Der Vertrag soll in Kraft treten einen Monat nach dem Tage, an welchem die feierliche und amtliche Veroeffentlichung mit der Unterschrift Seiner Majestaet des Deutschen Kaisers im Deutschen Reiche erfolgt und diese Seiner Majestaet dem Emir aller Provinzen Afghanistans, Habib-Ullah-Khan, zur Kenntnis gebracht sein wird.

Zu Urkund dessen haben Seine Majestaet der Emir aller Provinzen Afghanistans, Habib-Ullah-Khan, im Namen Seines Reiches, und der Kaiserlich Deutsche Geschaeftstraeger, Wirklicher Legationsrat Nadolny, im Namen der Kaiserlich Deutschen Regierung diesen Vertrag in zwei gleichlautenden Exemplaren abgeschlossen, unterzeichnet und mit ihren Siegeln versehen.

5. *Convention concerning Afghanistan, Signed on August 31, 1907, between Great Britain and Russia.*

The High Contracting Parties, in order to ensure perfect security on their respective frontiers in Central Asia and to maintain in these regions a solid and lasting peace, have concluded the following Convention:—

Article I

His Britannic Majesty's Government declare that they have no intention of changing the political status of Afghanistan.

His Britannic Majesty's Government further engage to exercise their influence in Afghanistan only in a pacific sense, and they will not themselves take, nor encourage Afghanistan to take, any measures threatening Russia.

The Russian Government, on their part, declare that they recognise Afghanistan as outside the sphere of Russian influence, and they engage that all their political relations with Afghanistan shall be conducted through the intermediary of His Britannic Majesty's Government; they further engage not to send any Agents into Afghanistan.

Article II

The Government of His Britannic Majesty having declared in the Treaty signed at Kabul on the 21st March 1905, that they recognise the Agreement and the engagements concluded with the late Amir Abdur Rahman, and that they have no intention of interfering in the internal government of Afghan territory, Great Britain engages neither to annex nor to occupy in contravention of that Treaty any portion of Afghanistan or to interfere in the internal administration of the country, provided that the Amir fulfils the engagements already contracted by him towards His Britannic Majesty's Government under the above mentioned Treaty.

Article III

The Russian and Afghan authorities specially designated for the purpose on the frontier or in the frontier provinces, may establish direct relations with each other for the settlement of local questions of a non-political character.

Article IV

His Britannic Majesty's Government and the Russian Government affirm their adherence to the principle of equality of commercial opportunity in Afghanistan, and they agree that any facilities which may have been, or shall be hereafter obtained for British and British-Indian trade and traders, shall be equally enjoyed by Russian trade and traders. Should the progress of trade establish the necessity for Commercial Agents, the two Governments will agree as to what measures shall be taken, due regard, of course, being had to the Amir's sovereign rights.

Article VI

The present arrangements will only come into force when His Britannic Majesty's Government shall have notified to the Russian Government the consent of the Amir to the terms stipulated above.

6. *Letter from King George V to His Majesty, the Amir of Afghanistan, Buckingham Palace, September 24, 1915.*

I have been much gratified to learn from my Viceroy of India how scrupulously and honourably Your Majesty has maintained the attitude of strict neutrality which you guaranteed at the beginning of this War, not only because it is in accordance with Your Majesty's engagements to me, but also because by it you are serving the best interests of Afghanistan and of the Islamic religion.

I am confident that Your Majesty will continue to preserve unchanged this friendly attitude towards me and my Government till victory crowns the arms of the Allies, a prospect which daily grows nearer.

You will thus still further strengthen the friendship I so greatly value, which has united our peoples since the days of your father, of illustrious memory, and of my revered predecessor, the great Queen Victoria.

7. *British* Aide-Mémoire *Presented by Henry R. C. Dobbs to the Afghan delegates on July 24, 1920.*

Note on proposals of British and Afghan Governments discussed by delegates of two States at the Conference held at Mussoorie between months of April and July 1920 as a preliminary to definite negotiation of a treaty of friendship.

1) It was agreed that it is in the mutual interests of both Governments that the Afghan State shall be strong and prosperous.

2) British Government will be prepared to reiterate understanding given by them to respect absolutely integrity and independence of Afghanistan both in internal and external affairs, and to restrain to the best of their ability all persons within the British boundaries from actions obnoxious to the Afghan Government.

3) British Government expects that Afghan Government will similarly undertake to prevent to the best of their ability all action within the boundaries of Afghanistan, whether by their own subjects or by British subjects, who are, or may be in the future, refugees from the British Dominions, or by subjects of other nations which may tend to stir up strife or produce enmity against British Government within the boundaries of India. British Government expects that Afghan Government will undertake in particular to restrain their subordinate officials and others from inciting frontier tribes within the British boundaries against the British, to prevent to the best of their ability passage through Afghan territory to the British frontier of arms and ammunition, and of persons raising agitation against British Government, to prohibit preparation within Afghan territory for making raids into British territory, to punish persons found guilty of committing such raids, and to abstain themselves from all interference with tribes or persons on the British side of frontier, and from all kinds of political propaganda within the British Empire.

4) If the Afghan Government were willing to give formal understanding as set forth in the foregoing paragraph, then British Government, in the event of a treaty of friendship being signed, and in order to show their sympathy for desires of Afghan Government to develop their country, would be willing to consider as part of a treaty of friendship the grant, for so long as Afghan Government performed its undertakings to the satisfaction of the British Government, of assistance and concessions to Afghanistan on the following lines:—

a) A yearly subvention of 18 lakhs of rupees.

b) Reasonable assistance towards education in Europe, at such places as might be agreed upon between the two Governments, of a moderate number of Afghan youths, to be selected by the Afghan Government with due respect to their educational qualifications.

c) Reasonable assistance to be granted gradually, as financial and other circumstances might permit, towards the construction in Afghanistan of railways, telegraph lines, and factories, and towards the development of mines.

d) Technical advice regarding irrigation.

e) The manufacture and supply of specially prepared paper for the printing of Afghan currency notes, and (if necessary) provision of special machines for the note printing.

f) Technical advice regarding establishment of an Afghan Government or commercial bank, and regarding possibility of improving the system of commercial credit in Afghanistan.

g) The restoration of the privilege of importing arms and ammunition and military stores through India to Afghanistan, provided that the Government of Afghanistan shall first have signed the Arms Traffic Convention, and provided that such importation shall only be made in accordance with the provisions of that Convention.

h) The grant, in respect of all goods imported into India at British ports for re-export to Afghanistan and exported to Afghanistan by routes to be agreed upon between the two Governments of a rebate at the time and place of export of the full amount of the Customs duties levied on such goods subject to a deduction of not more than one-eighth of such duty as recompense for the work of the Customs registration, and provided that such goods shall be transported through India in sealed packages which shall not be broken before their export from India.

i) An understanding to levy no Customs duties on such goods of Afghan origin or manufacture as may be lawfully imported into India, provided that such goods shall not be exempted from levy of the present Khyber toll and from levy of octroi in any Indian municipality in which octroi is or may be hereafter levied.

j) An understanding to permit export from Afghanistan through India in bond and in sealed packages by routes to be agreed upon between the two Governments of opium and charas produced and manufactured in Afghanistan, provided that such opium and charas shall not be despatched from India to any destination to which British Government are under an obligation prohibiting or limiting despatch of opium or charas.

k) The facilitating of the interchange of postage articles between India and Afghanistan and arranging in accordance with a separate postage agreement establishment of offices of exchange of their frontiers, provided that neither Governments shall be permitted to establish a post office in the territory of the other Government.

l) Permission to establish at Peshawar and Quetta trading agencies of Afghan Government, provided that personnel and property of agency shall be subject to operation of all British laws and orders and to jurisdiction of British courts, and that they shall not be recognised by British authorities as having any official or privileged position.

m) Permission to establish Afghan Consulates at Calcutta, Bombay and Karachi, provided Afghan Government permit establishment of British Consulates at Jalalabad, Ghazni and Kandahar.

The Consuls of both Governments with their staffs to enjoy all the privileges conceded by international practices to such officials.

5) In the event of conclusion of a treaty of friendship, British

Government would be prepared on its signature to make following gifts to the Afghan Government as immediate and tangible tokens of sincerity of their intentions either following:—

A) (*a*) One hundred and sixty miles of steel telegraph posts with a double wire to be handed over either at Chaman or at Peshawar.

b) Ten new large motor lorries with spares.

c) Twenty new touring cars with spares, American make, owing to difficulty in obtaining prompt delivery of new English cars.

d) Three hundred soldiers' pats, bivouac tents.

Or the following:—

B) Four hundred and sixty steel telegraph posts with a double wire.

(N.B.—This would be sufficient for construction of a telegraph system from the British frontier to Kabul, and from Kabul to Kandahar; but it must be explained that immediate delivery could be made only of 160 miles, which would suffice for the line from the British frontier to Kabul. The balance of 300 miles could not be made available in less than a year from now, owing to shortage of material in India.)

The following points are reserved for consideration at the time of negotiating a treaty of friendship:—

a) Permission to export from Afghanistan rouble notes through India to countries outside India where their entry is permitted.

b) Representation of Afghan Government in London.

8. *Translation of Letter from Amir Amanulla Khan, Amir of Afghanistan and Its Dependencies, to His Excellency the Viceroy, March 3, 1919.*

After compliments.—I am desirous of informing my friend, His Excellency the Viceroy of the great and mighty British Government in the Indian Empire, with much despair and regret, of the particulars of a crime full of poignant grief, namely, the crime of the unjust and unlawful assassination of my late father, His Majesty Siraj-ul-Millat-wad-din Amir Habibulla Khan, King of the Government of Afghanistan, who was killed by a pistol shot at 3 A.M. in his royal bed on Thursday, the 18th Jamadi-ul-Awal 1337 Hijra, corresponding to the 20th February 1919, during his stay at a place called Kalla Gosh in his royal dominions by the hand of a treacherous perfidious traitor. I have no doubt that Your Excellency, my friend, will be much touched by the news of this painful event, for the observance of all the conditions of neutrality and the upright conduct and friendly relations displayed during the past and present by His Majesty my late father, the martyr, towards my esteemed friend's mighty Government were clearly proved and require no mention. I, Your Excellency's friend, had been appointed by order and command of His late Majesty, my assassinated pious father, as his plenipotentiary in the capital of Kabul, and consider myself in every way his heir and successor as Amir and the rightful caller to account and avenger at this time of my father's blood. The people and populace of the capital of Kabul and its surroundings, Saiyads, Ulemas, military and civil classes, traders, artisans, Muhammadan and Hindu subjects of Afghanistan itself, as well as all foreign subjects who were in the capital, unanimously and unitedly, with great enthusiasm and of their own free will and consent, swore allegiance to me, your friend; and putting my trust in God I placed on my head the crown of the Amirship of my Government of Afghanistan in the capital of Kabul amid the loud acclamations of the people and troops. And this by the grace of God. Later on our Government Armies in camp at Jalalabad also took their stand on the path of Right, which was wholly on our side, and proved their fidelity and loyalty by deposing and divesting of office my uncle Sardar Nasrulla Khan, who had as usurper declared himself Amir without any right at Jalalabad, and by submitting to me their oaths of allegiance. Thereupon my uncle Sardar Nasrulla Khan abdicated the throne of the kingdom, and my brothers Sardars Inayatulla Khan and Hayatulla Khan and other members of the Royal family, who had sworn allegiance to him, considered that allegiance illegal and submitted their oaths of allegiance to me at Kabul and acknowledged and recognised my succession as Amir and King. Therefore relying upon the friendship and sympathy that exist and will continue to exist between us, I have considered it necessary to do myself the great honour of informing my friend.

Nor let this remain unknown to that friend that our independent and free Government of Afghanistan considers itself ready and prepared at every time and season to conclude, with due regard to every consideration for the requirements of friendship and the like, such agreements and treaties with the mighty Government of England as may be useful and serviceable in the way of commercial gains and advantages to our Government and yours.

For the rest kindly accept considerations of my friendly esteem.

9. *Letter from His Excellency the Viceroy to Amir Amanulla Khan, April 15, 1919.*

After compliments.—I have received from you with deepest regret the lamentable news of the untimely death of your revered father His Majesty the late Amir Habibulla Khan Siraj-ul-Millat-Wad-din. United from of old by ties of friendship, the British Government and the Government of Afghanistan are now united in a common sorrow. For while Afghanistan mourns the loss of a great ruler who ever sought the welfare of his countrymen and by his wise statesmanship preserved it from the horrors which the war, just ended, has brought upon so many nations, the British Government mourns the loss of a staunch friend who throughout his reign maintained firm the alliance between the two Governments.

I thank you for informing me that you have been unanimously acknowledged as Amir by the populace of Kabul and its surroundings, Saiyads, Ulemas, Military and Civil classes, that your uncle Sardar Nasrulla Khan has abdicated, and that your brothers Sardars Inayatulla Khan and Hayatulla Khan and other members of the Royal family, together with the troops at Jalalabad, have sworn allegiance to you.

I note with pleasure that you say that you have sent me this information relying upon the friendship and sympathy which exist and will continue to exist between the two Governments. That friendship is based on the treaties and engagements concluded with the British Government by the late Zia-ul-Millat-Wad-din and confirmed by the late Siraj-ul-Millat-Wad-din, and I understand from what you say that the Government of Afghanistan intends to act upon them as in the past.

You say moreover that the Government of Afghanistan considers itself ready at every time and season to conclude with due regard to the requirements of friendship such agreements and treaties with the British Government as may be to the commercial advantage of the two Governments. From this it seems possible that the commercial requirements of Afghanistan are thought to call for some agreement with the British Government subsidiary to the treaties and engagements abovementioned. At this period of mourning I refrain from pursuing the matter further. But the Government of Afghanistan may rest assured that I shall be prepared at all times to invite His Majesty's Government to give careful consideration to anything it may wish to put forward and that it will be my constant endeavour in the future as in the past to foster friendly relations between the two Governments.

10. *Translation of Proclamation by Amir Amanulla Khan (undated).*

In the name of God, most merciful and compassionate.
O high-minded nation!
O courageous army!
This weak creature of the Creator of the Universe, *viz.*, your Amir, Amir Amanulla, gives you joyful tidings that thank God—again thank God—the Government of this great nation of ours and the sacred soil of our beloved country have in a very admirable way remained peaceful and safe from the horrors of such a disturbance as was calculated to make our enemies—near and far—happy and joyful and our friends much concerned. And this by the grace of God.

Listen, the facts are as follows:—

You have already been informed by proclamations, *firmans* and notices of the details of what has happened.

The happy news now is this. The bold and courageous army of our

Government at Jalalabad displayed the greatest sense of honour and courage in the discharge of all their obligations. On Thursday the 25th Jamadi-ul-Awal 1337 Hijra (27th February 1919), all the officers and soldiers who had accompanied His late Majesty, my father, the martyr, assembled on the parade ground of the cantonment at Jalalabad, swore allegiance to me with the band playing, a salute of guns and great rejoicings. Thereafter they arrested and imprisoned all persons who were entrusted with the safeguarding of His late Majesty and who were on special duty in the Royal bedroom at the time of the assassination and demanded their being called to account and punished by my uncle, who, without any religious or worldly right, had acted as usurper and declared himself as Amir. Since no false claimant can establish his illegal claim, my uncle, who had no right, voluntarily abdicated the Amirship and recognised me as Amir. The deeds of his allegiance and those of my brothers, Sardars Inayatulla Khan and Hayatulla Khan and other members of the Royal family have been received by me. Copies of these are herewith sent for your perusal and information.

O high-minded nation of Afghanistan! Let us offer thousands of thanks and praises most humbly to the imperishable God of the Earth and Heavens with our burning hearts and bleeding eyes that He has saved our sublime Government from the horrors of commotion and confusion and has inspired our Islamic Government with more strength, power and freedom. Please do not for a moment think that this King of yours expresses his thankfulness for his success in securing the throne. No, I express my thankfulness to God for safeguarding peace and prosperity of yourselves, my beloved nation, for saving the Muslims of the great nation of my beloved country Afghanistan at these perilous and hazardous times from various troubles and misfortunes and their painful consequences and for giving us a new lease of life.

O courageous army of the Government of Afghanistan! I offer thousands of thanks and endless praise to God, the Most Holy—Glory be to Him—that your soul-consuming bullets and your heart-piercing steel spearheads which were kept ready for the protection of the honour of the faith and nation of our country have by the grace of God been prevented from being used for our self-destruction and against each other. Understand it well and carefully realise that this is due to the special favour and mercy of God Almighty and the spiritual blessings of the Prophet which have been showered on our Government and nation. It is the eternal will of the unchangeable Creator—Exalted be His Glory—that all hardship and oppression may be removed from the heads of your nation; and that Afghanistan may be protected from the mischief of enemies of the faith and the country.

O nation with a nice sense of honour.

O brave army.

While my great nation were putting the Crown of the Kingdom on my head, I declared to you with a loud voice that I would accept the Crown and throne only on the condition that you should all co-operate with me in my thoughts and ideas. These I explained to you at the time and I repeat here a summary thereof:—

1) *Firstly* that the Government of Afghanistan should be internally and externally independent and free, that is to say, that all rights of Government that are possessed by other independent Powers of the world should be possessed in their entirety by Afghanistan.

2) *Secondly* that you should unite with me with all your force in avenging the unlawful assassination of my late father, the martyr, who was spiritually a father to all of you.

3) *Thirdly* that the nation should be free, that is to say, that no individual should be oppressed and subjected to any highhandedness or tyranny by any other individual. Of course obedience to the sacred law of Muhammad and Civil and Military laws is looked upon as a glorious honour for which we, the great nation of Afghanistan, are by disposition and nature well-known.

I would not accept your Crown except on these conditions. All of you, members of the high-minded strong nation, accepted these conditions with enthusiasm and acclamation, and I also put that great supreme Crown on my head with extreme honour and with determined resolution and purpose thus putting my head under the heavy weight of *"imamat* and *amarat"* (religious leadership and rulership). I hope that you, my faithful prudent and high-minded nation, will pray to the Creator of the Earth and the Heavens to favour me with strength to be successful in my undertaking and in doing all that may be necessary for your welfare and prosperity; and that you will co-operate with me manfully in the execution of my thoughts and ideas. O nation! at present I abolish at the outset the system of "begar" (impressed labour) in the country. Henceforward no labour will be impressed and not a single individual will be employed by force from among you on making roads, working on public works, tree cutting, etc., and by the grace of God our sublime Government will adopt such measures of reform as may prove serviceable and useful to the country and nation so that the Government and nation of Afghanistan may make a name and gain great renown in the civilized world and take its proper place among the civilized Powers of the world.

For the rest I pray to God for His favours and mercy and seek His help for the welfare and prosperity of you Muslims and all mankind. From God I seek guidance and the completion of my wishes.

Notes

Abbreviations

D.A.A. Deutsches Auswärtige Amt, Bonn, Germany
I.O.   India Office, London
N.A.I. National Archives of India, New Delhi, India
U.M.   University of Michigan, Ann Arbor, Michigan

Notes

Introduction

[1] See p. 36.

[2] See chap. 7. See also N.A.I., Foreign and Political Department, Frontier B, Nos. 15-138, Oct., 1919, Notes, App. I.

[3] N.A.I., For. Pol., Secret, Nos. 213-239, Aug., 1882, K.W. 1, p. 2.

[4] *Ibid.*, Nos. 128-159, May, 1909. See also Angus Hamilton, *Afghanistan* (London and New York, 1906), pp. 360 ff.

[5] See chap. 6.

[6] N.A.I., For. Pol., Frontier, Nos. 6-195, Sept., 1919, Notes 49, 57.

[7] See p. 118.

[8] Johannes Humlum, *La géographie de l'Afghanistan* (Copenhagen, 1959), p. 17.

[9] See chap. 1.

[10] For A. N. Kuropatkin's plan of invasion see chapter 3. A similar project was suggested by Staff Captain Rittich (see D.A.A., Stabskapitän Rittich, "Zur Afghanistan Frage," *Afghanistan*, Sept. 15, 1905—Oct. 31, 1906, Bde. 14-15 [University of Michigan Library, Microfilm, Reel 71, p. 43]).

[11] Olaf Caroe, *The Pathans, 550 B.C.-A.D. 1957* (London, 1958), pp. xiv-xv.

[12] Mir Munshi, Sultan Mahomed Khan, ed., *The Life of Abdur Rahman* (2 vols.; London, 1900), II, 170-171.

[13] For Afghan trade see Hamilton, *op. cit.*, pp. 288 ff.; Eberhard Rhein and A. Ghanie Ghaussy, *Die wirtschaftliche Entwicklung Afghanistans, 1880-1965* (Opladen, 1966).

[14] N.A.I., For. Sec. F, Feb., 1903, Nos. 13-14.

[15] *Ibid.*, Dec., 1905, Nos. 33-72.

[16] See chap. 6.

[17] Mir Munshi, *op. cit.*, II, 117 ff.

[18] See chap. 5.

[19] That the Amir was his own man was especially apparent during the negotiations with the Dane Mission in 1905 and those that followed the Third Anglo-Afghan War (see chaps. 3, 6, 7).

[20] See chapter 5 for the declaration of neutrality in World War I.

[21] Hamilton, *op. cit.*, pp. 288-307; Mir Munshi, *op. cit.*, II, 75; Rhein and Ghaussy, *op. cit.*, pp. 19-21.

[22] See chap. 5. See also Werner Otto von Hentig, *Mein Leben eine Dienstreise* (Göttingen, 1962).

[23] N.A.I., For. Pol., Secret File 502-F, 1923, Nos. 1-3, No. 3.

[24] The records of official correspondence in the private papers of British

statesmen are often incomplete. Singhal's assumption that Lord Curzon wanted to reconsider the engagements with Afghanistan because he wanted the subsidy to be reduced can be challenged on the basis of documentary evidence in the Archives of India.

[25] See N. A. Khalfin, *Soviet Historiography on the Development of the Afghan State in the XVIII–XX Centuries* (Moscow, 1960).

Chapter 1

[1] N.A.I., Foreign and Political Department, Secret, F, Nos. 243–250, June, 1880, No. 244.

[2] *Ibid.*, Sec., Supplementary Nos. 299–745, Dec., 1880, Nos. 324, 329, 374, 377, 403. Persia finally rejected the offer of Herat under Russian pressure.

[3] *Ibid.*, For. Sec., Nos. 304–340, June, 1880, K.W. of Nos. 308–310, Note by the Viceroy.

[4] *Ibid.*, Nos. 243–250, June, 1880, No. 244A.

[5] *Ibid.*, Nos. 145–174, May, 1900, No. 174. Gortchakoff's assurance was reiterated in 1872, 1873, 1874, 1876, 1878, and many times subsequently until the Russian Memorandum of 1900 reopened the question.

[6] C. U. Aitchison, *Treaties, Engagements and Sanads* (Calcutta, 1933), XIII, 77–78, 81–85. Persia was pledged by the Anglo-Persian Engagement of 1853 and the Treaty of 1857.

[7] N.A.I., For. Nos. 143–144, Aug., 1905, No. 143. The letter was written by Sir A. Lyall, foreign secretary, and transmitted by Lepel Griffin. It is generally known as the "Letter of July 1880" (see App. I, no. 3).

[8] *Ibid.*, For. Sec., Nos. 304–340, June, 1880, K.W. of Nos. 308–310, Note by the Viceroy.

[9] *Ibid.*, For. Sec., Supplement No. 330, July, 1880 (Memorandum to Marquis of Hartington, July 27, 1880).

[10] For a historical account up to 1900 see Dilip Kumar Ghose, *England and Afghanistan* (Calcutta, 1960); William Habberton, *Anglo-Russian Relations Concerning Afghanistan, 1837–1907*, Urbana, Ill., 1937; R. S. Rastogi, *Indo-Afghan Relations, 1880–1900* (Lucknow, 1965); and D. P. Singhal, *India and Afghanistan, 1876–1907* (St. Lucia, Queensland, 1963).

[11] See App. I, nos. 1, 2, 3.

[12] A lakh is 100,000 (for the Anglo-Afghan Agreement regarding the subsidy see App. I, no. 4).

[13] Aitchison, *op. cit.*, pp. 247 ff. The town is now named Khwāja Sālār (see *Qāmūs-i-Jughrāfiyā-ye-Afghānistān*).

[14] N.A.I., For. Sec., Nos. 573–577, Aug., 1892, No. 575, p. 7.

[15] Mir Munshi, Sultan Mahomed Khan, ed., *The Life of Abdur Rahman* (2 vols.; London, 1900), II, 112.

[16] N.A.I., For. Sec., Nos. 420–426, Aug., 1880, No. 420.

[17] *Ibid.*, For. Sec. F, Nos. 34–40, Aug., 1899, No. 34.

[18] Mir Munshi, *op. cit.*, II, 115 ff.

[19] N.A.I., For. Sec., Nos. 256–280, July, 1880, No. 261, p. 8.

[20] *Ibid.*, For. Sec. F, Nos. 48–72, March, 1895.

[21] *Ibid.*, For. Sec. E, Nos. 5–23, Dec., 1883, K.W. of Notes.

[22] Mir Munshi, *op. cit.*, II, 243. Cf. an announcement at durbar to that

effect (N.A.I., For. Sec. F, Nos. 169-176, Sept., 1899, No. 174). Nasrullah went to London and had an audience with Queen Victoria in July, 1895, but he was unsuccessful in obtaining permission to establish an Afghan agency in London (*ibid.,* For. Sec., Nos. 93-100, Dec., 1895; Mir Munshi, *op. cit.,* II, 142 ff.).

[23] N.A.I., For. Sec. F, Nos. 34-40, Aug., 1899, No. 34.

[24] Abd Allah Khan was Afghan Agent in Meshed (*ibid.,* For. Sec. War, Nos. 1-195, March, 1916, No. 71; For. Sec. F, Nos. 36-44, Oct., 1899). Haus Khan, alias Ghuz Muhammad Khan, was in Turkestan (*ibid.,* Nos. 1-7, Aug., 1913).

[25] *Sirāj al-Akhbār,* April 11, 1914, pp. 13 ff.

[26] N.A.I., For. Sec., Nos. 213-239, Aug., 1882, K.W. 1, pp. 7-8; Nos. 124-129, Jan., 1900, No. 124, p. 8.

[27] *Ibid.,* For. Sec. F, Nos. 76-83, Aug., 1899, No. 81A, pp. 5-6.

[28] *Ibid.,* For. Sec., Nos. 256-280, July, 1880, No. 263 (see App. I, no. 2).

[29] *Ibid.,* No. 265.

[30] *Ibid.,* For. Sec., Nos. 213-239, Aug., 1882, K.W. 1, p. 4.

[31] *Ibid.,* Nos. 573-577, Aug., 1892, No. 575, pp. 2-3; For. Sec. E, No. 423, April, 1883.

[32] By 1892, thirteen Englishmen were employed by the Amir at Kabul (*ibid.,* For. Sec. Frontier B, Nos. 151-157, Oct., 1892).

[33] *Ibid.,* For. Sec., Nos. 573-577, Aug., 1892, No. 575, p. 3.

[34] *Ibid.,* For. Sec. F, Nos. 384-387, Sept., 1895.

[35] Lord Ampthill, who was viceroy at the time, stated that "we ourselves are to a certain extent responsible for the neglect and contempt with which our Agent at Kabul is at present treated. We give him no information and we do not entrust him with any particular duties. I think that we should let the Agent be our means of communication on all minor matters and that we should at least keep him informed of all important communications which pass between ourselves and the Amir unless they are of so secret and delicate a nature as to render this inadvisable" (*ibid.,* For. Sec. F, Nos. 34-136, Jan., 1905). On the other hand, the Amir sent all his correspondence to the English Agent (*ibid.,* Nos. 28-37, May, 1904, No. 30, Notes).

[36] *Ibid.,* Nos. 384-398, Dec., 1884.

[37] *Ibid.,* Nos. 141-152, Feb., 1899, K.W. 2; Nos. 760-787, May, 1885, No. 761.

[38] *Ibid.,* Nos. 141-152, Feb., 1899, K.W. 2; Nos. 855-868, July, 1887, Lord Dufferin to the Amir, July 20, 1887.

[39] *Ibid.,* Nos. 141-152, Feb., 1899, K.W. 2; Nos. 241-292, July, 1889; Nos. 57-89, Nov., 1889.

[40] *Ibid.,* Nos. 475-488, June, 1892, No. 475.

[41] After trade in 1892 had reached a volume of 25,279 maunds, shipments decreased to 7,474 maunds in April. The volume of shipments at Qila Abd Allah gained correspondingly to this loss (*ibid.,* For. Sec. Frontier B, Nos. 169-170, Jan., 1893).

[42] *Ibid.,* For. Sec. F, Nos. 76-83, Aug., 1899, No. 81A, p. 2.

[43] *Ibid.,* pp. 6-7.

[44] *Ibid.,* Nos. 220-261, Oct., 1884, No. 259.

[45] *Ibid.,* For. Sec. Frontier B, No. 51, June, 1912.

[46] Mir Munshi, *op. cit.,* II, 138.

[47] N.A.I., For. Sec., Nos. 193–217, Jan., 1894, No. 207, p. 38.
[48] *Ibid.*, For. Sec. F, Nos. 313–324, March, 1898.
[49] *Ibid.*, Nos. 573–577, Aug., 1892, No. 575, p. 5.
[50] Mir Munshi, *op. cit.*, II, 260.
[51] *Ibid.*, pp. 260 ff.
[52] *Ibid.*, pp. 272 ff.
[53] *Ibid.*, p. 264.
[54] *Ibid.*, p. 266.
[55] *Ibid.*, p. 119.
[56] *Ibid.*, p. 237.
[57] *Ibid.*, p. 171.
[58] Britain would permit Europeans to cross into Afghanistan only if they produced an entrance permit from the Afghan ruler. At times, however, the government of India refused passage despite possession of a permit, if the visit was deemed not to be in the best interests of Britain. Herr Rosen, a German engineer, was, for example, denied entrance on this ground (N.A.I., For. Sec. Frontier B, Nos. 185–187, July, 1892).

Chapter 2

[1] N.A.I., Foreign and Political Department, Secret F, Nos. 213–239, Aug., 1882, K.W. 1, pp. 1–14. At various times the government of India received reports of the arrest and execution of British spies in Afghanistan (*ibid.*, Nos. 245–271, July, 1894; Nos. 20–40, June, 1892, No. 25).
[2] *Ibid.*, For. Sec., Nos. 199–236, Aug., 1892, K.W., p. 18.
[3] *Ibid.*, p. 16.
[4] *Ibid.*, For. Sec. F, Nos. 1–129, Nov., 1901, No. 9.
[5] Ayyub Khan lived in Indian exile with his family and a number of followers.
[6] N.A.I., For. Sec. F, Feb., 1904, Nos. 23–32, Notes, p. 2, Memorandum on Afghan Succession by Lord Curzon, Dec. 7, 1898.
[7] N.A.I., For. Sec. F, Nos. 101–121, Feb., 1891, Notes.
[8] *Ibid.*, Nos. 23–32, Feb., 1904, Notes, pp. 2–5.
[9] *Ibid.*, Nos. 1–129, Nov., 1901, Nos. 9, 22, 36, 40, 50, 63.
[10] *Ibid.*, Nos. 8–48, Dec., 1901, No. 37.
[11] *Ibid.*, Nos. 95–103, June, 1902, No. 95.
[12] *Ibid.*
[13] *Ibid.*, Nos. 1–35, Jan., 1903, No. 25, Notes.
[14] *Ibid.* McMahon's award was unacceptable to both Persia and Afghanistan. The Amir objected to Clause IV, which required that a British irrigation officer be permanently stationed on the border (*ibid.*, Nos. 1–41, Nov., 1905, No. 34; Nos. 3–127, March, 1904, No. 93).
[15] *Ibid.*, Nos. 145–147, May, 1900, Notes; No. 147, Encl. 1, pp. 55, Précis by Parker.
[16] *Ibid.*
[17] *Ibid.*, p. 56; see also Nos. 145–147, May, 1900, No. 147, p. 22.
[18] *Ibid.*, No. 147, Encl. 1, p. 56, Précis by Parker.
[19] *Ibid.*, p. 59.
[20] *Ibid.*, p. 61.

NOTES TO PP. 35-45   219

[21] *Ibid.*, p. 64.
[22] Lieutenant Colonel A. C. Yate, a British officer, was arrested by Afghan soldiers when he strayed across the border (*ibid.*, Nos. 5-50, May, 1903).
[23] *Ibid.*, Nos. 83-162, Aug., 1903, No. 155, Notes.
[24] *Ibid.*
[25] *Ibid.*, No. 87.
[26] *Ibid.*, Nos. 40-183, Feb., 1904, No. 164.
[27] *Ibid.*, No. 148.
[28] *Ibid.*, No. 164.
[29] *Ibid.*, Nos. 31-149, July, 1904, No. 39, Notes, p. 6, and No. 107.
[30] *Ibid.*, No. 33, Notes.
[31] *Ibid.*, No. 41.
[32] *Ibid.*, Nos. 13-14, Feb., 1903, No. 14; Nos. 91-97, Nov., 1903.
[33] *Ibid.*, Nos. 5-50, May, 1903, No. 42, Notes. The Achakzai were Afghans of the ruling Durrani tribe. When their territory was annexed by Britain after the Second Anglo-Afghan War, many of them fled into Afghanistan. Regarding the tribes, see Olaf Caroe, *The Pathans, 550 B.C.-A.D. 1957* (London, 1958); James Spain, *The Pathan Borderland* (The Hague, 1963).
[34] N.A.I., For. Sec. F, Nos. 1-90, Nov., 1903, Notes.
[35] *Ibid.*, Nos. 13-14, Feb., 1903, No. 14.
[36] *Ibid.*, Nos. 1-7, Oct., 1902.

Chapter 3

[1] N.A.I., Foreign and Political Department, Secret F, Nos. 233-271, Oct., 1904, No. 233, Notes, p. 2.
[2] I.O., Hamilton Papers, 510/II, p. 432 (quoted in D. P. Singhal, *India and Afghanistan, 1876-1907* [St. Lucia, Queensland, 1963], p. 163).
[3] N.A.I., For. Sec. F, Nos. 143-144, Aug., 1905, No. 143, pp. 5-6 (see App. I, nos. 5, 6, 7).
[4] *Ibid.*, Nos. 233-271, Oct., 1904, No. 233, Notes, pp. 5-6.
[5] *Ibid.*, No. 239, p. 19.
[6] *Ibid.*, p. 20. Kuropatkin's plan had already been designed by 1886 (*ibid.*, No. 68, Sept., 1904).
[7] *Ibid.*, Nos. 233-271, Oct., 1904, No. 257, p. 28, as paraphrased by E. H. S. Clarke.
[8] *Ibid.*, Nos. 34-136, Jan., 1905, No. 42 and Notes.
[9] *Ibid.*, Notes, p. 4.
[10] *Ibid.*, No. 42, p. 2.
[11] *Ibid.*
[12] *Ibid.*, Notes, p. 4.
[13] *Ibid.*, No. 42.
[14] *Ibid.*, Notes, p. 5.
[15] *Ibid.*, No. 43.
[16] *Ibid.*, p. 2.
[17] *Ibid.*, p. 3.
[18] *Ibid.*, p. 7.
[19] *Ibid.*, No. 43, Notes, pp. 11, 13.
[20] *Ibid.*, No. 45.

21 *Ibid.*, No. 74.
22 *Ibid.*, No. 59.
23 *Ibid.*, p. 1.
24 *Ibid.*, p. 3.
25 *Ibid.*, p. 4.
26 *Ibid.*, p. 6.
27 *Ibid.*, No. 67.
28 *Ibid.*, No. 75, Encl. 1.
29 *Ibid.*, No. 114.
30 *Ibid.*, No. 112.
31 *Ibid.*, No. 116. In addition to Dane, the members of the mission were H. Dobbs, secretary; H. A. Grant, in charge of frontier matters and mission accounts; W. Malleson and Captain Brooke, in charge of military matters; Major Norman, camp commandant; Captain Turnbull, physician, and his medical assistant; Khan Bahadur Maula Bakhsh, translator; Rai Bahadur Kanshi Nand, to collect commercial information; Nawab Hafiz Abd Allah Khan; and Khan Bahadur Arbab Muhammad Azam Khan, Mohmand. The Amir's Council consisted of Sardar Nasrullah Khan, Sardar Abdul Kuddus Khan, Sardar Muhammad Asif Khan, Loinab Khushdil Khan, Muhammad Husayn Khan, and Muhammad Sulayman Khan (*ibid.*, Nos. 61-72, July, 1905, No. 61, pp. 4, 14).
32 *Ibid.*, Nos. 34-136, Jan., 1905, No. 118.
33 *Ibid.*
34 *Ibid.*, Notes.
35 *Ibid.*, No. 125, Notes.
36 *Ibid.*, p. 58.
37 *Ibid.*, p. 61.
38 *Ibid.*, Nos. 1-141, May, 1905, No. 3, Encl. 2.
39 *Ibid.*, Nos. 34-136, Jan., 1905, No. 126, Notes, pp. 62-63.
40 *Ibid.*; see also Nos. 1-141, May, 1905, No. 5, Notes.
41 *Ibid.*, Nos. 1-141, May, 1905, No. 4.
42 *Ibid.*, p. 10.
43 *Ibid.*, p. 13.
44 *Ibid.*, No. 5, Notes.
45 *Ibid.*, No. 12, Encl. 1.
46 *Ibid.*, Nos. 145-147, May, 1900, No. 147, Encl. 1, Précis by Parker.
47 *Ibid.*, Nos. 1-141, May, 1905, No. 24.
48 *Ibid.*, Encls. 3, 4.
49 *Ibid.*, No. 18, Notes.
50 *Ibid.*, No. 19, Notes.
51 *Ibid.*, No. 25.
52 *Ibid.*, Notes.
53 *Ibid.*, p. 15.
54 *Ibid.*, No. 37.
55 *Ibid.*, No. 34.
56 *Ibid.*, No. 50.
57 *Ibid.*, Notes.
58 *Ibid.*, No. 75.
59 *Ibid.*, No. 78.

⁶⁰ *Ibid.*
⁶¹ *Ibid.*, No. 83.
⁶² *Ibid.*, No. 94, Encl. 1.
⁶³ *Ibid.*, No. 112.
⁶⁴ *Ibid.*, Notes.
⁶⁵ *Ibid.*, No. 114.
⁶⁶ *Ibid.*, Nos. 143–144, Aug., 1905, App. to Notes.
⁶⁷ *Ibid.*, No. 144.
⁶⁸ *Ibid.*, Nos. 105–106, June, 1905, No. 105.
⁶⁹ *Ibid.*, No. 106.
⁷⁰ *Ibid.*, Nos. 1–141, May, 1905, No. 18, Notes.
⁷¹ *Ibid.*, Nos. 61–72, July, 1905, No. 64.

Chapter 4

¹ N.A.I., Foreign and Political Department, Secret F, Nos. 425–455, June, 1906, No. 454, Notes, p. 15.
² *Ibid.*, No. 98, May, 1907, App. to Notes.
³ *Ibid.*, Nos. 105–137, July, 1907, Nos. 106, Notes.
⁴ *Ibid.*, Nos. 176–179, Feb., 1907, No. 179, Notes.
⁵ *Ibid.*, Nos. 119–137, Feb., 1907, No. 125.
⁶ I.O., Dane Papers, MSS Eur. D. 659/6; see also Mary, Countess of Minto, *India, Minto and Morley, 1905–1910* (London, 1934), pp. 74 ff.
⁷ N.A.I., For. Sec. F, Nos. 105–137, July, 1907, No. 106, Notes.
⁸ *Ibid.*, No. 98, May, 1907, Notes.
⁹ Faqir Saiyid Iftikhar-ud-Din, *Report on the Tour in Afghanistan of H. M. Amir Habibullah, 1907* (Simla, 1908).
¹⁰ N.A.I., For. Sec. F, Nos. 353–366, June, 1906, No. 353.
¹¹ *Ibid.*, No. 355.
¹² *Ibid.*, No. 360.
¹³ *Ibid.*, No. 362.
¹⁴ *Ibid.*, No. 363, March 16, 1906.
¹⁵ *Ibid.*, Nos. 469–533, June, 1907, No. 469.
¹⁶ *Ibid.*, No. 484.
¹⁷ *Ibid.*, Nos. 491, 493.
¹⁸ *Ibid.*, No. 493, Notes.
¹⁹ *Ibid.*
²⁰ *Ibid.*, Nos. 26–145, Nov., 1907, App. to Notes (see App. II, no. 5, above).
²¹ *Ibid.*, No. 128.
²² *Ibid.*, No. 141.
²³ *Ibid.*, Nos. 94–128, Oct., 1908, Notes.
²⁴ *Ibid.*, Nos. 469–533, June, 1907, App. to Notes.
²⁵ *Ibid.*, Nos. 94–128, Oct., 1908, No. 94, Notes.
²⁶ *Ibid.*
²⁷ *Ibid.*, Nos. 98–99, Oct., 1908, No. 98.
²⁸ *Ibid.*
²⁹ *Ibid.*, Nos. 94–128, Oct., 1908, No. 97.
³⁰ *Ibid.*, No. 99.

[31] *Ibid.*, No. 111.
[32] *Ibid.*, Encl.
[33] *Ibid.*
[34] *Ibid.*, No. 118.
[35] *Ibid.*, No. 123.
[36] *Ibid.*, Nos. 167-220, Oct., 1908, App. I to Notes.
[37] *Ibid.*, Nos. 51-65, Dec., 1908, Nos. 55, 61.
[38] *Ibid.*, Nos. 1-65, Jan., 1904, No. 7, Notes; Nos. 618-640, June, 1908, No. 624, Notes.
[39] *Ibid.*, No. 624, Notes.
[40] British news writers resided in Kandahar from the days of Shir Ali Khan (1870-1879); when the British left this city in 1881, they again appointed a news writer.
[41] N.A.I., For. Sec., Nos. 18-68, Sept., 1907, No. 65, Notes.
[42] *Ibid.*, No. 67, Notes.
[43] *Ibid.*, For. Sec. Frontier B, Nos. 30-32, June, 1902, No. 30.
[44] *Ibid.*, For. Sec. F, Nos. 75-91, Nov., 1909, No. 75, Notes; Olaf Caroe, *The Pathans, 550 B.C.–A.D. 1957* (London, 1958).
[45] N.A.I., For. Sec. F, Nos. 1-9, June, 1911, No. 1, Notes; Frontier A, Nos. 59-65, Dec., 1903.
[46] *Ibid.*, For. Sec. F, Nos. 57-59, Jan., 1907, Notes.
[47] *Ibid.*, Nos. 20-21, Feb., 1909, No. 20.
[48] *Ibid.*, Nos. 22-24, Dec., 1910, No. 22.
[49] *Ibid.*, Nos. 162-188, Aug., 1906, No. 167, Notes.
[50] *Ibid.*, Nos. 78-127, Jan., 1908, No. 126.
[51] *Ibid.*, Nos. 235-554, June, 1908, Nos. 399, 401, Notes.
[52] *Ibid.*, Nos. 169-170, June, 1905, No. 169, Notes.
[53] *Ibid.*, For. Sec. I, Nos. 1-23, May, 1913, No. 1.
[54] *Ibid.*, No. 18, Notes.
[55] Mahmud Tarzi was a member of the ruling Muhammadzai clan and a descendant of Payanda Khan. Born in Ghazni in 1866, he inherited his literary talents from his father. Tarzi was the author or translator of some fifteen books on a variety of subjects, such has the Russo-Japanese War and the adventures of Jules Verne (see article in *Pioneer* [India], April 21, 1920, in N.A.I., For. Sec. F, Nos. 317-550, Oct., 1920, No. 455, Notes; Muhammad Haydar Zhūbel, *Negāhī be-Adabiyāt-i-Mu'āser dar Afghānistān* [Kabul, 1337/1959]. Cf. Vartan Gregorian, "The Emergence of Modern Afghanistan: Politics of Modernization, 1880-1930" [unpublished Ph.D. dissertation, Stanford University, June, 1964]).
[56] N.A.I., For. Sec. F, Nos. 247-249, Feb., 1904, No. 247.
[57] *Ibid.*, Nos. 224-235, July, 1904, Notes.
[58] *Ibid.*, Nos. 276-278, July, 1908, No. 276, Notes.
[59] *Ibid.*, No. 5, Sept., 1910; Frontier B, Nos. 92-93, Nov., 1910.
[60] *Ibid.*, Frontier B, No. 105, Nov., 1911. Cf. Turkish activity in Afghanistan and Central Asia (*ibid.*, No. 2, Feb., 1912).
[61] A list of Turkish nationals employed by the Amir in 1913 is given in *ibid.*, Nos. 71-73, May, 1913.
[62] *Sirāj al-Akhbār*, June 6, 1913, pp. 7-8. Cf. N.A.I., For. General A, Nos. 1-36, Jan., 1913, Nos. 31, 33.

NOTES TO PP. 82–87   223

[63] N.A.I., For. External B, Nos. 370–379, April, 1914, No. 374.
[64] *Ibid.* Cf. "Defects in our Agreement with England," *Golos Moskvi*, in *ibid.*, For. Sec. F, Nos. 58–59, Sept., 1910.
[65] *Ibid.*, Nos. 75–82, Oct., 1914, No. 82.

Chapter 5

[1] D.A.A., No. A 1212 (U.M. Microfilm, Reel 150, p. 204). Cf. Ulrich Gehrke, *Persien in der Deutschen Orientpolitik während des Ersten Weltkrieges* (Stuttgart, n.d.), Band 1 (I), p. 23.
[2] D.A.A., Telegram by Wangenheim, No. A 34018 (U.M., Reel 71, p. 327).
[3] *Ibid.*, No. A 17312 (U.M., Reel 139, p. 443).
[4] *Ibid.*, No. A 19498 (U.M., Reel 139, p. 471). Cf. Gehrke, *op. cit.*, Band 1 (I), p. 23.
[5] D.A.A., No. A 20636 (U.M., Reel 139, p. 511); Gehrke, *op. cit.*, Band 1 (I), p. 24.
[6] D.A.A., No. A 27438 (U.M., Reel 139, p. 783).
[7] D.A.A., No. A 9519 (U.M., Reel 140, p. 462); No. A 9366 (U.M., Reel 142, pp. 401–409).
[8] D.A.A., Wassmuss Report, No. A 9366 (U.M., Reel 142, pp. 401–409). Several Germans bragged about their secret mission, and some of them registered in a hotel in Constantinople as "members of an Expedition to A——" (*ibid.*, No. A 25924 [U.M., Reel 139, p. 697]). Cf. Gehrke, *op. cit.*, Band 1 (II), p. 43 n. 202.
[9] D.A.A., No. A 6526 (U.M., Reel 140, p. 296).
[10] Mahendra Pratap has described himself as "a landlord of Hathres, a younger son of Raja Ghanshiam Singh and an adopted son of Raja Harnarain Singh, whose ancestors were independent princes of India until the British conquest" ("My German Mission to High Asia," *Asia*, XXV [May, 1925]).
[11] D.A.A., Hentig Report, No. A 20844 (U.M., Reel 141, pp. 780 ff.). Hentig's group consisted of the Germans Dr. Becker and Lieutenant Roehr, the Turkish officer Kazim Bey, Mahendra Pratap, the Indian Muslim Barakat Allah, and six Afridis who were enlisted from German prisoner-of-war camps. Two Afghans from the United States, Abdur Rahman and Sobhan Khan, joined the expedition at their own expense (Werner Otto von Hentig, *Mein Leben eine Dienstreise* [Göttingen, 1963], pp. 93–94).
[12] D.A.A., No. A 28117/16 (U.M., Reel 141, p. 567). See App. II, no. 1.
[13] *Ibid.*, Niedermayer Report, No. A 30787 (U.M., Reel 141, pp. 616 ff.); Hentig Report, No. A 21209 (U.M., Reel 142, pp. 17 ff.).
[14] N.A.I., For. Sec. War F, Nos. 176–194, July, 1915, No. 178. Cf. Gehrke, *op. cit.*, Band 1 (II), p. 44 n. 204.
[15] N.A.I., For. Sec. War, Nos. 1–202, Jan., 1916, No. 134, Notes, p. 39.
[16] *Ibid.* See also I.O., No. P 4741, 1914; and I.O., Memo No. A 173.
[17] *Sirāj al-Akhbār*, Oct. 21, 1914, p. 1.
[18] I.O., No. P 2814, 1915.
[19] N.A.I., For. Sec. War, Nos. 1–202, Jan., 1916, No. 65.
[20] *Ibid.*, No. 60; I.O., No. P 2814, 1915.
[21] I.O., No. P 3078, 1915; N.A.I., For. Sec. War, Nos. 1–202, Jan., 1916, No. 171.

[22] N.A.I., For. Sec. War, Nos. 1–202, Jan., 1916, No. 67.
[23] D.A.A., Niedermayer Report, No. A 34142/15 (U.M., Reel 141, pp. 429 ff.); Winkelmann Report (pp. 449 ff.); Seiler Report (pp. 451 ff.).
[24] N.A.I., For. Sec. War, Nos. 1–327, Feb., 1916, No. 101.
[25] *Ibid.*, No. 165.
[26] *Ibid.;* I.O., Memo No. A 173.
[27] *Ibid.*
[28] When the commander of the troops threatened some of his elderly officers with dismissal, a British agent lost no time in telling these "senior" officers that their dismissal was favored by the Germans (*ibid.;* Hentig, *op. cit.*, p. 134).
[29] N.A.I., For. Sec. War, Nos. 1–195, March, 1916, No. 11, Notes.
[30] *Ibid.*, No. 184. See App. II, no. 6.
[31] *Ibid.*, No. 186.
[32] I.O., Memo No. A 173(*b*). Cf. Hentig, *op. cit.*, p. 137.
[33] Hentig, *op. cit.*, pp. 130 ff. Cf. Oskar von Niedermayer, *Im Weltkrieg vor Indiens Toren* (Hamburg, 1942), pp. 129 ff.
[34] Niedermayer, *op. cit.*, p. 148; Hentig, *op. cit.*, p. 138.
[35] Hentig, *op. cit.*, p. 140; D.A.A., Hentig Report, No. A 20844 (U.M., Reel 141, p. 791).
[36] It was originally planned to send the Amir, among other gifts, a photograph of the German Kaiser, together with a letter signed by the Emperor. The letter was written, but it carried the name of Wassmuss as leader of the Afghanistan Expedition (D.A.A., Nos. A 22087, A 52096 [U.M., Reel 139, p. 561]). A month later, in October, 1914, the Auswärtige Amt decided against sending a letter from the Kaiser, fearing that it might fall into the hands of the British (*ibid.*, No. A 26646 [U.M., Reel 139, p. 736]). Nevertheless, Hentig claimed to have handed the Amir a typewritten letter from the Emperor; the Amir expressed some doubts about its authenticity (Hentig, *op. cit.*, p. 141).
[37] N.A.I., For. Sec. War, Nos. 1–195, March, 1916, No. 112, Notes.
[38] *Ibid.;* Nos. 1–288, May, 1916, No. 252.
[39] *Ibid.*, Nos. 1–288, May, 1916, No. 252.
[40] *Ibid.;* Nos. 1–195, March, 1916, No. 103, Notes; Nos. 1–212, June, 1916, No. 5.
[41] *Ibid.*, Nos. 1–212, June, 1916, No. 95.
[42] *Ibid.;* Nos. 1–288, May, 1916, No. 214, Notes.
[43] *Ibid.*, No. 245.
[44] The British agent was a Pathan, or transborder Afghan.
[45] *Ibid.*, No. 245, Notes.
[46] *Ibid.*, No. 252, Notes.
[47] *Ibid.*, No. 274, Notes.
[48] *Ibid.*, No. 280, Notes.
[49] *Ibid.;* Nos. 1–212, June, 1916, No. 132.
[50] *Ibid.*, Nos. 1–212, June, 1916, No. 133.
[51] *Ibid.*, No. 39, Notes.
[52] *Ibid.;* Nos. 147–536, July, 1917.
[53] I.O., Seiler's Shorthand Diary, Memo No. A 176 (see App. I, no. 9).

NOTES TO PP. 94–101 225

⁵⁴ *Ibid.*
⁵⁵ *Ibid.*
⁵⁶ *Ibid.;* N.A.I., For. Sec. War, Nos. 1–212, June, 1916, No. 118.
⁵⁷ Ikbal Ali Shah related that the Amir raised a copy of the Koran in front of the Kabul Bridge and asked the assembled mullahs and notables to show him where it is written that one must wage war against friends ("Afghanistan and the German Threat," *Edinburgh Review,* 22 [1918], 59–72).
⁵⁸ I.O., Memo No. A 176, p. 2.
⁵⁹ D.A.A., Niedermayer Report, No. A 26086 (U.M., Reel 141, pp. 552 ff.).
⁶⁰ Niedermayer left by way of Russian Central Asia and made his way to Teheran and Kermanshah. He claims that his affiliation with a secret fraternity—the Bahai religion, according to Wassmuss (*ibid.,* No. A 20636 [U.M., Reel 139, p. 511])—was helpful while traveling. Hentig returned to Germany via China and the United States. Other members of the expedition remained in Herat until the Russian Revolution opened new possibilities for anti-British activities (N.A.I., For. Sec. War, Nos. 147–536, July, 1917).
⁶¹ N.A.I., For. Sec. F, Nos. 705–806, Oct., 1920, No. 705, Notes.
⁶² The Germans were permitted to demonstrate artillery practice by shooting at fixed targets, but they were never permitted to practice with Afghan soldiers (Hentig, *op. cit.,* p. 153).
⁶³ N.A.I., For. Sec. War, Nos. 1–300, Aug., 1916, No. 205, Notes.
⁶⁴ *Ibid.;* Nos. 1–212, June, 1916, No. 13, Notes.
⁶⁵ *Ibid.,* Nos. 1–212, June, 1916, No. 59, Notes.
⁶⁶ *Ibid.,* No. 127.
⁶⁷ *Ibid.;* Nos. 1–350, Oct., 1916, No. 126.
⁶⁸ *Ibid.,* Nos. 1–350, Oct., 1916, No. 126; Nos. 1–319, Oct., 1917, No. 319.
⁶⁹ *Ibid.,* Nos. 1–155, April, 1917, No. 22.
⁷⁰ *Ibid.,* No. 25, Notes.
⁷¹ *Ibid.,* No. 39, Notes.
⁷² *Ibid.*
⁷³ *Ibid.,* No. 41, Notes.
⁷⁴ *Ibid.,* No. 69, Notes.
⁷⁵ *Ibid.,* No. 61.
⁷⁶ *Ibid.,* For. Sec. F, Nos. 1–285, July, 1917, No. 155, Notes.
⁷⁷ *Ibid.,* No. 274.
⁷⁸ *Ibid.,* No. 155, Notes.
⁷⁹ *Ibid.,* Nos. 1–76, Jan., 1918, No. 15, Notes.
⁸⁰ *Ibid.,* For. Sec. War, Nos. 1–175, March, 1917, British Agent Report, July 8, 1916.
⁸¹ *Ibid.,* No. 35.
⁸² *Sirāj al-Akhbār,* July 16, 1916, pp. 10–13.
⁸³ N.A.I., For. Sec. War, Nos. 1–175, March, 1917, No. 130.
⁸⁴ *Ibid.*
⁸⁵ The *Sirāj al-Akhbār* was first published on October 10, 1911 (corresponding to 15 Shawwāl 1329/15 Mīzān 1290 shamsī).
⁸⁶ Muhammad Haydar Zhūbel, *Negāhī be-Adabiyāt-i-Mu'aser dar Afghā nistān* (Kabul, 1337/1959), pp. 49 ff.; N.A.I., For. Sec. F, Nos. 317–550, Oct.,

1920, No. 455, Notes; Vartan Gregorian, "The Emergence of Modern Afghanistan: Politics of Modernization, 1880–1930" (unpublished Ph.D. dissertation, Stanford University, June, 1964), pp. 379–420.

[87] Pratap's letter to the editor explains the purpose of his mission (*Sirāj al-Akhbār*, May 4, 1919, p. 11).

[88] No figures are given anywhere, but circulation cannot have exceeded 1,000 copies.

[89] N.A.I., Home and Pol. Dept., Secret, Deposit, No. 21, July, 1916.

[90] *Sirāj al-Akhbār*, April 16, 1915, p. 7, gives a Pashtu poem by Saleh Muhammad which has a Pan-Islamic message.

[91] Note by A. H. Grant, July 21, 1915 (N.A.I., Home Sec. Dept., No. 21, July, 1916).

[92] *Ibid.*, No. 31, Oct., 1916.

[93] *Sirāj al-Akhbār*, Aug. 15, 1916, pp. 4–9.

[94] D.A.A., No. A 221 (U.M., Reel 150, pp. 325 ff.). See App. II, no. 4.

[95] *Ibid.*, No. A 28117/16 (U.M., Reel 141, pp. 576 ff.). See App. II, no. 3.

[96] *Ibid.*, No. A 29968 (U.M., Reel 141, pp. 616 ff.); No. A 34596 (U.M., Reel 141, pp. 636 ff.).

[97] *Ibid.*, No. A 34590 (U.M., Reel 141, pp. 635 ff.).

[98] *Ibid.*, No. A 10636 (U.M., Reel 142, pp. 60 ff.).

[99] N.A.I., For. Sec. War, Nos. 1–187, Dec., 1919, No. 154.

[100] *Ibid.*, For. Sec. F, Nos. 705–806, Oct., 1920, No. 705, Notes.

[101] *Ibid.*

[102] *Ibid.*

[103] *Ibid.*

[104] *Ibid.*

[105] *Ibid.*, No. 706, Notes.

[106] *Ibid.*, No. 705, Notes. The subsidy had been increased in October, 1915, to 20½ lakhs, and Lord Chelmsford announced in a letter of July 8, 1918, that Britain would pay 1 crore of rupees as a special present to the Amir (I.O., Memo No. A 178).

[107] N.A.I., For. Sec. F, Nos. 705–806, Oct., 1920, No. 705, Notes.

Chapter 6

[1] N.A.I., Foreign and Political Department, Secret, Fontier B, Nos. 7–16, June, 1917, Report by Dr. W. M. Smith.

[2] R. N. G. Scott, *The Fall of Amanullah*, N.A.I., IV, No. 86, Secret 44.

[3] *Ibid.* An extract from the Herat Newsletter of February 10, 1916, said that Amanullah addressed the Barakzai Khawanin, telling them that from his mother's side he considered himself a Barakzai and asking for information about their well-being (N.A.I., For. Fron. B, Nos. 13–14, April, 1916).

[4] Scott, *op. cit.*

[5] Intelligence collected by Khan Sahib Tasadduk Husayn, superintendent of police on special duty during the Anglo-Afghan peace conference at Rawalpindi (N.A.I., For. Fron. B, Nos. 15–138, Oct., 1919, App. I to Notes).

[6] *Ibid.*, For. Fron. B, No. 5, Oct., 1919.

[7] *Ibid.*

[8] Scott, *op. cit.;* W. K. Fraser-Tytler, *Afghanistan* (London, 1950), p. 195; Sir Percy Sykes, *A History of Afghanistan* (London, 1940), II, 268–269.
[9] N.A.I., For. Fron. B, Nos. 92–101, Sept., 1919, No. 98. See App. II, no. 8.
[10] *Ibid.,* For. Sec. F, Nos. 705–806, Oct., 1920, No. 720.
[11] *Ibid.,* For. Fron. B, Nos. 18–191, Sept., 1919, No. 147, Report of British Agent, April 15, 1919.
[12] *Ibid.,* No. 142. Cf. I.O., Parliamentary Papers, *Afghanistan,* Hostilities, 1919, No. 3, p. 5. See App. II, no. 9.
[13] N.A.I., For. Fron. B, Nos. 18–191, Sept., 1919, No. 121. See App. II, no. 10.
[14] *Ibid.,* Encl. 1.
[15] *Ibid.;* For. Sec. F, Nos. 1–235, July, 1919, No. 1, Notes. Cf. I.O., Memo No. A 183, *Afghanistan, 1919, Diary of Events,* p. 41.
[16] I.O., Memoranda Nos. A 177, A 183.
[17] N.A.I., For. Sec., Nos. 1–200B, Aug., 1919, Appendix to Notes, Intercepted or Captured Documents.
[18] *Ibid.,* For. Sec. F, Nos. 1–235, July, 1919, No. 12, Chief Commissioner, Peshawar, Telegram P 1240-R, May 4, 1919.
[19] *Ibid.,* No. 19.
[20] *Ibid.,* No. 7.
[21] *Ibid.,* No. 9, Telegram P 574-S, May 4, 1919.
[22] I.O., Memoranda Nos. A 177, A 183.
[23] *Ibid.*
[24] *Ibid.*
[25] N.A.I., Home and Pol. A Dept., Nos. 255–281, Sept., 1919, No. 280.
[26] *Ibid.,* For. Sec., Nos. 1–200B, Aug., 1919, No. 16, May 10, 1919.
[27] *Ibid.,* No. 11, Telegram P 6623, May 15, 1919.
[28] *Ibid.,* No. 15, Telegram P 2053, May 17, 1919.
[29] *Ibid.,* No. 20, Telegram P 698-S, May 21, 1919.
[30] *Ibid.,* Telegram P 680-S, May 18, 1919.
[31] *Ibid.,* No. 18, Telegram P 1412-R, May 21, 1919.
[32] *Ibid.,* Telegram P and R 702-S, May 21, 1919.
[33] *Ibid.,* No. 66, Telegram P 2138, May 23, 1919.
[34] I.O., Parliamentary Papers, *Afghanistan,* Hostilities, 1919, No. 16, p. 10.
[35] N.A.I., For. Fron. B, Nos. 92–101, Sept., 1919, No. 41, Telegram P 721-S, May 23, 1919; I.O., Memo No. A 179. Some of the early Soviet-Afghan correspondence is given in L. B. Teplinskiy, *Sovetsko-Afganskiye Otnosheniya, 1919–1960* (Moscow, 1961), pp. 165 ff.
[36] N.A.I., For. Fron. B, Nos. 92–101, Sept., 1919, No. 72, Telegram P and R, May 24, 1919; Telegram P 801-S, June 4, 1919.
[37] *Ibid.,* For. Sec., Nos. 1–200B, Aug., 1919, Nos. 23, 47; For. Fron. B, Nos. 81–83, Oct., 1915, Notes.
[38] *Ibid.,* For. Sec. F, Nos. 1–235, July, 1919, No. 34.
[39] *Ibid.,* No. 189.
[40] *Ibid.,* For. Sec. Nos. 1–200B, Aug. 1919, No. 136, Telegram P 11-S, May 31, 1919.
[41] *Ibid.,* No. 134.

[42] *Ibid.*, No. 147.
[43] *Ibid.*, No. 148.
[44] *Ibid.*, For. Sec. F, Nos. 705–806, Oct., 1920, No. 723, Notes.
[45] *Ibid.*
[46] *Ibid.*
[47] *Ibid.*, For. Fron. B, Nos. 1–200B, Aug., 1919, No. 42, Telegram P and R 685-S, May 19, 1919, Intercepted Documents.
[48] *Ibid.*, For. Sec. F, Nos. 705–806, Oct., 1920, No. 721, Notes.
[49] Amanullah had continued the boycott of the British railroad terminal at Chaman which was begun by Abdur Rahman.
[50] N.A.I., For. Sec. F, Nos. 705–806, Oct., 1920, No. 721, Notes.
[51] *Ibid.*, For. Fron. B, Nos. 92–101, Sept., 1919, Telegram P and R 792-S, June 2, 1919. Cf. I.O., Parliamentary Papers, *Afghanistan,* Hostilities, 1919, No. 51, p. 27.
[52] N.A.I., For. Fron. B, Nos. 201–420, Aug., 1919, No. 264; text in Telegram P and R 69-S, June 14, 1919.
[53] *Ibid.*, No. 277.
[54] *Ibid.*, June 19, 1919.
[55] *Ibid.*, No. 396, July 4, 1919.
[56] *Ibid.*, For. Sec. F, Nos. 705–806, Oct. 1920, Nos. 723, 730, Notes.
[57] *Ibid.*
[58] *Ibid.*, For. Fron. B, Nos. 201–420, Aug., 1919, No. 360, Telegram 954-S, June 29, 1919.
[59] *Ibid.*
[60] *Ibid.*, No. 415, Telegram P 9174, July 7, 1919.
[61] *Ibid.*
[62] *Ibid.*, Nos. 18–191, Oct., 1919, No. 50, July 16, 1919.
[63] G. N. Molesworth, *Afghanistan 1919* (New York, 1962), gives a good but not unbiased account of the military operations during the Third Afghan War.
[64] N.A.I., For. Fron. B, No. 18–191, Oct., 1919, No. 73, Telegram P 1066-S, July 20, 1919.
[65] *Ibid.*, No. 81.
[66] *Ibid.*, Nos. 13–191, Oct., 1919, No. 77.
[67] *Ibid.*, For. Sec. F, Nos. 6–195, Sept., 1919, No. 132.
[68] *Ibid.*, No. 112, Telegram P 2962-R, July 25, 1919.
[69] The British negotiators at the Rawalpindi conference were Sir Hamilton Grant, chief British representative; Captain Gillies-Reyburn, aide-de-camp to chief; J. L. Maffrey, political adviser; Brigadier General F. J. Moberley, military adviser; Nawab Sir Shams Shah, Muslim representative; Baba Sir Gurbakhsh Singh, Sikh representative; Major C. P. Paige, assistant to military adviser; G. Cunningham, secretary; Nawab Maula Bakhsh, in charge of general arrangements; Khan Bahadur Mozaffar Khan, in charge of Afghan party.

The Afghan negotiators at the conference were Ali Ahmad Khan, commissary for Home Affairs, president; Civil General Sardar Muhammad Yunus Khan; Ghulam Muhammad Khan, commissary for Commerce; Civil Colonel Abdul Aziz Khan, late Afghan envoy; Muhammad Rafiq Khan, superintendent of correspondence (replaced by Sardar Abdur Rahman Khan, late Afghan envoy); Dr. Abdul Ghani, chief of compilation department; Civil Colonel Divan Niranjan Das, head tax department; Abdul Hadi Khan, chief clerk; Civil Colonel Mirza Ghulam Muhammad Khan, Mir Munshi.

Ali Ahmad had accompanied Inayatullah and Habibullah to India in 1905 and 1907, respectively. He was arrested by the soldiers in Jalalabad after the Amir's murder because he made a speech recognizing Nasrullah as amir. Released by Amanullah.

Muhammad Yunus Khan was with Habibullah in India in 1907. He was governor of Kandahar in 1913. He had been sent from Jalalabad to Kabul to induce Amanullah to renounce the throne; he was temporarily detained.

Abdul Aziz was Afghan envoy in India in 1915–1919.

Muhammad Rafiq Khan lived in Indian exile until 1904; later he accompanied Habibullah to India.

Abdul Ghani was director of public instruction in Afghanistan and principal of Habibiya College. Arrested in 1909 in connection with the plot on Habibullah's life, he was released by Amanullah in March, 1919.

Ghulam Muhammad Khan was the brother of the Afghan postmaster in Peshawar.

See N.A.I., For. Sec. F, Nos. 201–422, Aug., 1919, No. 270.

[70] *Ibid.*, For. Fron. B, Nos. 6–195, Sept., 1919, No. 129, Telegram P and R 1101-S, July 29, 1919.

[71] *Ibid.*, Nos. 15–138, Oct., 1919, No. 26.

[72] *Ibid.*

[73] *Ibid.*, No. 39.

[74] *Ibid.*

[75] *Ibid.*, Nos. 6–195, Sept., 1919, No. 137, Telegram P 29-PC, July 30, 1919.

[76] *Ibid.*, Telegram P and R 1101-S, July 29, 1919.

[77] *Ibid.*, Nos. 15–138, Oct., 1919, No. 78.

[78] *Ibid.*

[79] *Ibid.*, Nos. 6–195, Sept., 1919, No. 176, Telegram P 61-PC, Aug. 5, 1919.

[80] *Ibid.*, No. 168, Telegram P and R 1123-S, Aug. 4, 1919.

[81] *Ibid.*, No. 173, Telegram P, Aug. 5, 1919.

[82] *Ibid.*, Nos. 15–138, Oct., 1919, No. 128. See also App. I, no. 10; C. U. Aitchison, *Treaties, Engagements and Sanads* (Calcutta, 1933), XIII, 286–288.

[83] N.A.I., For. Pol. Sec. F, Nos. 15–138, Oct., 1919, No. 128.

[84] *Ibid.*, Nos. 6–195, Sept., 1919, No. 25.

[85] *Ibid.*, Nos. 18–191, Oct., 1919, No. 30.

[86] *Ibid.*, No. 70.

[87] *Ibid.*, No. 181.

[88] *Ibid.*, No. 127.

[89] *Ibid.*, No. 132.

[90] *Ibid.*, Nos. 151, 184.

[91] *Ibid.*, No. 155.

[92] *Ibid.*, Nos. 15–138, Oct., 1919, No. 108, Sept. 6, 1919, Report by Sir H. Grant.

Chapter 7

[1] N.A.I., Foreign and Political Secret F, Nos. 18-191, Oct., 1919, No. 141. Cf. I.O., Memo No. A 190.

[2] N.A.I., For. Pol. Sec. F, Nos. 18-191, Oct., 1919, No. 141.

[3] I.O., Memo No. A 190.

[4] Ibid.

[5] N.A.I., For. Sec. F, Nos. 317-550, Oct., 1920, No. 324, Notes.

[6] Ibid., No. 329.

[7] Ibid.

[8] Ibid., No. 330, Notes.

[9] Ibid., No. 340.

[10] I.O., Memo No. A 190.

[11] Nasrullah, who was imprisoned in Kabul, contrived to send a messenger to the British Agent of Khaybar, urging the British to continue the war and advance upon Kabul. Nasrullah promised, if he was restored to power, to cede large areas of Afghanistan to the British (N.A.I., For. Sec. F, Nos. 6-195, Sept., 1919, Nos. 49, 57).

[12] Ibid., Nos. 317-550, Oct., 1920, No. 341.

[13] Ibid., No. 343.

[14] Ibid., No. 353.

[15] Ibid.

[16] Ibid., No. 355, Notes.

[17] Ibid., No. 356, Notes.

[18] Ibid.

[19] Ibid., Nos. 357, 358.

[20] Ibid., No. 363.

[21] Ibid., No. 368, Notes.

[22] Ibid., No. 377, Notes.

[23] In addition to the Foreign Minister, the delegation included Ghulam Muhammad, minister of Commerce; Abdul Hadi, officer in charge of Frontier Affairs; Divan Niranjan Das; Finance member; and Colonel Pir Muhammad (ibid., No. 380).

[24] Ibid., Nos. 201-422, Aug., 1919, No. 281. Cf. L. B. Teplinskiy, *Sovetsko-Afganskiye Otnosheniya, 1919-1960* (Moscow, 1961).

[25] I.O., Memo No. A 187, Bolshevism in Central Asia and Afghanistan. Barakatullah was interviewed in Moscow by a reporter from *Isvestia* on May 8, 1919, and gave his impressions of Afghanistan (N.A.I., For. Sec. F, Nos. 77-171, Feb., 1920, No. 142).

[26] I.O., Memo No. A 184, p. 10; *Times* (London), Oct. 15, 1919.

[27] I.O., Memo No. A 184, p. 10.

[28] Ibid.

[29] Ibid.

[30] Ibid.; *Times* (London), Nov. 2, 1919.

[31] N.A.I., For. Sec. F, Nos. 77-171, Feb., 1920, No. 109.

[32] Ibid., No. 161, Notes.

[33] I.O., Memo No. A 187. Bravin later defected and remained in Afghanistan where he was later assassinated.

NOTES TO PP. 144-151   231

³⁴ N.A.I., For. Sec. F, Nos. 77-171, Feb., 1920, No. 151.
³⁵ *Ibid.*, No. 153, Notes.
³⁶ *Ibid.*, No. 142, Notes.
³⁷ *Ibid.*, No. 160.
³⁸ *Ibid.*, No. 159.
³⁹ *Ibid.*, No. 113.
⁴⁰ *Ibid.*, No. 167. Malleson was sent to Transcaspia to intercept Turco-German missions to Afghanistan and to assist anti-Bolshevik forces. After he received orders to withdraw from Russian soil, he remained in Meshed and attempted to foil Russo-Afghan cooperation by telling each side about the perfidy of the other (Sir Wilfred Malleson, "The British Military Mission to Turkestan, 1919-1920," *Journal of Central Asian Studies*, 9 [Jan. 24, 1922], pt. 1, pp. 96 ff.).
⁴¹ I.O., Memo No. A 184, Afghan Aggression, No. 14597.
⁴² *Ibid.*, Pan-Islam, 14920 M, Oct. 30, 1919.
⁴³ *Ibid.*
⁴⁴ I.O., Memo No. A 184, Afghan Missions to Bokhara and Khiva, No. 12418, Sept. 9, 1919.
⁴⁵ *Ibid.*, Memo No. A 185, Bolshevik Missions to Kabul, No. 15338 M, Nov. 9, 1919.
⁴⁶ *Ibid.*, No. 15500 M, Nov. 14, 1919.
⁴⁷ *Ibid.*, Memo No. A 187.
⁴⁸ *Ibid.*
⁴⁹ N.A.I., For. Sec. F, Nos. 1-18, Dec., 1920, No. 2. Cf. Nos. 1-582, Nov., 1920, No. 209.
⁵⁰ Malleson Intelligence Report, Moscow to Bogoyavlenski, Tashkent (*ibid.*, Nos. 77-171, Feb., 1920, No. 98).
⁵¹ *Ibid.*, Nos. 1-18, Dec., 1920, No. 14.
⁵² *Ibid.*, No. 16.
⁵³ *Ibid.*, For. External B, No. 23, Dec., 1920, p. 43, Malleson, Telegram P MD, 3099, Jan., 1920.
⁵⁴ *Ibid.*, For. Sec. F, Nos. 18-191, Oct., 1919, No. 155.
⁵⁵ I.O., Memo No. A 190, No. 14.
⁵⁶ N.A.I., For. Fron. B, Nos. 15-138, Oct., 1919, No. 131.
⁵⁷ *Ibid.*, For. Sec. F, Nos. 317-550, Oct., 1920, No. 368.
⁵⁸ *Ibid.*, No. 402.
⁵⁹ *Ibid.*, No. 406.
⁶⁰ Dobbs's assistants were S. E. Pears, revenue commissioner of Peshawar; Lieutenant-Colonel S. F. Musprat, General Staff, India; and Nawab Sir Abdul Kayyum. The Afghan Foreign Minister's council included Ghulam Muhammad Khan, minister of Commerce; Abdul Hadi Khan, Foreign Department; Divan Niranjan Das, Finance member; and Colonel Pir Muhammad (see I.O., Memo No. A 190; cf. N.A.I., For. Sec. F, Nos. 317-550, Oct., 1920, Nos. 379, 380).
⁶¹ N.A.I., For. Sec. F, Nos. 317-550, Oct., 1920, No. 405.
⁶² *Ibid.*, No. 409.
⁶³ *Ibid.*, No. 415.
⁶⁴ *Ibid.*
⁶⁵ *Ibid.*, No. 431.

⁶⁶ *Ibid.*, No. 434.
⁶⁷ *Ibid.*, No. 439.
⁶⁸ *Ibid.*, No. 453.
⁶⁹ *Ibid.*
⁷⁰ *Ibid.*
⁷¹ *Ibid.*, No. 447, Notes.
⁷² *Ibid.*, Home and Political Department, Deposit No. 11, May, 1920.
⁷³ *Ibid.*, For. Sec. F, Nos. 317–550, Oct., 1920, No. 455.
⁷⁴ *Ibid.*, No. 470.
⁷⁵ *Ibid.*, No. 462.
⁷⁶ *Ibid.*, No. 476.
⁷⁷ *Ibid.*
⁷⁸ *Ibid.*, No. 502.
⁷⁹ *Ibid.*, No. 525.
⁸⁰ *Ibid.*, Nos. 1–147, Jan., 1921, No. 27.
⁸¹ *Ibid.*, No. 35.
⁸² *Ibid.*, No. 55.
⁸³ *Ibid.*, No. 49.
⁸⁴ *Ibid.*, No. 56.
⁸⁵ I.O., Memo No. A 190, pp. 9–10.
⁸⁶ N.A.I., For. Sec. F, Nos. 1–147, Jan., 1921, Nos. 86, 86a.
⁸⁷ *Ibid.*, No. 86, Notes.
⁸⁸ *Ibid.*, No. 107, Notes.
⁸⁹ I.O., Memo No. A 190, pp. 8–9.
⁹⁰ *Ibid.*, For the text of the *aide-mémoire*, see App. II, no. 7.
⁹¹ I.O., Memo No. A 190, p. 9.
⁹² N.A.I., For. Sec. File 224-F, Nos. 1–22, 1923, No. 1.
⁹³ *Ibid.*; I.O., Memo No. A 190, p. 10.
⁹⁴ *Ibid.*
⁹⁵ *Ibid.*
⁹⁶ *Ibid.*
⁹⁷ *Ibid.*
⁹⁸ *Ibid.*
⁹⁹ N.A.I., For. Sec. File 224-F, Nos. 1–22, 1923.
¹⁰⁰ The purpose behind such a move on the part of the government of India was to allay the fears the Amir might have had that action against the tribes was really the beginning of an invasion of Afghanistan. By informing the Amir of prospective military actions, India impaired the effectiveness of her forces, for the Amir would lose no time in informing the tribes of the British intentions.
¹⁰¹ N.A.I., For. Sec. File 502-F, Nos. 1–3. 1923, Summary of Events, 1920–1924.
¹⁰² See Afghan-Italian Treaty, App. I, no. 15.
¹⁰³ Omitting the *s* in the name "Dobbs," *Jenāb-i dobb* meant "this is for the bear."
¹⁰⁴ See App. I, no. 12.
¹⁰⁵ W. K. Fraser-Tytler, *Afghanistan* (London, 1950), p. 199.
¹⁰⁶ N.A.I., For Sec. File 224-F, Nos. 1–22, 1923, No. 2.

Bibliography

Bibliography

ARCHIVAL SOURCES

NATIONAL ARCHIVES OF INDIA, NEW DELHI, INDIA

Foreign and Political Proceedings and Consultations (1880–1923). These files contain all the correspondence of Britain, India, and Afghanistan. Most important are the Notes, which include Précis, Memoranda, Résumés, Keep-withs, and other material not found anywhere in England.

Record of Intelligence Party. Afghan Boundary Commission. Vols. 1, 2: Diary of Major Maitland; vol. 3: Diary of Captain Peacocke and Report on Passes over the Range North of Herat Valley; vol. 5: Miscellaneous Reports and table of corrected elevations. Simla: Government Central Press, 1888.

Report on the Tour in Afghanistan of H. M. Amir Habibullah, 1907. Faqir Saiyid Iftikhar-ud-Din. Simla: Government Central Press, 1908.

Military Report on Afghanistan, 1914. General Staff Branch.

The Fall of Amanullah. R. N. G. Scott. IV, No. 86, Secret 44. Archives Library.

Biographical Accounts of the Chiefs, Sardars and Others in Afghanistan, 1888. No. 53, Category III. Archives Library.

Summary of Events in Afghanistan. Compiled by the General Staff. Vol. 1: June 1, 1920, to July 1, 1922; vol. 2: July 1, 1922, to June 30, 1923; vol. 3: July 1, 1923, to June 30, 1924.

INDIA OFFICE, LONDON

Political and Secret Subject Files. Afghanistan, Iran, Turkey, and India. 1900–1922.

Political and Secret Department Memoranda, 1898–1923. Vol. 2, Bound Collections, A 146–194.

Private Papers

Amir Habibullah. Specimen of letters in German and Hindi. MSS Eur. E. 204.

Lord Curzon Collection. Correspondence and Papers of George Nathaniel Curzon, Marquis Curzon of Kedleston. 3 secs. MSS Eur. F. 111.

Sir Louis Dane Collection. Correspondence and Papers of Sir Louis Dane. MSS Eur. D. 659.

Parliamentary Papers

Battles. Official names of battles fought by Military Forces of the British Empire, 1914–1918, and in the Third Afghan War. Vol. XX, p. 593, no. 1138.

Afghanistan. Papers regarding hostilities, 1919. Proclamation of Amir Amanullah Khan. Vol. XXXVII, p. 1183, no. 324, F. 837.

Anglo-Afghan Trade Convention, Kabul, June 5, 1923. Vol. XXV, p. 17, no. 1977, F. 876.

Treaty between the British and Afghan Governments. Treaty Series No. 19 (1922). Vol. XXV, p. 7, no. 1786, F. 870.

Convention between Great Britain and Russia. Vol. CXXV, pp. 477, 489, no. 3750, F. 680.

DEUTSCHES AUSWÄRTIGE AMT, BONN, GERMANY

Akten des Auswärtigen Amtes, Abt. A. (Microfilm Depository, University of Michigan, Ann Arbor).

Weltkrieg Nr. 11e. Unternehmungen und Aufwiegelungen gegen unsere Feinde in Afghanistan und Persien. Bände 1 bis 32.

Entwürfe von Allerh. Handschreiben an den Emir von Afghanistan und an indische Fürsten.

Unternehmungen und Aufwiegelungen gegen unsere Feinde in Afghanistan und Persien. Besetzung der Oelfelder am Karunfluss.

Afghanistan 1. Allgemeine Angelegenheiten. Bände 1 bis 18.

Persien, Afghanistan und Indien. Band 30.

OESTERREICHISCHES HOF UND STAATSARCHIV

Liasse Krieg, 1914–1918. Claar [journalist] Berichte, 1915–1918. I/850–865.

Englisch-russisches Abkommen, 1907. VIII/175.

Englands Haltung, 1914–1918. I/823–828.

Beteiligung Oesterreich-Ungarns und Deutschlands an der Reorganization der Türkei, 1914–1918. XII/467.

Haltung der Türkei, 1914–1918. I/941–948.

AFGHAN REFERENCE WORKS

Afghān Qāmūs. 'Abd Allāh Afghānī Nawīs. Pashtu Academy. Kabul: Government Printing Press, 1958. 3 vols.

Aryāna Dā'erat al-Ma'āref. Kabul: Anjuman-i-Dā'erat al Ma'āref, 1950–1962. 4 vols.: Alif-Jim.

Lughāt-i-'Amyāne-ye-Fārsī-ye-Afghānistān. 'Abd Allāh Afghānī Nawīs. Kabul, 1337/1959.

Mu'ārefī-ye Rūznāme-hā, Jarāyed, Majalāt-i-Afghānistān. Māyl Harawī. Kabul, 1341/1963.

Negāhī be-Adabiyāt-i-Mu'āser dar Afghānistān. Muḥammad Haydar Zhūbel. Kabul, 1337–1959.

Qāmūs-i-Jughrāfiyā-ye-Afghānistān. Kabul: Aryāna Dā'erat al-Ma'āref, 1340/1962. 4 vols.

Sālnāme-ye-Majale-ye-Kābul (later named *Da Afghānistān Kālanī*). Kabul, 1311/1933–1343/1965.

AFGHAN NEWSPAPERS

Sirāj al-Akhbār (Kabul), 1911–1918.
Ittihād-i-Mashriqī (Nangrahar), 1920.
Amān-i-Afghān (Kabul), 1919–1923.

BOOKS AND ARTICLES

Aitchison, C. U. *Treaties, Engagements and Sanads.* Vol. XIII: Persia and Afghanistan. Calcutta, 1933.
Caroe, Olaf. *The Pathans, 550 B.C.–A.D. 1957.* London, 1958.
Central Asian Research Centre. *Bibliography of Recent Soviet Source Material on Soviet Central Asia and the Borderlands.* London, 1957–1962.
Degras, Jane T. *Soviet Documents of Foreign Policy.* London, 1948. 3 vols.
Dvoryankov, N. A., et al. *Sovremennyy Afganistan.* Moscow, 1960.
Ellis, C. H. *The British "Intervention" in Transcaspia, 1918–1919.* Los Angeles, 1963.
Fletcher, Arnold. *Afghanistan: Highroad of Conquest.* Ithaca, N.Y., 1965.
Fraser-Tytler, W. K. *Afghanistan.* London, 1950.
Gehrke, Ulrich. *Persien in der Deutschen Orientpolitik während des Ersten Weltkrieges.* Stuttgart, n.d. Band 1 (I, II).
Ghose, Dilip Kumar. *England and Afghanistan.* Calcutta, 1960.
Gregorian, Vartan. "The Emergence of Modern Afghanistan: Politics of Modernization, 1880–1930." Unpublished Ph.D. dissertation. Stanford University, June, 1964.
Griesinger, W. *German Intrigues in Persia, Afghanistan, and India.* London, 1918.
Habberton, William. *Anglo-Russian Relations Concerning Afghanistan, 1837–1907.* Urbana, Ill., 1937.
Hamilton, Angus. *Afghanistan.* London and New York, 1906.
Hentig, Werner Otto von. *Mein Leben eine Dienstreise.* Göttingen, 1963.
Hoetzsch, Otto. *Documente aus den Archiven der Zaristischen und der Provisorischen Regierung.* Berlin, 1934.
Humlum, Johannes. *La géographie de l'Afghanistan.* Copenhagen, 1959.
Ikbal Ali Shah. "Afghanistan and the German Threat," *Edinburgh Review* (New York), 22 (1918) 59–72.
Kapur, Harish. *Soviet Russia and Asia, 1917–1927.* Geneva, 1966.
Khalfin, N. A. *Proval Britanskoy Agressii v Afganistane.* Moscow, 1959.
———, *Soviet Historiography on the Development of the Afghan State in the XVIII–XX Centuries.* Moscow, 1960.
Klimburg, Max. *Afghanistan: Das Land im historischen Spannungsfeld Mittelasiens.* Vienna, 1966.
Malleson, Sir Wilfred. "The British Military Mission to Turkestan, 1918–1920," *Journal of Central Asian Studies,* 9 (Jan. 24, 1922), pt. 1.
Masson, W. M., and Romodin, W. A. *Istoriia Afganistana.* Moscow, 1964.
Minto, Mary, Countess of. *India, Minto and Morley, 1905–1910.* London, 1934.
Mir Munshi, Sultan Mahomed Khan, ed. *The Life of Abdur Rahman.* London, 1900. 2 vols.
Molesworth, G. N. *Afghanistan 1919.* New York, 1962.

Niedermayer, Oskar von. *Im Weltkrieg vor Indiens Toren*. Hamburg, 1942.
O'Dwyer, Sir Michael. *India as I Knew It, 1885–1925*. London, 1925.
Pikulin, M. G. *Afganistan: Ekonomicheskiy Ocherk*. Tashkent, 1956.
Pratap, Mahendra. "My German Mission to High Asia," *Asia*, XXV (May, 1925), 382–455.
Rastogi, R. S. *Indo-Afghan Relations, 1880–1900*. Lucknow, 1965.
Rhein, Eberhard, and A. Ghanie Ghaussy. *Die wirtschaftliche Entwicklung Afghanistans, 1880–1965*. Opladen, 1966.
Ronaldshay, Earl of. *The Life of Lord Curzon*. London, 1928.
Samra, Chattar Singh. *India and Anglo-Soviet Relations, 1917–1947*. Bombay, 1959.
Schwager, Joseph. *Die Entwicklung Afghanistans als Staat und seine zwischenstaatliche Beziehungen*. Leipzig, 1939.
Singhal, D. P. *India and Afghanistan, 1876–1907*. St. Lucia, Queensland, 1963.
Spain, James. *The Pathan Borderland*. The Hague, 1963.
Sykes, Sir Percy. *A History of Afghanistan*. Vol. II. London, 1940.
Teplinskiy, L. B. *Sovetsko-Afganskiye Otnosheniya, 1919–1960*. Moscow, 1961.
Wilber, D. N. *Afghanistan*. New Haven, 1962.
———. *Annotated Bibliography of Afghanistan*. New Haven, 1962.

Index

Index

Abdul Hadi, 155
Abdul Kayyum, 112, 151–153
Abdul Kuddus Khan, 4, 10, 52, 61, 75, 91, 104, 151; corresponds with British, 125–126; incites tribes, 125; moves troops to Kandahar, 111, 120, 122
Abdul Majid Khan, 103
Abdur Rahman, 3, 4, 14–16, 24–25, 28, 30, 37, 39, 43, 47, 62, 63, 76–77, 79, 96, 101, 117; and subsidy, 19; as Absolute Amir, 7; as nation builder, 19; death of, 28; letter of, to Griffin, 172; policy of, 2, 17, 18, 20, 23–25; rise to power of, 23; views neighbors, 24
Afghan agents: in Bukhara, 18, 32; in India, 21, 40, 52, 66–67, 111, 114–117, 124, 127, 138, 150; in Meshed, 71; in Peshawar, 113, 119, 124
Afghanistan: as buffer state, 5, 17, 42; economic self-sufficiency of, 6; foreign policy of, 17, 18; topography of, 4
Afridis, 78, 79, 97–99, 117–118, 124, 128, 140
Aga Khan, 116
Ahmad Shah, 1
Aide-mémoire: for Louis Dane, 46–48; presented by Dobbs to Amanullah, 205–208
Ali Ahmad Khan, 121, 182; at Rawalpindi, 126–128, 132; offers peace conditions, 128–129; protests bombings, 127–128; signs treaty, 130
Aman-i-Afghan, 163
Amanullah, 4, 7, 90, 115, 118, 119, 133–135, 139; and Afghan War, 114, 117–122, 126, 133; aspirations of, 111; assumes power, 108; grievances of, 114; letter to Chelmsford, 109–110; letter to Grant, 136; letter to Lenin, 116; policy of, 139–140; proclamation of, 210–212; protests bombings, 117; punishes assassins, 109
Ampthill, Lord: on British agent in Kabul, 217 n. 35; on Dane Mission, 40–45
Anglo-Afghan Agreements (1880–1893), 7, 16, 28–31, 39, 47, 50, 52, 61
Anglo-Afghan Treaty of 1921, 167
Anglo-Afghan Wars: First (1839–1842), 1; Second (1878–1879), 1, 39; Third (1919), 4, 7, 108, 165, 167; causes of Third War, 109, 113, 122–123, 127, 133–135
Anglo-Iranian Agreement of 1919, 155
Anglo-Persian engagements (1853, 1857), 216 n. 6
Anglo-Russian Convention of 1907, 67, 68–74 *passim*, 80, 82, 134, 204; Afghan reaction to, 73–76
Arms and ammunition: British aid in, 161; British prohibit import of, 31, 39, 130, 182; German aid in, 90, 179; import of, 16, 19, 54, 57–58, 63, 78, 120, 123, 163, 165, 177, 185–186, 207; Soviet aid in, 143–144; stealing of, 78–79
Auckland, Lord, 1
Ayyub Khan, 4, 16, 19, 218 n. 5

Bagh, 112; occupied by Afghans, 113
Bagh-i-Baber, 89
Balfour, 60; on Afghan army, 51

INDEX

Balkan War, 80, 81
Baluchistan, 123
Barakatullah, 89, 98, 100, 142, 144–145, 223 n. 10; as prime minister of India, 148; in Moscow, 144–145
Basmachis, 167
Benckendorff, Count, 67, 68, 81
Bethmann-Hollweg, 199, 200
Bibi Halima, 4, 91
Bogoyavlenski, 143
Bolshevik mission to Kabul, 137, 144. *See also* Soviet Russia
Boundary of Afghanistan: demarcation of, 79, 129, 131, 132, 176, 177, 183, 184; question of, 137; Russo-Afghan, 32, 36, 44
Bravin, K., 144, 230 n. 33
Bray, Denys, 97, 104–106, 119, 120
British, 1, 2, 5, 7, 8, 14; aerial bombings, 122; agent at Kabul, 15, 20, 21, 48, 52, 62, 63, 71, 72, 75–78, 89, 91, 92, 95, 97, 99, 100, 104, 109, 110, 120, 124, 132, 172, 174, 217 n. 35; demands from Afghanistan, 3, 4, 6; forward policy, 15, 17, 24, 25, 29–31; troops, 22, 23
Buffer state, 5, 17, 42
Bukhara, 18, 32, 98, 140, 144, 146, 149, 153, 155, 161, 190, 192, 231 n. 44; Amir of, 153, 157, 167; conference at, 146; Revolutionary State of, 163; Young Bukhara party, 144
Butler, S. H., 76

Caliphate (Khalifate), 100, 128, 134, 140, 149, 153, 155, 192
Central Asia, 1, 166
Central Asian Federation, 106
Central Powers, 83, 85, 86, 90, 94, 96, 104
Chaman, 29, 56, 98, 120, 123, 126, 151, 176, 177, 228 n. 49; boycott of, 120, 228 n. 49
Char Bagh, 146
Chelmsford, Lord, 99, 105, 109–110, 112, 114, 116, 120–122, 124–125, 129, 137–139, 141, 147–149, 156, 157; letters of, to Amanullah, 112, 120, 122, 124, 139, 156, 209–210; on policy for Mussoorie, 120, 121, 124–125, 129, 137–139, 141, 148–149; on reward for Habibullah, 105; suggests Anglo-Russian treaty, 147
Chicherin, G. V., 142, 188
Clarke, E. H. S., 38, 45, 51, 56–57, 63, 66, 69, 71
Communism, 127
Council of Advisers, 8, 55, 76
Curzon, Lord, 22, 28–29, 30–31, 35, 37, 39–41, 51–54, 57–59, 62, 63, 65, 72, 79, 136, 163–164; on Afghan treaty, 51–54, 57, 58; on Habibullah succession, 28–29

Dakka, 64, 111, 113, 128, 131; in Afghan War, 114, 117, 119, 122–124
Dane, Louis W., 35, 36, 39–64 *passim*; mission of, 65, 66, 68, 76, 77, 125, 129, 178, 215 n. 19, 220 n. 31
Dobbs, Sir Henry: at Kabul, 160–162, 164; and members of mission, 231 n. 60; and mission of 1903, 3, 36–37; at Mussoorie, 149–156 *passim*; suggests meeting, 137–138; with Dane mission, 50
Dufferin, Lord, 22, 23, 24
Durand Agreement of 1893, 23, 37–40, 58, 61, 79, 175–177
Durand Line, 131

Economy of Afghanistan, 6, 7, 9,
Edward VII, 58, 66
Egypt, 112
Elgin, Lord, 79
Enver Pasha, 83, 90, 160, 167

Ferghana, 140, 148, 149, 153
France, 193

George V, 91–93, 136, 205
Germany, 67, 83, 88, 117, 159, 160; Afghan treaties with, 93–94, 106, 201–204; Foreign Office of, 94, 96, 103
Ghazni, 147, 159, 189, 207
Ghilzay, 113
Ghulam Muhammad Khan, 149, 152, 153

INDEX 243

Ghulam Nabi, 131
Ghulam Sadiq, 188
Grant, A. H., 50, 88, 91, 97, 132–133, 136, 137, 182; at Rawalpindi, 126–130 *passim;* on policy, 137, 140; on the *Serāj al-Akhbār,* 102; on the tribes, 98, 126
Granville-Gorchakoff Agreement, 15, 67
Grey, Sir Edward, 67
Griffin, Lepel, 14, 20, 171, 173

Habibullah, 4, 7, 8, 28–30, 37, 108, 119, 126, 133, 136, 201, 204, 208, 209; accession of, 28, 30; British bomb tomb of, 117; Dane Mission to, 30, 37, 40, 49, 50; death of, 107, 208; policy of, 54, 81, 86, 87, 91–93, 95, 100, 101, 105
Haig, T. W., 87–88
Hardinge, Lord, 67, 85, 86, 87, 99
Hayatullah, 209–211
Hejaz revolt, 100
Helmand, 123
Hentig, Otto von, 85, 89, 93–94, 103, 180, 181, 199, 200, 201; members of group, 223 n. 11, 225 n. 60
Herat, 4, 5, 14, 18, 23, 35, 36, 47, 55–56, 60, 88, 98, 104, 146, 172, 173, 175, 182, 189, 216 n. 2; governor of, 34–36, 40, 87, 88, 89; Shrine custodians of, 146
Hijrat movement, 155, 158
Hindu Kush, 4, 5, 14
Hindustani Fanatics, 116
Holy Places, 112
Humphrys, F., 149

Inayatullah, 61, 90, 108, 109, 209–211
India, 94, 101, 112; Provisional Government of, 148; revolutionaries of, 137
Isolationism, 20, 22, 23
Isvolsky, 68
Ittihād-i-Mashriqī, 141

Jalalabad, 29, 107, 108, 147, 184, 207, 209, 211; bombed, 117; war moves to, 113, 114, 116, 117, 122

Jamshidis, 80
Japan, 40, 42, 47, 50, 52; Russo-Japanese War, 40, 68, 101
Jemal Pasha, 155, 159–160, 164
Jihad (holy war), 6, 7, 8, 52, 88, 90, 95, 98–100, 112, 116, 117, 119, 126, 139, 146; explained by Abdur Rahman, 24, 27

Kabul, 97, 114, 161; mission to, 157, 159–161, 163, 165, 167
Kafiristan, 123
Kandahar, 5, 14, 19, 29, 56, 60, 100, 114, 122, 147, 159, 161, 171, 184, 189, 207
Karahan, L. M., 188
Kazim Bey, 85, 89, 142, 144, 223 n. 11
Khiva, 140, 153, 161, 190, 192, 231 n. 44
Khutbah, 153
Khyber (Khaibar), 48, 113, 123, 166; Rifles, 111, 115
Kitchener, Lord, 37, 41–43, 45, 57, 66, 69
Klein, Captain, 84
Kolchak, 142, 144
Kuropatkin, A. N., 40
Kurram, 118
Kushk, 128, 140

Lamsdorff, Count, 33, 67
Landi Khana, 111, 112
Landi Kotal, 113
Lansdowne, Lord, 28, 40, 67
Lenin, 116, 142, 143, 190
Loe Jirgah, 8, 91
Lytton, Lord, 14

Maconchy, E. W. S. K., 30
Mahendra, Pratap, 85, 89, 100, 101, 145, 148, 199, 200, 223 n. 10
McMahon, A. H., 31, 65, 66, 73, 218 n. 14
Maffey, John, 118–119, 131
Mahsuds, 73, 98, 99, 117, 118, 152, 154, 158
Majlis-i-Shura, 90
Malleson, Major General, 116, 145, 231 n. 40

244 INDEX

Maymana (Meimane), 49, 64, 146, 189
Maywand, Battle of, 16
Mazar-i-Sharif, 49, 64, 146, 189
Merv, 145
Meshed, 18
Military aid to Afghanistan, 139, 158, 161
Minto, Lord, 65, 70–73, 76, 79–80
Mohmands, 48, 63, 72, 79, 80, 97, 118, 124, 128
Mornington, Lord, 1
Muhammad Wali Khan, 110, 142, 143, 162, 164, 188, 191–194, 197
Mullahs, 7, 8, 66, 67, 82, 90, 100
Musahiban, 108, 109
Mussoorie Conference, 3, 136, 141, 148–151, 154, 205
Mustafa Kemal Ataturk, 155, 159

Nabokoff, C., 88
Nadir Khan, 10, 90, 109, 111, 113, 117, 122, 137, 141, 151
Naqib of Baghdad, 81, 116–117
Narimanov, N. N., 142
Nasrullah, 4, 8, 50, 67, 75, 76, 79, 81, 90, 95, 97–99, 103, 108, 109, 179, 181, 200, 209, 210, 217 n. 23, 230 n. 11
Neutrality (bi-tarafi), 106, 168
Newswriters, 54, 62, 64, 72, 77–78, 100, 222 n. 40
Nicholson, Sir A., 68
Niedermeyer, Oskar von, 83–85, 87–90, 93–96, 103, 104, 106, 132, 142, 180, 181, 225 n. 60
North West Frontier (of India), 22, 134, 167
Novoe Vremya, 33, 68, 72

Obeidullah, 123, 148
Orakzais, 99, 117
Ottoman Empire, 68, 77, 81, 101, 133, 141. *See also* Turkey
Oxus River, 17, 55, 57, 60, 82, 125–126, 178

Pan-Islamism, 6, 24–26, 81, 101, 102, 133, 144–146

Panjdeh, 16, 51, 140, 144, 148; Afghans forced out of, 146, 148; Afghans penetrate into, 145
Paschen, Wilhelm, 93
Pathan (Frontier Afghans), 6. *See also* Tribes
Peace Conference: at Paris, 104–106; at Rawalpindi, 126–127, 130. *See also* Rawalpindi Peace Conference
Persia, 14, 25, 31, 68, 80, 85, 94, 101, 102, 110, 149, 155, 174, 179; Persian treaties with: Afghanistan, 194–196; Britain, 142
Peshawar, 18, 22, 113, 119, 122, 148, 149, 155, 187; in the Afghan War, 113, 119, 122; postmaster of, 113, 119
Prideaux, Major, 97

Railways, 29, 46, 57, 74; Afghan boycott of, 22; Afghan opposition to, 5, 22, 23; Afghan desire for, 55, 56, 66, 149; British insistence on, 22, 23, 42, 45, 48, 69, 124, 156; Russian plans for, 22, 42, 68; Soviet Russia suggests, 143
Raskolnikoff, F., 162
Rauf Bey, 84, 85
Rawalpindi, 22; negotiators at, 228–229 n. 69; Peace Conference of, 120, 122–124; Treaty of, 182–183
Representatives of Afghanistan, 45, 47. *See also* Afghan agents
Ripon, Marquess of, 20–21, 174
Roberts, Lord, 23
Roos-Keppel, Sir George, 76, 98–99, 112, 113, 115, 117
Rowlatt Bill, 114, 115, 127
Russia, 1, 5, 7, 8, 14, 18, 19, 50, 70, 94, 98, 174; advances of, 16, 22, 31, 40; Afghan policy toward, 7, 14–15, 50, 53; Japanese war with, 40, 68, 101; memorandum of, 31, 67, 80, 216 n. 5; policy of, 3, 5, 17, 24, 25; pressures Afghanistan for relations, 31–37, 70, 80

Saleh Muhammad, 10, 111, 112, 122
Salisbury, Lord, 31
Samarkand, 47, 88, 98, 146

INDEX 245

Schreiner, Jacob, 104
Secretary of State for India, 30, 45, 46, 58–60, 62, 114–115, 124, 138, 157, 158
Seiler, Captain, 87; diary of, 178–182
Sèvres, Treaty of, 158
Sharif of Mecca, 100
Shiah, 77
Shinwari, chiefs of, 119
Shura, 104
Sirāj al-Akhbār, 8, 81, 82, 100–103, 134; Indian policy on, 101–102
Sistan, 123
Soviet Russia, 116, 119, 163, 174; Afghan Treaty with, 157, 158, 162, 164–165, 188–191; mission of, 143–144; relations opened with, 116, 142–144, 146–147, 162; Revolution of, 104, 105, 133. *See also* Anglo-Russian Convention
Spin Boldak Fort, 122, 125, 126, 131
Subsidy: British, 4, 6–7, 18, 19, 37, 39, 40, 44, 45, 47, 54–58, 63, 88, 91, 106, 120, 123, 124, 129, 130, 139, 155, 156, 158–159, 160–161, 163, 165–166, 174–175, 182, 206, 226 n. 106; of Central Powers, 90, 179; of Soviet Union, 191
Sultan Galiev, 142–143
Sultan of Turkey, 88, 116
Suritz, Z., 146, 148, 155, 157, 162, 164
Sykes, Sir Percy, 61

Talaat Pasha, 160
Tarzi, Mahmud, 3, 8, 19, 81, 90, 100, 101, 103, 111, 116, 120, 132, 136, 141, 149, 150, 151, 153, 164, 222 n. 55
Tashkent, 98
Times of India, 141, 143–145, 147
Telegraph in Afghanistan, 191
Torkham, 111, 112

Trade: British-Afghan, 45, 48; Russo-Afghan, 32, 36–37
Treaties: Anglo-Afghan, 70, 138, 171–178, 182, 183; Franco-Afghan, 193; German-Afghan, 179, 201; Italo-Afghan, 194; Perso-Afghan, 194; Soviet-Afghan, 188; Turco-Afghan, 191
Tribes, Afghan-Pathan Frontier, 19, 62–63, 65, 78, 96, 98–99, 115, 122, 125, 137, 141, 154, 155; problem of, 78, 115, 122, 125, 137, 154–155
Turkey, 8, 25, 104, 119, 127, 163, 165, 191–193; activities of, in Afghanistan, 80–81, 88, 97; Allied peace terms with, 149, 154; and treaty with Soviet Union, 161; Italian war with, 80, 81, 84, 101; Treaty of Sèvres with, 158

Ulema of India, 117
Ulya Hazrat, 108

Viceroy of India. *See* Ampthill, Chelmsford, Curzon, Dufferin, Elgin, Hardinge, Lytton, Minto, Ripon
Voice of the Poor, 144

Wagner, Kurt, 98
Wakhan Corridor, 4, 16
War party, 8, 90, 91, 108
Wassmuss, Wilhelm, 84, 85
Waziristan, 73, 97, 99, 128, 148, 176; Anglo-Afghan disputes over, 151–153, 159, 160, 162, 163, 166; Mahsuds, 73; Wana Waziris, 159
World War I, 8

Yangi Kila, 60, 80
Yate, A. C., 37–38, 48, 219 n. 22
Young Afghans, 8

Zar Shah, 111, 112, 114
Zimmermann, 200

www.ingramcontent.com/pod-product-compliance
Lightning Source LLC
Chambersburg PA
CBHW021701230426
43668CB00008B/694